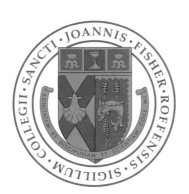

Lavery Library

St. John Fisher
College

Rochester, New York

The Administration of Justice: Current Themes in Comparative Perspective

The Administration of Justice

CURRENT THEMES IN COMPARATIVE PERSPECTIVE

EDITED BY

Jeremy Sarkin
&
William Binchy

FOUR COURTS PRESS

Set in 10.5 pt on 12.5 pt Bembo for
FOUR COURTS PRESS LTD
7 Malpas Street, Dublin 8, Ireland
e-mail: info@four-courts-press.ie
http://www.four-courts-press.ie
and in North America by
FOUR COURTS PRESS
c/o ISBS, 920 N.E. 58th Avenue, Suite 300, Portland, OR 97213.

A catalogue record for this title
is available from the British Library.

ISBN 1–85182–837–0

Printed in England
by Antony Rowe Ltd, Chippenham, Wilts.

Contents

Contributors

WILLIAM BINCHY is Regius Professor of Laws at Trinity College Dublin.

NEIL BOISTER is Senior Lecturer in Law at the University of Canterbury.

DECLAN BUDD is a Judge of the High Court of Ireland and President of the Irish Law Reform Commission.

PAUL CARNEY is a Judge of the High Court of Ireland.

ESTELLE FELDMAN is a Research Associate at the School of Law, Trinity College Dublin.

NIAL FENNELLY is a Judge of the Supreme Court of Ireland.

ADRIAN HARDIMAN is a Judge of the Supreme Court of Ireland.

CHRISTOF HEYNS is Professor of Law at the University of Pretoria.

J.M. HLOPHE is Judge Present of the Cape High Court, Cape Town.

ELIZABETH MAYER was DAAD Lektor in Law and German at Trinity College Dublin from 1995 to 2001.

BRIAN MC CRACKEN is a Judge of the Supreme Court of Ireland.

FRANCIS MURPHY was a Judge of the Supreme Court of Ireland until his retirement in 2002.

RODERICK MURPHY is a Judge of the High Court of Ireland.

YVONNE MURPHY is a Judge of the Circuit Court of Ireland.

AINDRIAS Ó CAOIMH is a Judge of the Court of Justice of the European Communites. Formerly he was a Judge of the High Court of Ireland.

KEVIN O'HIGGINS is a Judge of the High Court of Ireland.

MOHAMED NAVSA is a Judge of Appeal at the Supreme Court of Appeal, Bloemfontein.

JEREMY SARKIN is Senior Professor of Law at the University of the Western Cape.

ALEX SCHUSTER BL is Lecturer in Law at Trinity College Dublin.

ESMOND SMYTH is President of the Circuit Court of Ireland.

ESTHER STEYN is Senior Lecturer in Law at the University of Cape Town.

D.H. VAN ZYL is a Judge at the Cape High Court, Cape Town.

Preface

The administration of justice is a subject that can benefit greatly from a comparative perspective. It is not static, being constantly reshaped by social, economic, cultural and philosophical influences. New concepts, strategies and solutions may be found outside one's own legal system. Some of these travel well and thrive when transplanted; others are so distinctly connected to their particular system that they can never flourish on a foreign soil.

Irish and South African judges, legal practitioners and academics have been engaging in a process of dialogue in recent years at the initiative of the Law Faculty of the University of the Western Cape and the Law School of Trinity College Dublin. An earlier set of papers was published by Round Hall Sweet & Maxwell in 2002, entitled *Human Rights, The Citizen and the State: South African and Irish Perspectives*. The present volume contains papers delivered at the University of the Western Cape on 14 September 2001. A certain degree of updating has been possible in respect of some of the contributions. No doubt, with the rich jurisprudence flowing from the Constitutional Court of South Africa and the radical changes in the structure of litigation taking place in Ireland, lawyers from both jurisdictions have much more to learn from each other's legal systems in future years.

Estelle Feldman contributed hugely to the task of editing the papers.

We are very grateful to Four Courts Press for the help we have received in the publication process, especially from Michael Adams and Anthony Tierney.

Jeremy Sarkin
William Binchy

I   THE JUDICIAL ROLE

Native and foreign judges and laws in Ireland: a post-colonial reflection

ADRIAN HARDIMAN

Nearly eighty years after Ireland achieved legislative independence, a legal visitor from any country in the common law world would find our courts and judgments comfortingly familiar. Apart from the physical appearance of the courts, judges and lawyers, he would recognise the forms of citation and argument and the structure of judgments. Unless perhaps he was from Great Britain itself he would have at least a general familiarity with the main features of the constitutional jurisprudence and the provisions of the Constitution itself. If the visitor looked a little more closely at Irish law he would note that a considerable, though decreasing, number of the statutes in force were enacted by the Westminster Parliament prior to 1921; up to a few years ago these included some of the principal statutes dealing with the staples of the criminal law. And common law principles are daily applied and developed in substantially the same manner as in the country of their origin.

CONSTITUTIONAL TREATMENT OF PRE-INDEPENDENCE LAW

It was not perhaps obvious that a country which gained its independence by force of arms would follow this path. The Irish War of Independence between 1919 and 1921, and the preceding, suppressed but inspirational, insurrection of 1916, were the culmination of a national revival which placed great emphasis on the distinctive history of Ireland as opposed to Great Britain and on its ancient language, customs, laws, and even dress. The language revival movement, in particular, underpinned the movement for national independence. Eoin MacNeill, who was the founder of the Irish Volunteers which was the military wing of the independence movement, was also the leading academic authority on ancient Irish history and laws.

At the height of the War of Independence, in July 1920, the revolutionary parliament (Dáil Éireann) decided to establish its own 'Courts of Justice and Equity'. This policy was executed with a considerable degree of success throughout the war and its immediate aftermath. The legal code administered was: 'The law, as recognised on the 21st January, 1919, until amended ... except such portion thereof as was clearly motivated by religious or political animosity'. There was, however, a provision allowing citations to be made to any court from: 'The early Irish law codes or any commentary upon them in so far

3

as they may be applicable to modern conditions'. This dualist statement of the sources of law to be administered by the republican courts illustrates the difficulties of the legal advisers to the Dáil

Dáil Éireann had ratified the establishment of the Irish Republic proclaimed in 1916, and had repudiated foreign government. This was done at its first meeting on 21 January 1919. But it had no opportunity to pass laws of its own or to produce any detailed constitutional instrument. A reference to the early Irish law codes must be regarded mainly as a pious gesture to nationalist sensibility, especially as many of these codes and commentaries existed only in old Irish. Nevertheless they were in fact cited on a number of occasions and Mr Justice Creed Meredith, subsequently a judge of the Supreme Court established under the Free State Constitution, at least once purported to apply early Irish law.[1] As we shall see below, any broader application of Brehon law would have had revolutionary effects, especially in the area of marriage and family law.

The War of Independence ended with a treaty to which was attached as a schedule the 1922 Constitution of the Irish Free State. It contained, in Article 73, a provision carrying into effect in the Free State the laws in force immediately prior to its establishment. The Irish Free State itself was a self-governing Dominion within the British Commonwealth. This status was unacceptable to many nationalists, some of whom carried their opposition to it to the point of civil war in 1922/23. During the course of this conflict a judge of the Republican Supreme Court granted a conditional order of habeas corpus to an anti-treaty prisoner, directing his production by the Minister for Defence and a prison governor. Some days later the provisional government rescinded the decree of Dáil Éireann establishing the republican courts and declared it to be of no effect.

This brought to an end the brief existence in the modern era of early Irish or 'Brehon' law as a recognised source of binding adjudication. This position was confirmed in 1937, on the adoption of our present constitution. Article 50 provided:

> Subject to this Constitution and to the extent to which they are not inconsistent therewith, the laws in force in Saorstat Éireann immediately prior to the date of the coming into operation of this Constitution shall continue to be a full force and effect until the same or any of them shall have been repealed or amended by enactment of the Oireachtas.

With the abolition of the only courts prepared or entitled to recognise Brehon law, the remaining sources of law were the common law, the surviving statutes of the old Irish Parliament which existed up to 1800 and the statutes of the United Parliament of Great Britain and Ireland which existed to 1922.

---

1 See D. McArdle, *The Irish Republic* (London, 1937), p. 376.

The policy behind Article 73 of the Free State Constitution, which brought about this state of affairs, was explained by a judge of impeccable nationalist credentials in the 1931 case of *The State (Kennedy v. Little)*:[2]

> It seems to me to have been intended to set up the new State with the least possible change in the previously existing law, and that Article 73 should be so construed as to effectuate this intention ... I am of opinion that the fullest possible effect should be given to Article 73, and that the previously existing laws should be regarded as still subsisting unless they are clearly inconsistent with the Constitution.

Another judge in the same case said he thought that the court: 'should be very slow to do anything that would have the effect of depriving the State of the benefit of the vast body of statutory law which regulated hundreds and thousands of necessary matters in the body politic at the date of the coming into operation of the Constitution'.

The same reasoning was adopted in stark language by a judge of the old regime in the very short period between the adoption of the Free State Constitution and the creation in 1924 of a new system of courts and judicature by the Irish Free State. In *R (Armstrong) v. County Court Judge of Wicklow*[3] Lord Justice Ronan referred to Article 73 and said: 'But for that article there would be no law at all in the country'.

A FOOTNOTE TO HISTORY

The abolition of the republican courts prompted a remarkable dissent from a significant figure. George Gavan Duffy, one of the signatories to the Anglo-Irish treaty, was then Minister for Foreign Affairs in the Free State cabinet. He resigned in protest at the abolition of the Court saying:

> Ministers must feel some diffidence about championing against their own justices the judges of the old regime most of whom, a year or two ago, would have welcomed an opportunity of lodging our present rulers in jail ... [T]he war record of that judiciary is still branded on the public memory ... but the vital point is that no government may annihilate its judges at the moment when their most sacred jurisdiction over the executive itself is being involved.

In a totally changed political environment, and after the adoption of the 1937 Constitution, Gavin Duffy became President of the High Court and the judge, according to our leading constitutional scholar, 'to whom almost all the assertive

---

2 [1931] IR 39.   **3** [1924] 2 IR 139.

interpretation of the Constitution in the first fifteen years after its enactment can be attributed'.[4]

A LONGER RETROSPECT

The Brehon law thus reconsigned to history had played a decisive role in Ireland's early historical period and afterwards for the first 400 years of our long colonial experience. The final and decisive extension of English rule to all parts of Ireland in the late sixteenth century was determined upon in part because Brehon law was thought inconsistent with civilisation as understood by Elizabethan England. It was the law of a society which was rural, tribal, hierarchical, familial and mobile, in contrast to the centralised, unitary, settled, individualist and expanding society which extirpated it. Most fatally of all, the older law rejected primogeniture, the very basis of stability in Tudor society, and rejected too the notion that all land belonged ultimately to a single monarch, acknowledging only one natural and immutable territorial unit, the *tuath* or territory of a petty tribal king. There were about 80 to 150 such units at any time in Ireland between the beginning of the historical period and the Anglo-Norman invasion of 1169. Their average population was perhaps 3,000 to 6,000. Information about the society and economy which then prevailed is largely gathered from the law texts. The picture that emerges is of a self-sufficient mixed agricultural economy based on stock rearing and cereal cultivation. There was a limited import and export trade.

Despite the very fragmented nature of the political units both the language (Gaelic or Irish) and the law appears to have been universal throughout Ireland. The law texts which survive are medieval redactions of texts originally committed to writing in the sixth to eighth centuries AD. These are mainly in old or middle Irish, written in the Latin script introduced into Ireland after the coming of Christianity in the fifth century AD. The earliest texts are often in mnemonic poetical form suggesting that they were originally transmitted orally and only later reduced to writing. The law was expounded by a professional, often hereditary learned class divided into judges (*brithem*) and advocates (*aigne*). These were members of a broader class of expert or skilled persons (*aos dána*) which included also clerics, poets, physicians, druids, wrights and blacksmiths.

Both lawyers and physicians were trained at specialised schools. Descriptions of these survive from the late sixteenth century testifying to the fact that in 'Their common schools of leach-craft and law ... they begin as children and hold on 16 or 20 years ... they speak Latin like a vulgar language and con (learn) by wrote the aphorisms of Hypocrates and the Civil Institutions ... being for the most part lustie fellows of 25 years and upwards'.[5]

---

4 John Kelly, *The Irish Constitution* (1st ed., Dublin, 1980), Preface.   **5** Edmund Campion, *History of Ireland* (1571).

This reference to Latin and the civil institutions raises an important point. The Irish law texts themselves are archaic in the sense that they redact laws already old when first written down. Because they were customary, rather than statutory, in nature they were not repealed or amended but they were glossed and interpreted. The glosses, commentaries and academic teaching material of later years, right up to the early modern period, gives some idea of how they changed in practice. When it is remembered that more than 1100 years elapsed between the introduction of Christianity, and thus of manuscript writing, and the extirpation of the Brehon laws, it can be imagined that change was dramatic.

With Christianity, Ireland was exposed to canon law, which was significant for native legal development in two ways. Firstly, as elsewhere in early medieval Europe and later, bishops, often referred to as 'ordinaries', exercised a considerable jurisdiction of their own both spiritual and temporal. There is, in fact, considerable evidence of Brehons functioning also as judges in the bishops' courts. Secondly, interaction of this kind caused the early Irish lawyers to become familiar with the Latin language and the civil institutes of Justinian and other aspects of Roman law. Collections of civil law maxims, in a sort of phonetic Latin with Irish explanations, are found in late Irish law manuscripts. There are also examples of rules expressly based on Roman law rules being imported such as *Si sua res predit, Si non sua reddit duplex*: the taker of a thing without just cause was bound to restore double the value.[6]

ASPECTS OF BREHON LAW

Brehon law reflected a society in which individuals were minutely distinguished as to their ranks and functions. There were some sixteen divisions of society other than the Aos Dána, ranging from a provincial king, i.e. an over-king of a considerable number of *tuaithe* down to the rank of slave. All free persons had a set value or 'honour price' which was vital in determining the amount he was liable for, or entitled to receive, in all the various contingencies which the law provided for.

The law itself was remarkable for the small part played in its enforcement by centralised authority. Compensation or redress by personal service was the usual remedy for delicts regardless of whether they would now be classed as civil or criminal in nature. These were generally enforceable not only against the person himself but against his clan (*fine*). In relation to most transactions which we would now regard as civil, enforcement was facilitated by the requirement of a giving of pledges or the taking of sureties. For example, contracts required pledges or sureties from third parties varying in amount depending on its value. If one wished to engage in a sort of activity which gave rise to an

---

6 E. O'Curry, *Brehon law transcripts*, p. 676.

obvious danger to neighbours, such as bee-keeping or cattle-driving, sureties in advance were also required. Only in the case of default in one's obligations, or a particularly heinous crime for which the injured party or his kin rejected compensation, were penalties such as execution or banishment enforced. A person in default of his obligations could also lose his status or honour price, even be relegated to the rank of slave.

It was a remarkable feature of Brehon law at all times that liability for crimes or torts was collective as well as individual. In other words, liability extended in the hope of finding someone able to meet it, either on the basis of kinship to the perpetrator or residence in the same district, though these might over-lap totally. This custom of *cin comhfhocuis* (*kincogus* in medieval English) is well testified to in medieval sources including Anglo-Irish treaties as early as the thirteenth century and legislation of the sixteenth century. The grand jury of Kilkenny in 1537 stated that in cases of homicide: 'the hole kindred of the dead man' would force 'the hole kindred of the murderer to come before the said Irishe judge' when they would all be compelled to contribute to the payment of the *eraic*. They said that the same applied in civil disputes and instanced a case where a man's horse was seized for a debt owed by his brother. According to a 1537 presentment of the grand jury of Waterford, if a thief was unable to pay the *eraic* 'the Lord or Lady taketh of the poor thief five marks, and of the rich thief much more; and if he had nothing, he shall be hanged; his friends shall be warned to redeem him by a certain day or else to be hanged.'

Despite the essentially private nature of these transactions, it is to be noted that a portion, varying in amount, of the sums recovered by complainants were payable to the king or lord, presumably as a fee for maintaining the justice system, or for being ready to enforce decrees in the last resort.

Personal injuries

The law relating to injuries to the person may perhaps serve as an example of the texture of Brehon law. Firstly, accidental injury attracted compensation at half the rate of deliberate injury. There were seven types of injury which did not incur compensation at all including 'injury by a proper physician – acting with the authorisation of the patient's family and provided a joint or sinew be not cut'.

No compensation was payable for an injury from which the patient recov-ered within nine days, unless there was a lasting blemish or disability. If the victim were in need of nursing after that period the culprit had extensive oblig-ations for which he would have to provide pledges or sureties. He would have to bring the injured person to an approved house for nursing and provide nurs-ing at his own expense. He would have to provide suitable food and accom-modation for the victim and accompanying persons depending on his status. There were detailed regulations as to the type of nursing and maintenance. Defendants were required to provide a substitute to do the normal work of the victim. An injury which did not detract from the person's capacity for work, action or movement did not entail a right to a sick maintenance but only to lump sum compensation. This was also payable in all other cases.

The lump sum compensation was intended to cover: 'The fear of death, the gravity of the sickness and the extent of blemish'. The types of injury were minutely distinguished: there were six classes of tooth injury, twelve classes of internal injury and seven principle classes of fracture. A physician was entitled to a stated proportion of lump sum compensation or fine. Permanent disability or cosmetic injury was compensated separately by additional payments. In the later historical period, after perhaps 700 AD, the detailed provisions about sick maintenance were replaced by money payments.

Exclusion of liability

There was a considerable jurisprudence relating to the exclusion of liability for personal injuries. People attending at dangerous activities or places, (e.g., a blacksmith's forge, where flailing is going on, a mill, a building operation) had no right to compensation unless they could prove a defect in the equipment. Other activities such as tree felling were exempt if warning was given. The ferryman was liable only if he set out in poor weather or with his craft over-loaded. People attending a fair (*aonach*) are deemed to have willingly exposed themselves to the risk of being killed or injured by horses or chariots.

There were also detailed exemptions for injuries to boys playing sports. There was no liability for injuries received during hurling, jumping, swimming, hide and seek or juggling. Military type games (*flanchulichi*) such as stone or spear throwing did attract liability, as did a contest of 'few against many'. There was no liability either if one fell from another person's horse, or was injured by a stone thrown up by a horse, by a cow after calving or by a dog in a dog fight.

Judges

The judges or Breitheamhs are divided into three kinds. In the post-Christian period the highest class of judge required to be competent in traditional law, canon law and poetry which might be regarded as the heritage of his district. There was a single judge in each *tuaidh* and references to multiple judge courts in ordinary cases at first instance appear to refer to experts acting as assessors or jurors with the Breitheamh. This, in fact, seems to have been the rule rather than the exception: of the relatively small number of actual decided cases recorded only two were apparently decided by a jurist sitting alone. The status of the Breitheamh was a high one, exemplified in the provision that in the absence of the queen he sat beside the king at formal celebrations.

The qualities of a judge are often described in the texts: 'Three things required, of a judge: wisdom, sharpness, knowledge'. These qualities were enforced by the requirement that the judge give a pledge in advance in support of his judgment. The maxim 'to every judge his error' meant that he was responsible for any mistake of law and had to pay a fine for an erroneous judgment. On the other hand he was entitled to receive compensation if his judgment were impugned but upheld.

A corrupt, as opposed to a merely erroneous judgment could lead to a judge losing his office and his honour price. A specific example is a judgment given after hearing only one side (*leth-tacrae*). An unjust judgment was one of the 'three ruins of a Tuath' and a false judgment secured by bribery was described as one of 'the three injustices which God most avenges'. Specific types of cases required more than one professional judge, at least on appeal.

It appears that many cases were decided by the graduates of the law schools who had not been appointed as judges of a *tuath*, or by an official judge not acting as such. In these cases his fee was a proportion of the claim or award. Sixteenth-century sources described this as one twelfth each, from the plaintiff and the defendant. An advocate, by contrast, was entitled to one third of the plaintiff's award, apparently on the basis of no foal no fee.

Modern practitioners would recognise quite readily certain surviving documents which correspond to bills of costs and costs awards. In a document of the second half of the sixteenth century there are listed the 'twelfths' paid to judges by one Dábhí at the various stages of an action. These amount to one pound and sixteen shillings. He then had to pay five shillings and four pence for food and wine for the judges, four shillings and four pence for expenses involved in redeeming securities given for the payment of the 'twelfths' and two shillings and eight pence notorial fees. In a slightly earlier document there was a case arising from the theft by one Domhnall Dearg (Red Donal) of two pigs from Domhnall Óg O Ceamaidh. The plaintiff was awarded half a mark for each of the two pigs, three *uinge* (one shilling and eight pence) as expenses for witnesses to bring the theft home to the defendant (*fiacha faisnéise*) and a further *uinge* as the Brehon's fee.[7]

Distraint

We have already seen that the law was mainly enforced by private action, and the role played by pledges and sureties in this. However, where no pledges had been exchanged because no delict had been foreseen, a plaintiff was entitled to distrain, i.e. to seize the property of the proposed defendant. The defendant could redeem his property by giving pledges, thus exposing himself to legal process. There is detailed regulation of the notice period before distraint, the manner of distraint (which had to be carried out in the presence of a lawyer), and the responsibility for the goods distrained. The goods were said to 'decay' that is to pass bit by bit into the possession of the distrainer if there was delay in giving pledges. Distraint could also take place against a person's surety or

---

7 Mac Niocaill, 'Notes on litigation in late Irish law' (1967), 2 *Irish Jurist* (n.s.), 299 at 307.

other person responsible for him in which case all notice periods are doubled.

A particular custom existed in relation to a person whose rank exempted him from distraint. Here, the proposed plaintiff had to fast against the *nemed* or a noble person by camping on his doorstep and abstaining from food. The *nemed* was then himself prohibited from eating during the period of the fast. The fast could be ended by giving pledges in the usual way. Later, the plaintiff became entitled to distrain after a three days' fast.

Marriage, relationships and divorce

These matters were the subject of a special text, Cáin Lánamna or Law of Sexual Unions. Seven main types of union were distinguished, the first three being marriages of the highest and most onerous grade. These were distinguished according to whether they were '*lánamnas comthinchuir*, or unions of joint property, *lánamnas mná* for *furthinchur* or union of a woman on the man's property, or *lánamnas fir* for *bantinchur*, or union of a man on the woman's property'. In the event of divorce (*imscarad*) the nature of the original marriage was significant in determining the division of property.

The law also recognised other forms of union which might be engaged in instead of, or as well as, the above. The first of these was a less formal union where the man visited the woman at home with the consent of her *fine* or family. Again, the woman might depart from her *fine* with the man, without objection being given by them. Alternatively, she might either be 'visited' secretly or abducted without the consent of the *fine*. By reason of these different types of union, polygamy was possible and apparently widespread, as evidenced by the number of references to an *adaltrach*, a word usually translated as concubine.

There is ample evidence of objections by the Christian Church to these polygamous unions, but the law texts also contain strong justifications of it. A later text acknowledges the controversy that exists: 'There is dispute in Irish law as to which is more proper, whether many sexual unions or a single one: for the chosen people of God (*i.e.* the old testament Hebrews) lived in plurality of unions, so that it is not easier to condemn it than to praise it.'[8]

There were elaborate provisions for divorce. Seven grounds for a man divorcing his wife and fourteen grounds for a woman divorcing her husband were provided. A woman could be divorced for infidelity, thieving, procuring an abortion, or killing a new born child. She could also be divorced 'Bé loites cách rét' which literally translates as 'because she destroys or messes up everything'. The commentators suggest that this relates to incapacity in the ordinary, and considerable, domestic work attributed to women and their responsibility for the domestic economy.

A woman who is repudiated for another could divorce her husband, with the option of remaining in his house if she wished. She could also divorce him

---

8 *Bretha Crólige.*

for impotence, homosexuality or becoming so fat as to be incapable of intercourse. Failure to support her, leaving the household, sterility or disclosure of
the intimate details of their marriage were also grounds for divorce at the suit
of the woman. The apparently fairly enlightened treatment of women in this
context has led some readers of early Irish law to regard it as liberal in its treatment of women generally. However, like all early legal systems, Brehon law
did not attribute equal independent status to women, but regarded them as persons whose status depended on their family connections, whether through
fathers, husbands or sons. There were certain exceptions to this position in the
case of queens, and women who were members of the Aos Dána, usually as
physicians or wrights. There is a mythological reference to a woman
Breitheamh, but none in the law texts.

Land holding
The nineteenth-century translators of the word *fine* favoured 'tribe' to express
its meaning. In fact, it referred to a family or kinship group, usually all the
descendants of the same great-grandfather. This, probably, was as far back
as kinship could be ascertained with certainty. In any event, this mistransla-
tion led a number of commentators, starting with Frederick Engels, to conclude that all land and other property was held in common, i.e. that early
Ireland was a sort of communist state. This view cannot be reconciled with
the surviving texts, which feature very considerable emphasis on inheritance,
adverse possession, duties to fence and otherwise distinguish one's land and
cattle from that of others, acquisition of land by purchase or otherwise and
loss of it through legal process and numerous other incidents of individual
proprietorship.

Some land was held by the *fine* which distributed it to its individual members who then owned it individually but could not usually alienate it without the consent of the other family members. This land was however exclusive to the *fine*, and not to the broader community. Individual persons could
also acquire land of their own and apparently did so often. However, such a
person was not free of obligation to the *fine*: it retained a right to a portion
of it or its value if it were sold or bequeathed. If it was acquired wholly with
the surplus of his share of the kin's land, he could only retain one third of
its value; if acquired as a result of his own endeavours he could dispose of
half of it. If, however, land was acquired by the practice of a profession or
skill, the owner could dispose of two thirds of it, with the remainder owing
to the *fine*.

A portion of the land in each *tuadh* was set aside for the king, who in turn
transferred some of it to his brithen, poet, physician and other attendants. In
later Brehon times a good deal of land belonged to the Church which had tenants of its own. Moreover, a class of landlords developed granting land to clients

of their own: there are highly practical measures for the recovery of part or all of this land in the event of 'eisc, meisce or leisce', that is, absence, drunkenness or laziness.

While there is no evidence of the holding of land in common by any group broader than the *fine*, there is a great deal of evidence of co-operative agriculture, notably ploughing and pasturing. The pasturing arrangements are especially detailed. The number of cattle which each farmer in the arrangement was entitled to graze depended on the amount of land he was able to contribute to the *comingaire* or joint herding. This involved pasturing several men's cattle on one man's land at a time, and there were strict regulations concerning the separation of such lands. Many of the types of litigation relating to land holding and agricultural activities would be familiar to a lawyer with a country practice today. Adverse possession (*rodúrad*), trespass by cattle or other animals and over holding on agricultural tenancies are all expressly provided for.

'THE FIRST ADVENTURE OF THE COMMON LAW'

This rather smug phrase was used by an English legal historian to describe the imposition of the common law in Ireland after the Norman invasion of 1169. The Norman incursion into Ireland was, from the point of view of the Norman knights involved, certainly an adventure, but the blithe spirit of brave and expectant venturing was of course wholly absent from the point of view of the great majority of the Gaelic occupants of the territory. For them, the experience was to be, at best, one of constant embattlement, tense negotiations, strategic alliances and episodic open warfare and at worst, expropriation, extermination or banishment.

For our purposes, Ireland's 800-year long colonial experience must be drastically telescoped. The colonial era falls conveniently into two long phases of almost equal length: that between 1169 and about 1600, and the period from then until 1922. Speaking very broadly indeed, the first period featured the incursion int Ireland, at the request of an embattled Irish king, of a large number of noble Normans with their retinues and armies. Though they had the permission of the king of England, Henry II, for this enterprise it was in no sense an invasion by the English state. When, however, the first invaders established themselves widely throughout the east and southeast of Ireland, the English king himself arrived in the country in October 1171 with a large army. He assumed to himself the conquests of his subjects and regranted them to the Norman lords. He kept for the crown the main east coast towns. He also received the submissions of a large number of Irish regional kings outside the north of the country.

Although the Norman conquest of Ireland in the twelfth century was rapid, it was far from thorough. A generation later, and increasingly as time went by, it was undermined by two separate developments. First, it simply fell back from the remoter areas due to the inability to maintain the large military force which had it supported in the first place. More insidiously from the English point of view, a considerable number of the Norman lords, their families and humbler retainers simply became assimilated to Irish ways and began to speak the Irish language, inter-marry with the Irish nobility and adopt Irish ways of dress, agriculture and warfare. These people became known to the crown officials as 'Degenerate English'. The area of the country under effective English rule shrank continuously and eventually became restricted to an area of varying size around Dublin known as the Pale.

The native Irish law from the first attracted the strong condemnation of the English authorities. In many respects it was inconsistent with the common law and, in particular, the English concept of criminal law and of land tenure. King Edward I of England was not untypical in describing it as 'detestable to God and contrary to all laws'. The Brehon law was regarded as insidious in its effect on the colony, in particular, because an astute person and particularly a great lord could play off one system against the other. It would be erroneous to think of Ireland in this early colonial period as divided between an area of English law and another of Irish law. There is evidence that the Brehons continued both to practice and adjudicate throughout the country. The circuits of the king's courts were episodic and depended very much on the changing military situation. When they could sit in the main towns, their determinations were often contrary to the Irish dispensation.

The English law which was brought to Ireland was strongly based on the notion that all land was ultimately the possession of the king and all persons who owned land held it ultimately from him. The crown was entitled to personal services, rent charges and most importantly to levies and charges, which could be crippling, in the event that land was inherited by a minor or a woman. To assist the levying of these charges, and to permit profit taking by the crown, land in such circumstances was taken in to wardship. To police this, in turn, it was necessary to enforce the rule that land devolved on the eldest son or, in default, any available heiress.

In Irish law primogeniture was unrecognised. The successor to a king was selected from among his *fine* but by a process of selection carried out within the kin group. This could occur before the king's death in which case a designated heir was described as the *tánaiste*. Very shortly after the conquest, both Irish lords and, increasingly, Norman nobles adopted the Irish rather than the English custom of inheritance to avoid land going to minors or heiresses, or to manifestly unsuitable elder sons thereby avoiding the crown's rights and powers of partition. Secondly, the Irish method with dealing with crimes was scarcely recognisable as law at all to the English. In an era when death or mutilation was the penalty for most offences at common law, the Irish system of composition, as the English described it, seemed barbaric. Yet, in the century after the conquest and later, the Irish system was administered in most parts of Ireland, even by English courts since the common law prescriptions of death and mutilation seemed barbaric to the Irish.

Moreover, the country abounded in border areas, neither fully English nor fully Irish. In these 'marches' both legal systems existed and the lords, not unnaturally, adopted whichever was more advantageous. Since the Irish law permitted a lord to maintain forces of his own, described by the English as 'kernes and idlemen', both Irish and Norman lords were in practice in a position of much greater independence than their English equivalents who could maintain no considerable force without the consent of the king. For the time shortly after the conquest, the great Norman lords began to keep Brehons of their own: this is recorded for a surprisingly late date even in the case of such a continuously loyal family as the Butlers of Ormond.[10]

Finally, the more adaptable nature of marriage law under the Brehon system had obvious attractions to Norman lords. This, amongst other things, greatly improved their chances of producing a male heir. Ten legitimate children and perhaps thirty acknowledged children who were, in the terms of the common law, illegitimate were often attributed to such people by the somewhat aghast administration in Dublin, to whom so many offspring seemed further proof of degeneracy.

'SEPARATE DEVELOPMENT'

A combination of Gaelic revival and Gaelicisation of the Normans (who, in a memorable phrase, were said to have become more Irish than the Irish) defied crown power up to the middle of the fourteenth century. However, in 1361 a new viceroy, Lionel of Clarence, who was the second son of King Edward III, came to Ireland with a considerable army. He made a thoughtful and realistic assessment of the situation in the lordship of Ireland, as the English viewed it. He did not consider a full conquest or reconquest of Ireland feasible and instead decided to abandon the larger part of the country to the Irish and the Normans who had adopted Irish ways for the purpose of preserving the remainder for people of English speech, race and law.

But this involved a rigid separation between the two. This separation was given the force of law by the statutes of Kilkenny of 1366. These statutes recited that:

> Many of the English of the said land, forsaking the English language, manners, mode of riding, laws and usages, live and govern themselves

10 See C. Kenny, *King's Inns and the kingdom of Ireland* (Dublin, 1992), p. 67.

according to their manners fashion laws and language of the Irish enemies, and also have made divers marriages and alliances between themselves and the Irish enemies, whereby the said land, and the people
thereof, the English language, the allegiance due to our Lord the King,
and the English laws are put into subjection and decayed, and the Irish
enemies exalted and raised up contrary to reason.

The statutes therefore provided, *inter alia*, that any man of the English race taking
an Irish name, or using the Irish language apparel or customs should forfeit all
his lands; that to adopt or to submit to the Brehon law was treason; that the
English should not permit the Irish to pasture or graze upon their lands nor
admit them to any ecclesiastical benefices or religious houses, nor entertain their
minstrels or rhymers; and that any alliance with the Irish by marriage, nurture
of infants, fosterage or sponsorship should be punishable as high treason.

These statutes became part of the constitution of the English rule of Ireland
and were confirmed and reconfirmed at regular intervals over the next century
and a half. But they were almost wholly ineffective except in a small but constant number of individual cases. By 1388 we find Lionel's successor as viceroy
fostering his son to Conor O'Brien, lord of Thomond. The effect on the statutes
was principally on members of the landed classes who, if they could be found
to have become 'of the Irish nation' were liable to lose their lands and other
civil rights at common law. In the words of an Anglo-Irish authority:

> The statutes of Kilkenny amounted indeed to a real outlawry of the
> mere Irish in so far as they refused to become English in speech law
> address custom and name. Until the abolition of the statutes in 1613 it
> was always possible in law to deny the right of an Irish man of Irish
> Nation to freehold land property trade or office.[11]

Over the period between the statutes of Kilkenny and the final conquest of
Ireland in 1603 the native Irish and anglicised Normans continued to make
gains against the crown and Brehon law continued to flourish amongst them.
A further division between the old English, as the Gaelicised Normans were
called, and the crown occurred with the English Reformation enforced under
King Henry VIII, King Edward and Queen Elizabeth. The great bulk of them,
even those most loyal to the crown, persisted in the Catholic religion even after
it was declared illegal. But the growth of the power and wealth of England
under the reign of Queen Elizabeth, together with the military necessities arising from England's wars with the Catholic powers of Europe and Spain in particular, was to give rise to a re-examination of England's relationship with her
unsatisfactory colony which was to prove decisive.

11 E. Curtis, *Medieval Ireland* (London, 1936), p. 235.

THE NEW ENGLISH VIEW OF THE BREHON LAW

A state of war existed in Ireland between 1594 and 1603. From the Irish point of view the causes of this war were the continued encroachments on the solidly Gaelic province of Ulster and on Gaelic or Gaelicised lords in the rest of Ireland, notably in North Munster. Furthermore, in the expanding world of the late sixteenth century the Gaelic lords were conscious that they might find support, military and financial, particularly in Spain which was linked to them by religion and antagonism to England. Among the English, the view was taken that all sorts of compromises and arrangements with Gaelic Ireland had been tried and none had endured. An influential lobby, exemplified by two figures famous far beyond the bounds of Ireland, Sir Walter Raleigh and the poet Edmund Spencer, believed that the time was ripe for a new conquest because 'the blood of the first conquest has in a manner failed'.

In 1596 Edmund Spencer wrote *A View of the State of Ireland* which may serve as an example of the new approach. Written in the form of a dialogue, it has this to say about the Brehon law:

> It is a rule of right unwritten, but delivered by tradition from one to another, in which often times there appeareth great show of equity, in determining the right between party and party, but in many things repugnant quite both to God's law, and mans. As an example in the case of murder, the Brehon, that is their judge, will compound between the murderer and the friends of the party murdered, which prosecute the action, that the malefactor shall give unto them or to the child or wife of him that is slain a recompense which they call an Eriach. By which wild law of theirs, many murders amongst them are made up and smothered. And this judge being as he is called the Lords Brehon, ajudgeth for the most part, a better share unto his Lord, or the head of that sept, and also unto himself for his judgement a greater portion, than unto the Plaintiff or parties grieved.

It would be seen that Spencer was under a considerable misapprehension as to the Brehon laws, in particular in considering them unwritten.

As to the extent of the two legal systems at the time when he wrote Spencer had this to say:

> There being many wild countries in Ireland, which the laws of England were never established in, nor any acknowledgement or subjection made, and also even in those which are subdued yet the same Brehon law is practised amongst themselves by reason that dwelling as they do without any English man amongst them they may do what they list, and compound or conceal amongst themselves their own crimes of which may notice may be had ... by the rule of the laws of England.

Spencer goes on to explain the failure of previous agreements with Irish laws by the proposition that the rules of tanistrie prevent any of these agreements from having effect beyond the life of the chief who makes it so that: 'It is vain to speak of planting laws, and plotting policy, 'til they (the Irish) be altogether subdued'.

Spencer was adamant that this total subjection was necessary. He argued that reformation could not be brought about by law alone since the common law, to work effectively, required an honest and co-operative approach whereas the Irish in his view were dishonest and devious. They were unsuitable for jury service (jury trial being the characteristic mode of trial at common law) because:

> When the cause shall fall betwixt an English man and an Irish, or between the Queen and any freeholder of that country, they make no more scruple to pass against an English man, and the Queen, though it be to strain their oaths, than to drink milk unstained. So that before the jury go together it is all to nothing what the verdict shall be.

Furthermore, in a backhanded compliment to Irish legal ingenuity, he said:

> In all their dealings especially with the English they are most wilfully bent. For though they will not seem manifestly to do it, yet will some-one or other subtle headed fellow amongst them put some quirk, or devise some evasion, whereof the rest will likely take hold … for in the most apparent matter that may be, the least question or doubt that may be moved, they will make a stop unto them, and put them quite out of the way. Besides, that of themselves they are so cautelous and wily headed, especially being men of so small experience and practise in law matters, that you would wonder whenst they borrow such sub-tleties and sly shifts.

This attitude to the Brehon laws, and, indeed, to the Irish in general is in marked contrast to that shown in the late medieval period. Previously, the old English had shown a considerable tolerance toward Brehon law, often making treaties on the question of by which law and in which court the particular classes of case should be heard. In the frontier culture that existed during most of the medieval period notions such as collective responsibility were useful to the old English lords, who had little or no chance of bringing a particular delict home to its individual perpetrator. And since the old English tended to speak Irish and to have dealings and interbreeding with the Irish, a tolerance for Irish law naturally arose. Moreover, the old English themselves were not above taking refuge in Brehon law when the exactions of the Crown became excessive. The new English, on the other hand decided on a quite separate policy of conquest subjugation and even extirpation in which such adaptive strategies had no role.

THE END OF GAELIC RULE

The policy advocated by Spencer was indeed followed. Between 1598 and 1603 the country was subjected to a most destructive war featuring not merely conventional battles but a scorched earth policy, slaying of cattle and destruction of crops so that more people died of starvation and disease than in conflict. At the end of the war superficially generous terms were granted to the great Gaelic nobles but in fact their position was untenable. The great Gaelic lordships were broken up by a policy of encouraging subordinate chiefs and disappointed aspirants to the headships of the royal families to make proceedings in the common law courts. The lands of Hugh O'Neill, the chief lord of Ulster and earl of Tyrone in the English peerage, was broken up in this way.

The engineer of this policy was Sir John Davies. He encouraged Gaelic chiefs such as O'Neill's son-in-law, Ó Cahan, to take proceedings in the common law courts by effectively guaranteeing their success. A series of cases heard on assizes in Ulster between 1606 and 1610 dismembered the great lordships by converting the Gaelic forms of tenure from the chief into direct feudal tenures from the crown. Large estates were also granted to the bishops of the reformed Church and to the crown itself in the same way. Long before the process had finished, most of the surviving Irish lords saw the writing on the wall and took flight to Spain and other sympathetic continental powers.

Davies himself, indeed, might serve as an example of the new English colonist who finally destroyed Gaelic Ireland. He was a man of humble background whose early career had been marred by some unspecified misdemeanour which led to his being excluded from the Inns of Court in London. Like many another adventurer of the time he decided to go to Ireland where, in the frontier atmosphere that then prevailed, fame and fortune might be quite easily attained by those who are prepared to take the risks involved. He was successively solicitor general, attorney general, and Speaker of Parliament, all in Ireland and, for a short period before his death, lord chief justice of England. It was he who spotted the fatal weakness, from the Irish point of view, in the settlement of 1603. This was that, although their lands were confirmed to the great Irish nobles, they held them merely as tenants from the king, and the common law was to hold sway throughout the Gaelic areas. Davies then masterminded the legal actions described above whereby the lands were dismembered.

Davies was conscious in his own life time that he had participated in a revolution which had seen the death of Gaelic Ireland and its Brehon laws and the substitution of the Protestant ascendancy and the common law. He described the details of what had occurred in the Law Reports he made of the Ulster assizes between 1606 and 1610. In 1612 he published a more general work, *A True Discoverie of the reasons – why Ireland was never entirely subdued until the beginning of his present Majesties happy reign*. This book is a work of colonial self-justification. The natives were savages, their princes barbarians and their laws a brutal and illogical code. It was a kindness to extirpate their leaders and confer on them, albeit forcibly, the manifest benefits of the common law. That they could not actually avail of these benefits while they clung to Catholicism was irrelevant in Davies' eyes: they should simply convert to the established Church.

Davies' volume continued in print through a great many editions, until the end of the eighteenth century. It was the book to which the colonial island of the Protestant ascendancy looked for its justification across more than two centuries, and this justification rested upon a one-sided and perverse view of native Irish society, its institutions and laws.

Justice and its concomitants in a new constitutional dispensation

D.H. VAN ZYL

In any discussion of the administration of justice, the question must inevitably be asked: what does 'justice' mean? This concept is encountered in various contexts – legal, philosophical, religious, social and the like – and may in fact mean widely differing things to different people. To a politician or civil servant it may mean compliance with rules, regulations and legislative provisions. To a man of religion it may mean the observance of religious norms, precepts and principles. To a community leader it may mean the fair and appropriate allocation of employment, housing, food and clothing to the needy. To a lawyer it should mean justice, in the sense of what is fair and reasonable under the circumstances, and of what accords with the good faith demanded by public morals or, as it has evolved in modern times, public policy.

When I hence speak of the concomitants of justice, I am referring, in the main, to the values of fairness or equity on the one hand, and reasonableness on the other. One must add to them, however, the equally significant value of good morals (the *boni mores* of Roman and later law), which has developed into public opinion, public interest or, more correctly in modern jurisprudence, public policy. Hand in hand with it goes the value of good faith (*bona fides*), a concept which has developed particularly in the law of contract. These are concepts I have been attempting to apply in my judicial activities for many years and are, in my view, essential elements of the justice we as judges have sworn to maintain and uphold. Neither the *boni mores* nor the *bona fides*, however, have played as prominent a role in ancient law and its development as the values of justice, fairness (equity) and reasonableness. It is also significant that they are not spelt out in the new South African Constitution with as much clarity as are the values of justice, fairness (equity) and reasonableness.

The question may rightly be asked as to how it was possible to achieve justice in this sense prior to our new constitutional dispensation in South Africa. The answer is, simply, that justice, fairness and reasonableness constitute values that have been part and parcel of Western thought and of our Roman-European common law since time immemorial.[1] I speak here of the sources

---

[1] I prefer to speak of 'Roman-European' rather than 'Roman-Dutch' law, inasmuch as the law that was received in South Africa was not restricted to Roman-Dutch sources emanating from the province of Holland in the Netherlands. It included the Roman based law of other provinces, such as Friesland, Utrecht, Zeeland, Gelderland and Groningen. It also included Roman legal sources as

and later development of Greco-Roman and other early European sources of Western philosophy and legal thought. I refer also to the jurisprudence and legal heritage of many generations of English[2] and South African judges, academics and lawyers who have assisted in interpreting and developing our common law.

GREEK LEGAL THOUGHT

The concepts of justice and fairness or equity may be taken back to ancient Greek philosophy, where the source of virtually all Greek, and for that matter Western, thought has, justifiably, been identified with the name of the great philosopher and teacher, Socrates (*c*.469–399 BC). With his dialectic approach, by word of mouth rather than by doctrinal writing, he developed Western philosophy and thought as none of his predecessors or contemporaries had done. He left it to his students, however, to convey his pearls of wisdom and insight to later generations of philosophers and lawyers.[3]

Undoubtedly the most illustrious of his students was Plato (427–327 BC), who was fascinated by the central theme in his approach to life, namely 'know yourself' (*gnothi seauton*) with a view to achieving true happiness (*eudaimonia*).[4] This required never doing wrong and acquiring knowledge of what is morally right, just and good. In this way the soul (*psyche*), as the seat of human intellect, personality and responsibility, could develop virtue (*arete*) as a practical form of moral goodness, directed at attaining to the supreme good (*agathon*). Virtue in this form gave rise to the Socratic conception of the four cardinal virtues, first among which was wisdom, in the sense of theoretical or intellectual wisdom (*sophia*) as opposed to practical wisdom or prudence (*phronesis*). Next in line was justice (*dikaiosyne*), followed by courage or fortitude (*andreia*) and temperance or moderation (*sophrosyne*).

Although justice features here as only the second of the four prime philosophical virtues, Plato elevated it to one of the ultimate ideals of the knowledge

developed in many other parts of Europe, such as France, Italy, Austria, Germany and even Spain. This gave rise to what is known as the common law of Europe (*ius commune europaeum*). **2** I include the English judiciary, legal academe and legal profession inasmuch as English law was received in the Cape from 1806 to 1910 and continued to influence South African law for many years thereafter, even to the present time. This has given rise to South African law being described as 'mixed' or 'hybrid'. **3** Classic works on Socrates include those of E. Zeller, *Socrates and the Socratic schools* (1885), A.E. Taylor, *Socrates* (1932) and O. Gigon, *Sokrates* (1947). **4** On the relationship between Plato and Socrates see G.C. Field, *Socrates and Plato* (1913). Among the numerous works on Plato in general, reference may be made to: A.E. Taylor, *Plato: the man and his work* (1929); G.C. Field, *Plato and his contemporaries* (1930); G.M.A. Grube, *Plato's thought* (1935); I.M. Crombie, *An examination of Plato's doctrines* (2 vols, 1962); A.W. Gouldner, *Enter Plato* (1965); G. Vlastos (ed.), *Plato: a collection of critical essays* (1971); R.W. Hall, *Plato* (1981); R.M. Hare, *Plato* (1982); C.J. Rowe, *Plato* (1984).

and virtue required for the successful functioning of any state. This may be seen throughout his *Republic* (*Politeia*) and *Laws* (*Nomoi*). The first book of the *Republic* constitutes a dialogue on justice, while the remaining nine books are directed at the concept of an ideal state. The *Laws*, in turn, contain directives as to the functioning of the ideal state by means of highly moral legal enactments that require strict observance. Justice, as one of the ultimate ideals of knowledge and virtue, is in fact the cardinal virtue required for the successful functioning of any state. It may be achieved by the promulgation of laws that aim to destroy chaos and injustice and to replace it with order and reasonableness. By their very nature such law would promote a virtuous way of life.

In one of these dialogues[5] Plato tells us that 'it is just to give each man his due', whether such person be a friend or an enemy. Elsewhere[6] he states that 'justice (*dikaiosyne*) is virtue (*arete*) and wisdom (*sophia*), while injustice (*adikia*) is vice (*kakia*) and ignorance (*amathia*)'. In this regard he distinguishes between universal and individual justice, the former relating to justice in state context and the latter to justice between individual citizens. The distinction is strikingly described by Jones in the context of virtue and goodness:[7]

> Plato believed that justice might be self-regarding in so far as it was identical with harmony in the human soul, putting an end to 'inner faction, enmity and discord within the self'. If justice is harmony, or something which produces and maintains harmony, it implies a community or reciprocity of forces. In its widest sense, then, as used by Plato, justice represents such a balance of influences within a man's soul as makes for goodness; it becomes roughly synonymous with self-control or temperance, embracing all with which a man of virtue can be concerned, and possession of such practical good sense or prudence as is indispensable for the smooth working of any organised complex of relationships, whether the individual human personality, the family, or the city. But in any of its forms justice to Plato was impossible to conceive apart from goodness and wisdom; indeed it was the same thing as virtue which was the only true wisdom; and since the virtuous man was a happy man, it was happiness as well ...

Plato closely links the concept of truth (*aletheia*) with justice and other virtues. Justice, he says,[8] is the virtue of a judge, whereas that of an orator is to speak the truth. He illustrates this in another passage[9] by observing that pleasure, pain and fear should not be exchanged as if they were mere coins. Only the cardinal virtues of wisdom, courage, temperance and justice can serve as currency for such exchange. They constitute true virtue, which cannot exist

---

5 *Republic* 335B–E.   **6** *Republic* 350B–D.   **7** J.W, Jones, *The law and legal theory of the Greeks: an introduction* (1956), pp 3–4.   **8** *Apology of Socrates* D 18 par. 1.   **9** *Phaedo* B 69 par. 13.

in a vacuum. Like truth, they provide a form of purification for the soul and spirit of mankind.

Plato's thought was carried on and further developed by his most famous student, Aristotle (384–322 BC),[10] whose doctrine of ethics was closely related to his doctrine of politics and his thought on law.[11] His basic premise was that all men, communities and states seek after happiness (*eudaimonia*) in the sense of prosperity, well-being and general satisfaction. This was an activity of the soul (*psyche*) directed at achieving virtue and goodness. In this regard he distinguished between intellectual virtues, such as wisdom and prudence, and moral virtues, such as justice, courage, temperance, truth, friendship and the like. He regarded justice[12] as the most perfect of virtues and the very foundation of the well-ordered political life of any community. It occurred in the sense of general justice, closely approaching the concept of a virtue, and particular justice, which is subdivided into distributive, corrective (remedial) and compensatory (retributive) justice, all of which aim to achieve fairness and equality before the law.

Alongside justice Aristotle developed the concept of equity (*epieikeia*), which was required to supplement the general law should it fail to provide for the issue in question, or to temper the existing law should its strict application be prejudicial to any of the parties to litigation. The nature of equity appears strikingly from the following passage in Aristotle's *Rhetoric*:[13]

> Let us first then speak of the laws, and state what use should be made of them when exhorting or dissuading, accusing or defending. For it is evident that, if the written law is counter to our case, we must have recourse to the general law and equity, as more in accordance with justice … [T]hat equity is ever constant and never changes …

It is clear that Aristotle has a far more clearly defined view of equity than Plato. He refers to it in the sense of fairness, reasonableness or, simply, justice. He explains that justice in terms of the written law is not always just and may require the application of equity, which comes from the unwritten law of nature, to make it truly just. In his *Nicomachaean Ethics*,[14] however, he deals somewhat confusingly with the relationship between justice and equity, describing them as neither absolutely identical nor generically different. Although they are in substance the same, both being good, equity is, in certain respects, better or superior. From this it appears that Aristotle sees equity as a form of justice with a decidedly moral aspect, in that it is good or virtuous and a particularly

10 See in general W.D. Ross, *Aristotle* (1949); J.R. Bambrough (ed.), *New essays on Plato and Aristotle* (1965); D.J. Allan, *The philosophy of Aristotle* (1970); J.L. Ackrill, *Aristotle the philosopher* (1981); J.D.G. Evans, *Aristotle* (1987); J.M. Rist, *The mind of Aristotle: a study in philosophical growth* (1989). 11 On the ethics and morality of Aristotle see J. Burnett (ed.), *The Ethics of Aristotle* (1900); J. Walsh, H. Shapiro, *Aristotle's Ethics* (1967); W.F.R. Hardie, *Aristotle's ethical theory* (1968). 12 In book 5 of his *Nicomachean Ethics*. 13 *Rhetoric* 1.15.4–12 (1375a–b) (Loeb translation of J.H. Freese). 14 *Nicomachaean Ethics* 5.10.1–8 (1137a–1138a).

acceptable supplement to justice. In fact it may even be said that justice must be equitable and equity just.

ROMAN LEGAL THOUGHT

Justice (*iustitia*) and its concomitants, namely equity (*aequitas*), reasonableness (*ratio recta*), good faith (*bona fides*) and good morals or public policy (*boni mores*), were fully recognised and applied in Roman and later legal thought. It was particularly the great Roman orator, lawyer and jurist, Marcus Tullius Cicero (106–43 BC), who played an important role in this regard.[15] He was an enthusiastic supporter of Plato and his cardinal virtues, which he rendered in Latin as *sapientia* (wisdom) or *prudentia* (prudence), *iustitia* (justice), *fortitudo* (fortitude or courage) and *temperantia* (temperance, moderation or self-control). Like Plato, Cicero linked justice with ethical or moral values emanating from nature (*natura*), describing it as the greatest good (*summum bonum*) and the ultimate in moral goodness (*honestum*). The purpose of the *summum bonum* was to bring man back to his true nature (*natura*) and to a happy, peaceful and harmonious life. It was directed at the attainment of moral goodness (*honestum*) and virtue (*virtus*), in conformity with nature and reason (*ratio*), which form the basis of true law and of all human relationships. True law (*vera lex*) was, indeed, right reason (*recta ratio*) in conformity with nature (*naturae congruens*). As such it was 'one eternal and immutable law' (*una lex et sempiterna et immutabilis*).[16] Justice, in turn,[17] was directed at giving to each his own (*suum cuique tribuere*), in the sense of having the intention to give to each what he deserves (*animi affectio suum cuique tribuens*). Elsewhere[18] he gave prominence to the interests of the community (the *boni mores*) in his description of justice as a state of mind that attributes to each his own dignity while maintaining the common benefit (*habitus animi communi utilitate conservata suam cuique tribuens dignitatem*).

Another famous Roman lawyer and jurist, Domitius Ulpianus (Ulpian), who lived during the third century AD, defined justice[19] as the constant and perpetual desire to give to each his own right (*constans et perpetua voluntas ius suum cuique tribuere*). According to him,[20] the fundamental principles of law (*iuris praecepta*) were to live honourably (*honeste vivere*), not to harm another (*alterum non laedere*) and to render to each his own (*suum cuique tribuere*). In this regard he emphasised that law (*ius*) emanated from justice (*iustitia*) and constituted the art of what is good and fair (*ars boni et aequi*). In this sense justice developed a decidedly moral tone and may be said to have been consistent with good faith (*bona fides*) and good morals (*boni mores*).

---

15 See in general D.H. van Zyl, *Justice and equity in Cicero* (1991) and the authorities cited therein. **16** *De re publica* 2.22.33. Cf. *De legibus* 1 6.18, where he describes law as the ultimate reason embedded in nature (*ratio summa insita in natura*). **17** *De finibus* 5.23.65. **18** *De inventione* 2.53.160. **19** *Digest* 1.1.10 pr. **20** *Digest* 1.1.10.1 (also in the *Institutes* of Justinian 1.1.3).

LATER DEVELOPMENT

The moral aspect of justice, as developed by Plato, Cicero and Ulpian, likewise featured in the thought of the famous theologian, Thomas Aquinas
(1225–1274). He described it[21] as the state of mind (*habitus animi*) in accordance
with which a person has the constant and perpetual desire to give to each his
own (*secundum quem aliquis constanti et perpetua voluntate jus suum unicuique tribuit*).
This does not mean that he advocated a self-centred approach to law. On the
contrary, he gave full recognition to the interests of the community (the *boni
mores* of Roman times) and to reason (*ratio*) or reasonableness in his definition
of law (*lex*)[22] as a certain arrangement of reason (*ratio*) for the common good
(*quaedam rationis ordinatio ad bonum commune*).

Justice and equity feature strongly in the work of the great French human-
ist, Hugues Doneau (Hugo Donellus), (1527–1591). In his commentary on the
civil (Roman) law,[23] as the art of what is fair and good and reaches out to justice (*ars aequi et boni … ad justitiam ferens*). Justice is hence inextricably inter-
woven with equity.

One of the greatest Roman-European lawyers of all time, Huigh de Groot
(Hugo Grotius), (1583–1645), was strongly influenced by Cicero's conception
of natural law and legal principles, which provided the incentive for his internationally acclaimed work on the law of war and peace (*De iure belli ac pacis*).[24]
Like Cicero[25] he saw natural law (*ius naturale* or *ius naturae*) as a 'dictate of right
reason' (*dictatum rectae rationis*).[26] It was, he said, so eternal and immutable (*per-
petuum atque immutabile*) that even God, who was never unjust, could not change
it or issue orders in conflict with it.[27] Grotius likewise adopted a moral approach
in defining the science of law or jurisprudence (*iurisprudentia*) as the art of what
is good and fair (*ars boni et aequi*).[28] Equity (*aequitas*), in turn, was 'the corrective virtue of the will' (*virtus voluntatis correctrix*) which applied 'when the law
was defective as a result of its generality' (*in quo lex deficit ob universalitatem*).[29]

> Permit me to make a quantum leap to the twentieth century by ven-
> turing a comparative reference to the description of justice by John
> Rawls as 'the first virtue of social institutions, as truth is of systems of
> thought'.[30] This has a decidedly moral tone in the twentieth century
> idiom of the social justice, fairness, reasonableness and equality char-
> acterising truth and democratic values. It does not, however, ignore
> the fundamental importance of ancient values that have stood the test
> of time.

21 *Summa theologiae* 2.2.58.1.   **22** *Summa theologiae* 2.1.90.4.   **23** *Commentarii de jure civile* 1.13.12.
24 See the discussion on Cicero and Grotius in Van Zyl (note 16 above) 222–7.   **25** In *De re publica* 3.22.33.   **26** *De iure belli ac pacis* 1.1.10.1.   **27** *De iure belli ac pacis* 1.1.10.5 and 1.1.17.2.   **28**
De aequitate 2.   **29** *De aequitate* 3.   **30** John Rawls, *A theory of justice* (1972) 3.

SOUTH AFRICAN LEGAL THOUGHT: THE NEW CONSTITUTION

The transformational period of development in the political, social and legal spheres in South Africa is the product of a long and arduous struggle to achieve justice for all South Africans. The concept of justice, however, has undergone significant changes as far as its content and ambit are concerned. Its primary purpose, it would appear from legislation, jurisprudence and legal writing, is to create and maintain the peaceful and harmonious co-existence of all its peoples and communities who have chosen to be ruled by generally accepted democratic values. This entails giving full recognition to the promotion of justice for all and to the protection of fundamental human rights and freedoms.

The recently promulgated new Constitution has done just this. In its preamble[31] we are told that it has been adopted as 'the supreme law of the Republic' intent upon healing the divisions of the past and establishing a society based on democratic values, social justice and fundamental human rights. Its vision is to lay the foundations for an open and democratic society governed in accordance with the will of all its citizens, who enjoy equal protection by the law. It aims to improve the quality of life of such citizens and to free the potential of every individual.

The Constitution has a strongly moral basis, as appears from the reference to 'social justice' in the preamble. This is given content in the founding provisions, wherein the Republic of South Africa is described as 'one sovereign, democratic state' founded on values such as human dignity, the achievement of equality and the advancement of human rights and freedoms.[32] All its citizens are 'equally entitled to the rights, privileges and benefits of citizenship', but are likewise 'equally subject to the duties and responsibilities of citizenship'.[33]

These rights (and corresponding duties) are spelt out in the Bill of Rights embodied in chapter 2 of the Constitution. Its introductory section, section 7, is entitled simply 'Rights'. It proceeds, however,[34] to describe the Bill of Rights as 'a cornerstone of democracy in South Africa' which 'enshrines the rights of all people in our country and affirms the democratic values of human dignity, equality and freedom'. By the same token it has placed huge responsibilities on the executive and legislative arms of government by enjoining the State[35] to 'respect, protect, promote and fulfil the rights in the Bill of Rights'.

It is for the judicial arm of government, however, as represented by the courts in which judicial authority is vested,[36] to administer justice and ensure that the aforesaid democratic values, social justice and fundamental human rights are given practical protection and effect. The courts are expressly described[37] as 'independent and subject only to the Constitution and the law, which they must apply

---

31 Preamble to the Constitution of the Republic of South Africa, Act 108 of 1996. **32** Section 1(a). **33** Section 3(2)(a) and (b). **34** Section 7(1). **35** Section 7(2). **36** Section 165(1). Chapter 8 of the Constitution is titled Courts and Administration of Justice. **37** Section 165(2).

impartially and without fear, favour or prejudice'. They are required to be independent and impartial and to provide access to law and the legal process by
making provision for 'a fair public hearing'.[38] This duty goes hand in hand with
the 'right to a fair trial' accorded to arrested, detained or accused persons.[39] In
this regard a court, tribunal or forum interpreting the Bill of Rights is required
to 'promote the values that underlie an open and democratic society based on
human dignity, equality and freedom'.[40] In doing so it must 'promote the spirit,
purport and objects of the Bill of Rights'.[41] Courts are required to make 'just
and equitable' orders when dealing with constitutional matters.[42] This accords
with the inherent power of higher courts (the Constitutional Court, Supreme
Court of Appeal and High Courts) to protect and regulate their own process and
to develop the common law, 'taking into account the interests of justice'.[43]

Throughout the Constitution one finds further provisions relating to justice,
fairness and reasonableness. A good example arises from the introductory provision relating to just administrative action, namely: 'Everyone has the right to
administrative action that is lawful, reasonable and procedurally fair'.[44] Rights
like this, however, may be limited to the extent that it is 'reasonable and justifiable in an open and democratic society based on human dignity, equality and
freedom'.[45] This inevitably establishes a link between what is just, fair and reasonable. Reasonableness in fact creates an objective standard against which the
more subjective perception of what is just and fair may be measured. Equality,
in turn, relates strongly to equity or fairness, albeit in the context of dignity and
freedom accorded the members of an open and democratic society.

The link between equality and equity occurs prominently in section 9 of
the Bill of Rights which, as a result of the oppressive inequities caused by unfair
discrimination in the past, gives primacy of position to equality as the first of
the human rights requiring special protection. Therein we are told that '[e]very-
one is equal before the law and has the right to equal protection and benefit of
the law'.[46] Equality in this sense 'includes the full and equal enjoyment of all
rights and freedoms'.[47] It is a right that has expressly vertical and horizontal
application, in that neither the State nor any person may unfairly discriminate,
directly or indirectly, against anyone on one or more of a variety of grounds.
They include race, gender, sex, pregnancy, marital status, ethnic or social origin,
colour, sexual orientation, age, disability, religion, conscience, belief, culture,
language or birth.[48] There is a presumption of unfairness of discrimination on
any one or more of these grounds, unless the contrary is proved.[49] This places
a burden on the State or person engaging in such discrimination to prove that
it is fair. I am of the view that, in its constitutional context, this will mean prov-

---

38 Section 34.   39 Section 35(3).   40 Section 39(1)(a).   41 Section 39(2). These principles apply
also to State institutions (see sections 182–6 and 195–6).   42 Section 172(1)(b).   43 Section 173.
44 Section 33(1).   45 Section 36(1).   46 Section 9(1).   47 Section 9(2).   48 Sections 9(3) and
9(4).   49 Section 9(5).

ing that the discrimination is not only fair or equitable, but also that it is just or justifiable and reasonable.

What is just, fair and reasonable also comes strongly to the fore in the constitutional provisions relating to labour relations. The introductory provision[50] states simply that '[e]veryone has the right to fair labour practices'. This includes the right to engage in collective bargaining and to conclude collective agreements.[51] Inasmuch as national legislation in this regard may constitute limitations to these rights, such limitations must comply with the relevant limiting provisions.[52] This will inevitably bring into play considerations of justice, fairness and reasonableness.

A similar relationship between these complementary values comes to the fore in the provisions relating to the environment. In this regard it is provided that everyone has the right to an environment that is not harmful to his or her health or well-being, and that this environment should be protected by 'reasonable legislative and other measures'.[53] These measures are required to promote 'justifiable economic and social development'.[54] The result will be an environment that is just, fair and reasonable in the user-friendly sense.

The provisions on property likewise promote these values. No one, we are told, may be deprived of property except in terms of law of general application, subject thereto that no such law may permit the arbitrary deprivation of property.[55] Property may, indeed, be expropriated only 'for a public purpose or in the public interest'.[56] The amount of compensation payable for the property, and the time and manner of payment thereof, must be 'just and equitable, reflecting an equitable balance between the public interest and the interests of those affected, having regard to all relevant circumstances'.[57] The 'public interest' referred to here 'includes the nation's commitment to land reform, and to reforms to bring about equitable access to all South Africa's natural resources'.[58] In this regard the State is required to take 'reasonable legislative and other measures, within its available resources, to foster conditions which enable citizens to gain access to land on an equitable basis'.[59] A person or community whose tenure of land is 'legally insecure' or who has been dispossessed of property as a result of 'past racially discriminatory laws or practices' is entitled to 'legally secure' tenure or to restitution of the property, as the case may be. In the alternative 'comparable' or 'equitable' redress should be afforded.[60]

Similar provisions pertain to socio-economic rights, such as the right of access to adequate housing, health care, food, water and social security. In this regard the State is required to take 'reasonable legislative and other measures, within its available resources, to achieve the progressive realisation' of such rights.[61]

---

50 Section 23(1). **51** Sections 23(5) and (6). **52** Section 36. **53** Section 24(a) and (b). **54** Section 24(b)(iii). **55** Section 25(1). **56** Section 25(2)(b). **57** Section 25(3). **58** Section 25(4)(a). **59** Section 25(5). **60** Sections 25(6) and (7). **61** Sections 26(2) and 27(2).

A pragmatic approach to what is just, fair and reasonable appears from the provisions underlying the right to education. Everyone, it is said, has a right to a basic education and to further education which the State, 'through reasonable measures must make progressively available and accessible'.[62] In addition everyone has the right to be educated, in the official language of his or her choice, in a public educational institution 'where that education is reasonably practicable'. In order to ensure effective access to and implementation of this right, the State is required to consider 'all reasonable educational alternatives', taking into account equity, practicability and 'the need to redress the results of past racially discriminatory laws and practices'.[63]

There are a number of State institutions provided by the Constitution with a view to maintaining, as far as possible, justice, equity, reasonableness and truth in public life and in the community. Prominent among them is the Public Protector (previously known as the *Ombudsman*). He has the power to investigate any conduct in State affairs, or in the public administration in any sphere of government, that is alleged or suspected to be improper or to give rise to any impropriety or prejudice. He may report on that conduct and take appropriate remedial action.[64]

Likewise prominent is the Human Rights Commission. It is required to promote respect for human rights and a culture of human rights, to promote the protection, development and attainment of human rights and to monitor and assess the observance of human rights.[65] It has the power to investigate and report on these matters and, in cases of any violation thereof, to take appropriate steps to redress it.[66]

The public administration is said, at the outset, to be governed by 'the democratic values and principles enshrined in the Constitution'.[67] This includes that it must render services 'impartially, fairly, equitably and without bias'.[68] The chief organ of the public administration is the Public Service Commission. It is said to be independent and is required to be impartial and to exercise its powers and perform its functions 'without fear, favour or prejudice in the interest of the maintenance of effective and efficient public administration and a high standard of professional ethics in the public service'.[69] Other organs of State are required, by legislative and other means, to assist and protect the Commission to ensure its 'independence, impartiality, dignity and effectiveness'.[70]

The transformational period of the new constitutional dispensation has required an exposure of the truth and a reconciliation of conflicting interests as never before in the history of South Africa. The statutory institution of the Truth and Reconciliation Commission was a major achievement in this process. Although there was initially considerable resistance to the Commission and its activities, it did not take long for the general public to realise that the public

---

62 Section 29(1)(a) and (b).   **63** Section 29(2).   **64** Section 182(1).   **65** Section 184(1).   **66** Section 184(2).   **67** Section 195(1).   **68** Section 195(1)(d).   **69** Section 196(2)   **70** Section 196(3).

investigations and related amnesty hearings would play an important role in promoting the reconciliation that was so urgently needed in the country. The truth has certainly not been exposed in all its fullness, but enough has been done to provide a stimulus for placing the past in its correct context and creating a new South Africa where the ancient values of justice, equity and reasonableness reign supreme.

It would appear from the preceding discussion that, although the aforesaid values are, metaphorically speaking, as old as the hills, they are prevalent throughout the provisions of the Constitution and are fundamental to the administration of justice and the activities of the courts and State institutions. It is now up to the courts and such institutions to apply these values. There are a number of good examples of such application in practice, but there has also been a certain amount of reluctance or restraint in doing so. Only the future will tell whether or not justice and its concomitants will be given the full recognition they deserve.

Evaluating the proposal to amend the South African Constitution to change the length of service of Constitutional Court judges from a fixed 12-year term to an indefinite term based on age

JEREMY SARKIN

South Africa's 'interim' Constitution came into force as the basis for the first democratic election in 1994. This was the country's fourth Constitution: its antecedents were passed in 1910, 1961 and 1983.[1] These earlier Constitutions took little account of the multi-ethnic, multilingual and multicultural nature of South African society. Indeed, they catered almost exclusively for the white, Christian, Afrikaans-speaking, patriarchal minority.[2] It is not surprising therefore, that South Africa was a highly polarised and divided society.[3] Many people had been dispossessed of their land, had seen their language and cultures marginalised, and had suffered gross human rights violations.[4] The majority of South Africans had been denied access to a wide variety of amenities, institutions and opportunities, including restricted access to many places and types of employment, particularly in State institutions. The South African State systematically violated the rights of black people and subjected them to socio-economic deprivation.[5] Black South Africans were disenfranchised and many were forcibly removed from where they lived and had their citizenship removed.[6] State employees, and others acting with State sanction and assistance routinely carried out torture, assault and killings.[7] Many detentions[8] and deaths in custody

---

1 See Jeremy Sarkin, 'Innovations in the Interim and 1996 South African Constitutions' *The Review* (June 1998) 57.   2 See J. Sarkin, 'The effect of patriarchy and discrimination on apartheid South Africa's abortion laws', 4 *Buffalo Human Rights Journal* (1998) 141.   3 See J. Sarkin & Howard Varney, 'Traditional weapons, cultural expediency and the political conflict in South Africa: a culture of weapons and a culture of violence', 6 *South African Journal of Criminal Justice* 2 (1993).   4 See J. Sarkin, 'The development of a human rights culture in South Africa', 20 (3) *Human Rights Quarterly* (1998) 628, 644.   5 J. Sarkin 'Can South Africa afford justice? The need and future of a public defender system' 4, (2) (1993) *Stellenbosch Law Review* 261.   6 See D.D. Mokgatle, 'The exclusion of blacks from the South African judicial system', 3 *South African Journal on Human Rights* 44 (1987).   7 See Howard Varney & Jeremy Sarkin, 'Failing to pierce the hit squad veil: An analysis of the Malan trial', 10 *South African Journal of Criminal Justice* 141 (1997).   8 See J. Sarkin, 'Preventive detention in South Africa', in Andrew Harding & John Hatchard (eds), *Preventive detention and security law: a comparative survey* (Dordrecht, 1993), 209.

occurred. Freedom of expression and association were severely limited. As a result of parliamentary (rather than constitutional) supremacy, Parliament could enact law without the courts being able to play an effective oversight role.

The new constitutional order, the protection of individual rights and the establishment of new structures such as the Constitutional Court must be seen to be the result of several factors. These include the strength of the old order during the negotiating process, the old order's suspicion of the new environment, the adherence of the largest liberation organisation, the African National Congress (ANC), and other political parties to the notion of fundamental rights. There was also a strong belief among many South Africans that ethnicity and division ought not be part of a post-apartheid South Africa.[9]

Over a period of four years beginning in 1990, the former South African government and liberation movements successfully negotiated a two-phase transition to democracy. The first stage was the drafting of the interim Constitution[10] by 26 parties, many of whom had little apparent legitimacy and no mandate.[11] This Constitution came into force on 27 April 1994[12] and established the system for governing the country under a government of national unity. It also established new structures to protect and promote human rights such as the Constitutional Court, the Human Rights Commission, the Commission for Gender Equality and various other commissions. The interim constitution also set out the process for elected representatives to draft a final constitution after the first democratic elections. The drafting of the final Constitution by the Constitutional Assembly (CA)[13] was the second phase of the transition.[14]

After giving a background to the establishment of the Constitutional Court and some of the milieu that the court has operated in, this paper examines the

---

9 See J. Sarkin, 'The effect of constitutional borrowings on the drafting of South Africa's interim Bill of Rights and the role played by comparative and international law in the interpretation of human rights provisions by the Constitutional Court', *Journal of Constitutional Law* (1999). 10 Constitution of the Republic of South Africa Act 200 of 1993. 11 Political organisations at the negotiations included 'governments' and parties from the nominally independent homelands. The drafting of the interim Constitution took place with little public input and a degree of secrecy attributed by those involved to the need to reach a settlement. However, participants guaranteed that the drafting of the final Constitution would be a transparent affair which sought and used public input. 12 The change from parliamentary to constitutional supremacy is probably the most critical shift to occur during the transition to democracy in South Africa. Until the introduction of a justiciable Constitution in April 1994, Parliament was sovereign and there was no check on the limits of State power. 13 The Constitutional Assembly (CA) was composed of the 490 members of the National Assembly and the Senate (the second house of Parliament, now replaced by the National Council of Provinces). It was given two years to draft a constitution that accorded with the negotiated 34 constitutional principles contained in the interim (1993) Constitution. Adoption of the final Constitution required a two-thirds majority in the CA and certification by the Constitutional Court that the document complied with the 34 principles. 14 See section 68(1) read in conjunction with sections 40(1) and 48(1) of the Constitution of the Republic of South Africa Act 200 of 1993.

proposal to amend the Constitution to change the tenure of these judges of this court. At the moment, Constitutional Court judges may serve a maximum of 12 years or until they reach the age of 70, whichever comes first. The proposal is to appoint judges to serve until the age of 70, without regard to how many years they have been in the position.

This is a critical issue as the independence of the judicial arm of government from the executive and legislative arms is a key issue in any democratic State. This principle is particularly important in a constitutional democracy where a court has the power to overturn legislation and declare executive acts unlawful. It goes to the heart of the separation of powers as security of tenure, and length of tenure, is one of the essential conditions for the independence of the judiciary.[15]

THE COURTS DURING APARTHEID

South Africa has a two-tiered structure for the judiciary: Judges who sit on the superior courts such as the High Court[16] and the Supreme Court of Appeal,[17] and magistrates who sit in the magistrates' courts. During the apartheid years the judges were drawn from a very small segment of the population. All of the approximately 130 judges were white and, with one exception, all were male. At the end of 1988, all of the 144 regional court magistrates were white, while of 782 district court magistrates, 768 were white, 10 were Indian, 4 were coloured and not one was black.[18] Undoubtedly, the fact that the legal system was faced with a crisis of legitimacy[19] was due in part to its composition. Whatever their personal political preferences, judges spent their years on the bench submitting to the heavy hand of the executive.

Under apartheid, judges in South Africa were appointed entirely by the executive – by the State President on the recommendation of the Minister of Justice. Given 40 years of hegemonic white rule, the perception has been that on occasion judges were appointed for political reasons rather than merit.[20] On a number of occasions appointments were made from the ranks of the public service. As a result, commentators across an unusually broad section of the political spectrum called for a fairer process of appointment, one that would secure a wider variety of input and add representativity and credibility to the judiciary.

15 Articles 11 and 12 of Basic principles on the independence of the judiciary, UN Resolution 40/146 of 13 December 1985; article 1 of the Declaration of principles of judicial independence issued by the Chief Justices of the Australian States and Territories; and arts 18–20 of the Beijing statement of the principles of the independence of the judiciary in the Law Asia region.   **16** Formerly called the Supreme Court.   **17** Formerly called the Appelate Division.   **18** Hansard, 28 April 1989, cols 7097–8.   **19** See Charles Dlamini, 'The influence of race on the administration of justice in South Africa', *South African Journal on Human Rights* 37 (1988).   **20** See the Hoexter Commission Report into the Structure and Functioning of the Courts, RP 78/83 Part A 59.

Judges, however, attempted to explain their role in the positivist tradition as declarers of the law, not makers of the law. Criticism of the judges was often predicated on a wider view of the judicial function. The defenders of the system argued that the judges were independent of the executive and were unswervingly devoted to justice, following the dictates of their consciences whenever not precluded by the dictates of parliamentary sovereignty.[21]

Critics of the judiciary contended in strident terms that the judges have been largely executive-minded, sometimes more so than the executive itself.[22] These commentators alleged that the judiciary often failed to intercede in the interests of justice even when the law would have provided them with the latitude to do so. While there had certainly been cases of judges availing themselves of opportunities to advance the aims of justice and human rights, these were few and far between. Unquestionably, the majority of the population perceived the judiciary as acquiescing to the white legislature and helping to preserve the status quo.

RESTRUCTURING THE COURTS

During the negotiation process, most parties agreed that the composition, structure and functioning of the judiciary and legal system had to be dramatically altered. Some posited, however, that there needed to be an even more profound and radical transformation of the whole system. Most considered that the (white) judges were not suited to decide on constitutional issues because of their training, experience and temperament.

This provoked a debate about the need for a constitutional court. It was said by some that leaving the judiciary untouched and conferring added powers of judicial review would be to allow law enacted by a democratically-elected Parliament to be overturned by a court composed of a partisan and insulated minority. Others said it was premature to condemn the judiciary as being too slavish to the government to be able to play a positive role in the bill of rights era.[23]

There were some that argued for the decentralisation of the constitutional powers of the courts. Within this model, as in the United States, all courts have constitutional testing powers and can strike down legislation or administrative acts that overstep constitutional boundaries.

For South African critics of the decentralised model, the crux was that even if more judges were appointed, apartheid judges would be the benefi-

21 See generally A. van Blerk, *Judged and be judged* (Capetown, 1988).   22 Edwin Cameron, 'Legal chauvinism, executive-mindedness and Justice LC Steyn's impact on South African law', 1982 *South African Law Journal* 38.   23 M. Cowling, 'Judges and the protection of human rights in South Africa: Articulating the inarticulate premise', 1987 *South African Journal on Human Rights* 177 at 195.

ciaries of these enhanced judicial powers but were ill-suited to wield them. Proponents of a constitutional court therefore argued that only one court, meticulously selected and well-balanced, should have the powers of constitutional review.

Criticism of the centralised court idea came from a variety of sources. Some believed that such appointments would be more politically inspired than the elevation of judges to other courts. Others argued that granting all courts review powers would allow a rights culture to permeate the whole legal order. Confining review powers to the central court would prevent the infusion of this rights culture to the lower courts, so all courts should have these powers. It was further claimed that judges deciding constitutional issues should not be insulated from the cut and thrust of daily courtroom litigation, as this is an essential element of judicial experience and provides the necessary training and proficiency so necessary for constitutional adjudication. The ANC supported the creation of a constitutional court above all other courts to adjudicate only on constitutional and human rights issues.

Issues central to the establishment of a constitutional court included the length of tenure and what training the members of the court should have had. Should only legally trained individuals be considered for a seat, or should the inclusion of lay persons also be explored? Should academics be considered for appointment?

The method of judicial appointment was seen to be a critical part of the debate as has been suggested:

> [C]are must be taken that the pivotal question of the appointment of judges not be left aside ... [a] Bill of Rights enjoys little hope of being generally respected where appointment to the judiciary remains within the gift of the prime litigant in constitutional matters.[24]

One suggestion was an impartial committee drawn from members of the executive, the judiciary and the legal profession.[25] The ANC's Constitutional Committee suggested that the appointments should be done by the State President 'on the recommendation of a Judicial Service Commission, or by any other methods acceptable in a democracy, comprising of judges, practitioners and academics'. Other proposals included allowing parliamentary parties represented on a proportional basis to elect a committee to decide on appointments. Another suggestion was that a procedure be established which entails a two-stage scheme whereby one group nominates and the second body appoints the candidate.

---

24 Jeremy Gauntlett, 'Appointing and promoting judges: Which way now?', 1990 (April) *Consultus* 23 at 27. **25** Ibid.

THE INTERIM CONSTITUTION

In terms of the interim (1993) Constitution, the outcome of this debate was the creation of the Constitutional Court, above the Appellate Division, to adjudicate on constitutional and human rights issues only.[26] Under the interim Constitution, the Appellate Division was denied jurisdiction to adjudicate any matter within the jurisdiction of the Constitutional Court. In the final Constitution, however, all the higher courts are given powers of constitutional review, except the power to strike down a parliamentary statute which resides only with the Constitutional Court. In such a case, the court must affirm the decision of the lower court before the lower court's decision has the force of law.

The procedure for appointing judges to the Constitutional Court is set out in the interim Constitution. Discussions over the procedure generated great controversy during the multi-party talks that preceded finalisation of the Constitution. The controversy reflected recognition that the judicial appointments might determine the outcome of constitutional decisions. To protect the judicial structure and maintain public confidence in the legitimacy of the court's decisions, the drafters sought to avoid a politicised appointment system. The drafters therefore departed from the highly political appointment procedure followed in the United States.

The interim Constitution provided that the President of the Constitutional Court and the ten other judges are appointed for a non-renewable period of seven years, and must be South African citizens, who are 'fit and proper person[s]'. Further, the interim Constitution required that candidates either be judges of the Supreme Court, or have been advocates, attorneys or law lecturers for a minimum of ten years, or, as a result of training or experience, have expertise in the field of constitutional law. Not more than two judges could be chosen from this latter category of persons. In fact all eleven judges appointed were lawyers. The composition has, and will continue to have, profound repercussions for the type of decisions handed down. Non-lawyers might have ensured a movement away from a strict legalistic approach.

Under the Constitution, the President of the Court was appointed by the President of the country, 'in consultation with the Cabinet and after consultation with the Chief Justice'. The President, however, must have chosen the President of the Court from a list of four names supplied by the Judicial Services Commission (JSC). The first appointment to the office of President of the Court was exempted from this requirement, and the President was left free to appoint any person who met the requirements laid down for appointment.

President Mandela was also able to appoint four additional judges from the ranks of sitting judges, in consultation with the Cabinet and with the Chief

26 Section 98.

Justice. Sitting judges, therefore, make up a large component of the 11, but those selected represented the more progressive sector of the existing judiciary. This was one of the compromises agreed to during the negotiations.

Following the interim Constitution's requirements, the remaining six judges were appointed by the President, 'in consultation with the Cabinet and after consultation with the President of the Constitutional Court'. For the first set of appointments, the six were selected from a motivated list of ten submitted by the JSC. Had Mandela not wanted to appoint any of the nominees, he would have had to furnish reasons to the Commission, and the Judicial Services Commission would have been required to provide another list of names from which the President would have been obliged to appoint six judges.

In terms of the interim Constitution, the JSC was made up of four parliamentarians (senators), five executive appointments (four by the President in consultation with Cabinet), five members of the legal profession and three members representing key posts in the judiciary, a total of 17 permanent members.

THE FINAL CONSTITUTION

The final Constitution, negotiated between 1994 and 1996 and which came into force on 4 February 1997 changed a number of provisions of the interim Constitution relating to the Constitutional Court and the process by which judges are appointed. The provisions relating to tenure were also changed.[27]

The final Constitution increased the number of permanent JSC members to 23. Ten are parliamentarians,[28] five are executive appointments (four appointed by the President after consulting with political party leaders)[29] and the representation of the judiciary and the legal profession remains the same as it was in terms of the interim Constitution.

Provisions for judicial appointment in the interim Constitution were criticised for failing to balance government representation with that of civil society. The provisions in the final text now present the added problem that representation is too heavily weighted in favour of the legislative and executive arms of government.

A further difficulty is that under the 1996 Constitution, the State President is able to appoint the President and Deputy President of the Constitutional

---

27 See Jeremy Sarkin, 'The drafting of South Africa's final Constitution from a human rights perspective', 1999 *American Journal of Comparative Law* 601.   28 Four designated by the National Council of Provinces, the second house of Parliament, with a supporting vote of at least six provinces – section 178(1)(i) – and six by the National Assembly, at least three of whom must be members of opposition parties – section 178(1)(h). section 178(5) states that the parliamentary members may sit on the JSC only when judges are to be appointed and not when the body carries out its constitutional duties of giving advice on matters relating to the judiciary or administration of justice.   29 Section 178(1)(d)&(j).

Court[30] after merely consulting (and possibly rejecting) the advice of the leaders of political parties represented in Parliament and the JSC.[31] Similarly, when appointing the Chief Justice and Deputy Chief Justice, the President is simply required to consult the JSC but again may ignore its advice.[32] When other Constitutional Court judges are to be appointed,[33] the JSC must provide a list of three names more than there are vacancies.[34] This weakens the role of the JSC and increases the possibility of political appointments to the judiciary. Even more problematic is the fact that the President may refuse to appoint any of the JSC nominees. The situation is mitigated to some extent by a provision requiring the President to give reasons for such a decision,[35] and the stipulation that the President must then make the necessary appointment from a further list supplied by the JSC.[36] Fortunately, however, for the bulk of judicial appointments, the President must appoint judges recommended by the JSC.[37]

The final Constitution also changed the length of service of Constitutional Court judges. In terms of the interim Constitution these judges 'shall be appointed by the President for a non-renewable period of seven years'.[38] However, the final Constitution determines that a Constitutional Court judge is appointed for a non-renewable term of 12 years, but must retire at the age of 70. As far as other judges are concerned, the same section of the final Constitution provides that:

> Other judges hold office until they are discharged from active service in terms of an Act of Parliament.[176(2)]

THE ROLE OF THE COURT

The importance of these changes cannot and should not be underestimated, since the process of appointment to the Constitutional Court has played a pivotal role in determining the character and independence of the bench. The new process has marked a distinct departure from the judiciary of the apartheid order. The dominance of older white men has given way to diversity in age, gender, religion and outlook. This has had a major effect on the type of decision handed down by the court, although the narrow spectrum of political leanings among the justices of the Constitutional Court is of crucial significance.

---

30 Section 174(1) requires that Constitutional Court judges be South African citizens, a stipulation not made in respect of the appointment of other judges.   31 Section 174(3).   32 Section 174(3).   33 In terms of section 176(1) Constitutional Court judges hold office for a non-renewable 12-year term, but must retire regardless at the age of 70. In terms of section 174(5) at least four Constitutional Court judges must have been judges at the time they were appointed to the court.   34 Section 174(4)(a).   35 Section 174(4)(b).   36 Section 174(4)(c).   37 Section 174(6).
38 Section 99.

It is not surprising, therefore, that a high level of concurrence has characterised the decisions of the court to date.

In addition, several of the rulings indicate that the court will permit Parliament to decide policy and govern with very limited judicial hindrance. In the realm of overtly 'political' cases,[39] the Constitutional Court has shown itself to be eager to deliver decisions as quickly as possible. The Court has frequently allowed 'political' cases to come before it on direct access, a procedure denied to other important public interest cases, such as the case involving the right to legal representation.[40]

In addition, the Constitutional Court has indicated that it will not be robust in its determination of issues relating to resource allocation.[41] Thus, while second and third generation rights have found their way into the final Constitution, they will have little significance in practice, since the resource prioritisation necessary to give them effect will depend largely on government determination. Already, the court has indicated that, as far as some questions are concerned, it will play a hands-off role. This is highly problematic, because a dynamic and robust court is necessary to find a balance between competing rights and claims in a country undergoing transition. This deferential approach also has broad socio-economic implications because the legacy of apartheid continues to plague South Africa in the form of poverty, illiteracy, homelessness, and other social ills.[42] Without the court playing a dynamic role in the resolution of questions around socio-economic rights, much of this legacy of disadvantage will continue to remain the reality for most South Africans.

However, many of the decisions of the court are victories for democracy and human rights. Decisions handed down include the abolition of the death penalty and corporal punishment as sentencing options, the outlawing of civil imprisonment for debt. The court has also struck down laws that violate gender equality, has arbitrated on the role and powers of local and regional authorities, the role of traditional leaders and has upheld the constitutionality of new bail laws. The court has also determined that the old sodomy laws are unconstitutional, and has recognised the right of access to police dockets and the right to consult State witnesses.

Additionally, many decisions have related to the right to a fair trial, as well as to issues of equality, privacy, freedom of expression, provincial powers, and the application of the Bill of Rights in many different circumstances.

---

39 See Jeremy Sarkin, 'The political role of the Constitutional Court', 1997 *South African Law Journal* 134.   **40** See *S v. Vermaas; S v. Du Plessis*, 1995 (7) *Butterworths Constitutional Law Reports* 851 (CC).   **41** See Jeremy Sarkin, 'The Constitutional Court's decision on legal representation: *S v. Vermaas* and *S v. Du Plessis*,' (1996) *South African Journal on Human Rights* 55.   **42** See Jeremy Sarkin, 'The drafting of South Africa's final Constitution from a human rights perspective', 1999 *American Journal of Comparative Law* 601.

THE PROPOSED AMENDMENTS ON TERMS OF SERVICE

Various proposals have been made in the recent past to change the structure, tenure or other issues relating to the courts in general and the Constitutional Court specifically. One proposal has been that there ought to be an elimination of the separation between magistrates and judges. The draft Department of Justice white paper noted that:

> Over the years the public images of judges and magistrates have been very different in that the status of magistrates has been much lower than that of judges and that they have not enjoyed the reputation for excellence and independence that judges have.

It was therefore argued that:

> Magistrates play as important a role in the administration of justice as judges do. They deserve the same respect that is accorded to judges and the expectation of attaining appointment to the bench of the high court if they prove to be good judicial officers.

Nothing has come of this proposal partly because there was much heated opposition from sectors of the legal community. A further proposal called for the JSC to take over the work of the body that elects and oversees magistrates, the Magistrates Commission. An additional proposal made in 1999 was to merge South Africa' two highest courts: the Constitutional Court in Johannesburg and the Supreme Court of Appeal in Bloemfontein. After much heated debate this idea was shelved but may be resurrected again in the future.

In 2001 the Department of Justice proposed that the clause in the Constitution that lay downs conditions of service, including the length of the term of Constitutional Court judges, be scrapped. It argued that the Constitution ought not govern such issues and it ought to regulated by an Act of Parliament (the Judges Remuneration and Conditions of Employment Act, no. 88 of 1989).

The crucial issue is that while the Constitution in section 176 determines that Constitutional Court judges are appointed for a non-renewable terms of 12 years or until they reach the age of 70 whichever comes first, other judges, in terms of an Act of Parliament, simply serve until they reach the age of 70. Part of the reasoning for the need for this change seems to revolve around benefits for Constitutional Court judges on retirement. All other judges receive a gratuity and continue to receive a full salary after retirement. Constitutional Court judges simply receive a once-off payment.

It has been proposed that there ought to be parity amongst judges and therefore the Constitution ought to be amended to read 'judges hold office until they are discharged from active service in terms of an Act of Parliament'. If this amendment were to be enacted, Constitutional Court President Arthur Chaskalson would be allowed to carry on in that position after his 70th birthday. For this reason this proposed amendment is being called the Chaskalson amendment. If Chaskalson were to stay on, another constitutional amendment that is being proposed at the same time would see him not only be the President of the Constitutional Court, but also the Chief Justice since another amendment proposes combining the office of Chief Justice and President of the Constitutional Court. At present the Chief Justice is the head of the Supreme Court of Appeal in Bloemfontein. This position has been vacant since South Africa's first black Chief Justice Ismail Mahomed passed away. As there are different appointment routes and service conditions for these two offices, it has been argued that only type of tenure should exist for both positions. However, this does not make sense. Should an individual in the new judicial dispensation want to be both Chief Justice and President of the Constitutional Court, the more stringent appointment and tenure rules applicable to the Constitutional Court must apply. Additionally, it makes sense for a Chief Justice to serve a fixed term like all Constitutional Court judges to ensure independence and new vision on a regular basis. Although this may act as a disincentive for some who may otherwise be willing to serve in this position, there are many possible candidates and the person must fit the position.

COMPARATIVE PRACTICE ON TENURE OF CONSTITUTIONAL COURT JUDGES

State practice regarding length of office for constitutional court judges sees two situations, namely, life (sometimes with a mandatory retirement age) and fixed-term appointments. While the majority of countries have specified lengths of service, there are very few countries that offer life appointments for constitutional court judges. These include Belgium, Cyprus, Egypt, Turkey and Russia.

The Australian Constitutional Court consists of a President, a Vice-President, 12 additional members and six alternate members appointed by the Federal President. Their term of office continues until judges reach the age of 70.[43]

The Court of Cassation of Belgium is composed of judges appointed by the King. Their term of office is for life subject to a retirement age determined by law.[44] The Constitutional Court of Cyprus is composed of a Greek, a Turk and a neutral judge. The neutral judge may not be a citizen of Cyprus, the

---

43 Article 147(1) and (6) of the Constitution of Australia.   **44** Article 99 of the Constitution of Belgium.

United Kingdom or any of its colonies. Except for the neutral judge (who is appointed for a term of six years), other judges are in office until the age of 68.[45] The Egyptian Supreme Constitutional Court comprises of a quorum of seven judges. Judges must be at least 45 years old and they serve until retirement age, namely 64.[46]

The Constitutional Court of Turkey is composed of 11 regular judges and four substitute members appointed by the President. Their term lasts until the age of 65.[47] The Constitutional Court of the Russian Federation consists of 19 judges appointed by the Federal Council following nomination by the Federal President. These judges may not be replaced. Neither may they be relieved of their duties nor suspended except under procedures and grounds established by federal law.[48]

While a few States have life tenures for constitutional court judges, by far the majority of countries have fixed terms of tenure for constitutional court judges that range from six to 12 years. Countries which have fixed tenure for these judges include Bosnia and Herzegovina (five years for the first set of judges, but the next set of appointees are in position until the age of 70), Burundi (six years), Madagascar (6), Portugal (6), Morocco (7), Angola (7), Gabon (7), the Slovak Republic (7), Chile (8), Columbia (8), Croatia (8), Italy (9), Poland (9) Bulgaria (9), Burkina Faso (9), France (9), Romania (9), Thailand (9), Lithuania (9), Spain (9), Cameroon (11), the Czech Republic (11) and Germany (12 years).

The country that uses both systems is Bosnia and Herzegovina where the Constitutional Court has nine members, four selected by the House of Representatives of the Federation, two by the Assembly of the Republika Srpska, and three selected by the President of the European Court of Human Rights after consultation with the Presidency. The term of judges initially appointed, who are serving at present, is five years. They are not eligible for reappointment. Judges subsequently appointed serve until age 70.[49]

The Constitutional Court of Angola is composed of seven judges nominated by the President of the Republic, the National Assembly and the Supreme Court for a single term of seven years.[50] In Burundi the Constitutional Court is composed of an odd number of at least five judges appointed by the President for a term of six years without the possibility of reappointment.[51] The Constitutional Court of Madagascar consists of nine members, appointed by the President, the National Assembly and the Superior Council of Magistrates

45 Article 133(6) and (7).   **46** Articles 174–178 of the Constitution of Egypt. See also M.I.M. Aboul-Enein, 'The emergence of constitutional courts and the protection of individual and human rights: a comparative study' in E. Cotran & A.O. Sherif (eds), *The role of the judiciary in the protection of human rights* (London 1997), 283, 316–17.   **47** Articles 146 and 147 of the Constitution of Turkey.   **48** Article 121 of the Constitution of Russia.   **49** Article 6 of the Constitution of 1 December 1995.   **50** Article 135(1) & (2).   **51** Article 150 of the Constitution of Burundi.   **52** Article 107 of the Constitution of Madagascar.

for a single term of six years.[52] In Portugal, the Constitutional Court has 13 judges, 10 of whom are appointed by the Assembly of the Republic and three of whom are co-opted. Their term of office is also six years.[53]

The Constitutional Court of Morocco is composed of nine members appointed by the King and the President of the Chamber of the Republic. Their term of office is six years renewable. Half the posts are filled every three years.[54] The constitutional courts of Gabon and the Slovak Republic offer a term of seven years for judges.[55] In Gabon, the court comprises nine members whose term is renewable once.[56] That of the Slovak Republic consists of 10 judges appointed by the President. The Constitutional Court of Angola is composed of seven judges nominated by the President of the Republic, the National Assembly and the Supreme Court for a single term of seven years.[57]

The Constitutional Tribunal of Poland is composed of 15 judges elected by the House of Representatives for a non-renewable period of nine years.[58] The Constitutional Council of Cameroon is composed of 11 members appointed by the President of the Republic, also, for a non-renewable term of nine years.[59] The Constitutional Court of Romania is composed of nine judges appointed by the Chamber of Deputies, Senate and the President for a renewable nine-year term.[60] The Constitutional Court of Lithuania is composed of nine judges appointed by Parliament from candidates nominated by the President of the Republic, the Chairman of the Supreme Court and the Chairperson of Parliament. Their term of office is nine years, which is non-renewable.[61]

In Thailand the Constitutional Court consists of a President and 14 judges, five selected from judges of the Supreme Court of Justice, two selected from judges of the Supreme Administrative Court, five selected from those deemed qualified in law and three who are deemed qualified in political science.[62] These judges hold office for nine years and are appointed for one term only.[63]

The Constitutional Court of the Czech Republic is composed of 15 judges appointed by the President with approval of Senate for a term of 11 years.[64] In Chile, the Constitutional Court has seven members appointed by the Supreme Court, the President, the National Security Council and the Senate. The term of office is eight years subject to the retirement age of 75 years. Membership is partially replaced every four years.[65]

In Columbia judges are appointed to the Constitutional Court for a period of eight years and cannot be re-elected. They must retire at the mandatory retirement age set by law.[66] The Constitutional Court of Croatia

---

53 Article 224.   54 Article 77.   55 For the Slovak Republic, see article 134 of the Constitution. 56 Article 89 of the Constitution of Gabon.   57 Article 135(1) & (2).   58 Article 94(1).   59 Article 51(1) & (2).   60 Article 140.   61 Article 103.   62 Section 255.   63 Section 259.   64 Article 84(1) & (2).   65 Articles 75 and 81 of the Constitution of Chile.   66 Article 231 of the Constitution of Colombia.

is composed of 11 judges elected by the Chamber of Representatives for terms of eight years.[67] The Constitutional Court of Bulgaria consists of 12 justices. The National Assembly appoints four, four are appointed by the President and the remaining four are elected at a joint meeting of the justices of the Supreme Court of Appeals and the Supreme Administrative Court. Their term of office is nine years without the possibility of reappointment. Membership of the court is renewed once every three years in accordance with legal procedures.[68]

In Burkina Faso, the Supreme Court has a Constitutional Chamber. This Chamber consists of the President of the Supreme Court, three magistrates appointed by the State President and three persons named by the President of the Assembly of the Deputies of the People. Except for the President of the Court, members of the Constitutional Chamber are appointed for a single term of nine years. The membership is renewed by a third every three years.[69] The Constitutional Council in France consists of nine members whose term of office lasts nine years. Their term is not renewal.[70] Former presidents of France are, however, ex-officio members of the court for life.

The Constitutional Court of Romania is composed of nine justices appointed by the Chamber of Deputies, Senate and the President. Their term of office is a non-renewable term of nine years.[71] In Spain, the Constitutional Court is composed of 12 members appointed by the King for a term of nine years. Members retire, and new members are appointed, every three years to ensure continuity.[72]

The Constitutional Court of Slovenia is composed of nine judges elected by the State Assembly on the proposal of the President. Their term of office is nine years without the possibility of re-election.[73] The Italian Constitutional Court is composed of 15 judges appointed by the President of the Republic, Parliament, and the Ordinary and Administrative Supreme Courts. Their term of office is nine years, non-renewable.[74] The Federal Constitutional Court of Germany comprises of judges appointed by the *Bundestag* and the *Bundestat*. Their term of office is 12 years with no possibility of reappointment.[75]

This comparative survey shows a large number of constitutional States offer fixed term contracts for constitutional court judges. The length of the terms ranges from 6 to 12 years.

---

67 Article 123 of the Constitution of Croatia. **68** Article 147 of the Constitution of Bulgaria. **69** Article 153 of the Constitution of Burkina Faso. **70** Article 56 of the Constitution of France. **71** Article 140 of Constitution of Romania. **72** Article 159 of the Constitution of Spain. **73** Article 165 of the Constitution of Slovenia. **74** Article 135(1), (2) & (3). **75** See article 94 of the Constitution of Germany and D.C. Umbach, 'The independence of the judiciary and the rule of law' in Cotran & Sherif (eds), *The role of the judiciary*, op. cit., 246.

Table of the terms of South African Constitutional Court judges

Judge	Birth date	Beginning of term of office	Present tenure end date
Chaskalson	24/11/1931	07/1994	11/2001 (70)
Kriegler	29/11/1932	10/1994	11/2002 (70)
Ackerman	14/01/1934	08/1994	01/2004 (70)
Sachs	30/01/1935	10/1994	01/2005 (70)
Goldstone	26/10/1938	08/1994	07/2006 (12 years)
Langa	25/03/1939	10/1994	07/2006 (12 years)
Mokgoro	19/10/1950	10/1994	07/2006 (12 years)
O'Regan	17/09/1957	10/1994	07/2006 (12 years)
Madala	13/07/1937	08/1994	10/2006 (12 years)
Yacoob	03/03/1948	02/1998	02/2010(12 years)
Ngcobo	01/03/1953	08/1999	08/2011(12 years)

THE DEBATE IN SOUTH AFRICA

The amendment proposing changing the length of tenure of Constitutional Court judges is becoming very contentious. Various role players have come out either supporting or opposing this amendment.

South Africa's official opposition, the Democratic Alliance, has argued that it was decided by all the political parties during the negotiations that constitutional judges should serve a single term in order to 'underpin their independence and prevent atrophication, which has been a real problem in the United States'.[76] This party has therefore proposed that the terms of these judges should only be amended to allow Constitutional Court judges to serve until the age of 75, provided that they had not yet served their full 12 years and that their health permit it.

Some judges are also against the proposed change. Judge Bernard Ngoepe, Judge President of the Pretoria and Johannesburg High Courts, has signed a memorandum on behalf of the 55 judges in his division registering an objection to the amendment.[77] The memorandum argued amongst other things that:

> It has always been accepted that the Constitutional Court wields immense political power. Very importantly, as the apex Court, it has

---

76 *Business Day*, 21 August 2001. **77** Memorandum by the Pretoria and Johannesburg judges of the Transvaal Provincial Division and Witwatersrand Local Division re: the proposed amendment of the Constitution to give judges of the Constitutional Court the same tenure as other judges of the Supreme Court of Appeal and the High Court.

the final say on issues placed before it. As it has the last word on the interpretation and application of the Constitution, its pronouncements influence the nation's political course. Also, as its definitions and understanding of the values enshrined in the Constitution constitute a bench mark, its pronouncements materially influence the nation's moral course. The question which immediately arises is whether, in a democratic society, anybody who wields such political power and moral authority with a final say, should hold office for life.

The memorandum further argues:

it was agreed [during the negotiation process] that it was essential for the judges of that court to have limited tenure so that the jurisprudence of the court would not stagnate. There would be a regular replenishment of personnel who would be fully cognisant of changed and changing circumstances in the country. The provisions of both the Interim Constitution and the final Constitution reflect this agreement. Amendments to a Constitution are as a general rule undesirable. In a young democracy such as ours this is particularly true and more so when they relate to the tenure of public office bearers ... Such amendments create a very bad precedent. It must also be borne in mind that the tenure of the Constitutional Court judges was originally seven years and it was increased when the new Constitution was enacted. A second extension is now sought ... Our Constitutional Court is modelled on the Continental System (eg Germany, France and Spain) where the tenure of the judges is limited. Our Constitutional Court cannot be compared to the US Supreme Court which hears disputes of all kinds apart from constitutional disputes.

Responding to the memorandum, Acting Chief Justice Joos Hefer has noted that when the committee that prepared the amendment for Cabinet asked the various Judges President, all but Ngoepe had had no difficulty and that this decision was ultimately a political decision, not a judicial one (*Sunday Times*, 20 August 2001).

Justice Chaskalson has also responded to this document, noting that his major concern was for the institution and not for himself.[78] He stated that stability and continuity were crucial during the establishment of a new legal order and that judges serving on similar courts in the US and the United Kingdom and other Commonwealth countries had tenure similar to that proposed (*Sunday Times*, 20 August 2001). Chaskalson's two contentions can be countered by noting that in the main constitutional courts around the world have fixed periods of tenure as the norm. The argument around continuity

---

78 *Sunday Times*, 20 August 2001.

and stability has also been made in a newspaper editorial that argued that it takes time for such a court to settle down and develop its philosophy and that the envisaged changes would strengthen the institution and entrench continuity. The newspaper noted:

> on balance, the 'Chaskalson amendment' is a necessary change to the Constitution – a change that could strengthen the court and entrench the continuity that is essential to the development of sound constitutional jurisprudence. It takes time for an 11-judge court to settle down and develop its philosophy. The current rules effectively mean clearing the court out after 12 years, which would undo such progress, undermining that crucial continuity. Furthermore there is a short supply of jurists able enough for the job. The new amendment allows those that there are to hang around longer. The downside is, of course, that the amendment could be used to entrench weak, pliant judges. But that is a risk worth taking.[79]

THE ARGUMENTS

The major reasons advanced in favour of these amendments are to ensure stability and continuity of the Constitutional Court. However, a fixed period does not necessarily undermine stability and continuity. In fact, the negotiators of the final Constitution made changes to the provisions of the interim Constitution regarding the tenure of Constitutional Court judges specifically to achieve these goals. A 12-year period provides stability and continuity, since judges do not all retire at the same time. As the table indicates, not more than four judges retire at any one time. That situation is rare as, in general, judges will retire at somewhat regular intervals, allowing new judges to be appointed and work with members of the court who have already served for a number of years. Do individual judges serving on a multi-member court necessarily result in continuity? Is it not the values of the Constitution that ensure continuity? A useful amendment might be, after sufficient debate, the institution of a system of regularly-spaced retirements. This might take the form of one judge retiring every year, three justices retiring every four years.

While continuity is important, a Constitutional Court needs a regular influx of new blood. New members will bring in new views and opinions. The effect of making regular conditions of service apply to Constitutional Court judges would lengthen the terms of service for judges about to retire and allow the youngest judge to serve for more than 30 years. This would severely affect the dynamism and legitimacy that the court presently enjoys. In the United States,

---

79 'Viva Chaskalson amendment', *Mail & Guardian*, 17 August 2001.

for example, members of that country's highest court, the Supreme Court, have life tenure, and judges often serve for more than 35 years. This feature has had a severely negative effect on that court.

The strongest argument about the need for fixed terms for these types of judges relates to how much constitutional responsibility the judiciary should enjoy over institutions such as the executive and the legislature to ensure constitutional legitimacy. According to this argument, the legislature and the government are subject to popular review at regular and stipulated intervals, ranging from four to seven years. The period of time that presidents and other senior office bearers may remain in office is often limited to a fixed number of years. It follows that, since Constitutional Court judges participate in policy making and exercise creative choices between contending social and economic interests in the political cases that come before them, they should also be subjected to constitutional accountability for their judicial decisions through fixed term appointments.[80] It has been argued that appointing this kind of judge for life offends the principle of constitutional legitimacy. Constitutional Court judges do much more policy work and make many more decisions that effect the direction of a nation and other courts than other judges do. Their position and power is vastly different.

On the one hand, fixed term appointments for Constitutional Court judges removes judges who have built up expertise and experience in such matters. Fixed term appointments may in this way jeopardise a sense of institutional commitment and history and reduce public respect for the court. While a fixed term may see judges who are experienced and competent having to retire when they may usefully serve for more time, members of the court who are lazy, erratic, and incompetent will not take up space for many years.[81] Even good judges may become stale if they are appointed for many years.[82] Fixed term contracts therefore regularly renew the vigour, vision, enthusiasm and energy of the court. They also help to ensure that the court remains in touch with the community it serves. A problem with fixed term appointments for judges and prospective judges is uncertainty about the future once the contract has ended. In relation to the 12 year-term of the German Constitutional Court, which is very similar to the South African situation, McWhinney has wondered 'what can an ex-judge do, after retirement at the end of the twelve year term, if he or she is still young?'[83] However, should we change the tenure of the judges for this reason even if it were true? A person who has served in such a high-profile position is in a good position

80 E. McWhinney, *Supreme courts and judicial law making: constitutional tribunals and constitutional review* (Dordrecht, 1986), 51–7. **81** See *Report of the Canadian Bar Association Task Force on the Independence of Federal Administrative Tribunals and Agencies in Canada* (later referred to as the *Canadian Bar Association report*) (1990) 87. **82** *Canadian Bar Association report*, 87. **83** McWhinney (above n. 80) 55. **84** McWhinney, 55; *Canadian Bar Association Report*, 79–80.

to serve as a judge in another court, become a university professor or be appointed as an ambassador.

While it could be argued that appointment to the Constitutional Court requires interrupting other pursuits that may be more rewarding than a fixed term judicial appointment, nobody who has actually been eligible for office has done so. In theory, fixed term contracts might in theory limit the range of eligible candidates for appointment to the court, especially younger candidates, but in practice this has not been the case.[84] Judge Kate O'Regan was not yet 40 years old when she was appointed to the court, and she did not make any such objection.

It has been argued by some that all judges should have the same conditions of service, but this does not take into account the very different role played by the Constitutional Court. When negotiations on the political settlement which led to the transfer of power focused on the question of having a supreme Constitution and Bill of Rights, it was argued that a special court with special powers was needed to take on the new responsibilities of being able to test legislation and, if necessary, strike down laws or government action. It was argued that only the Constitutional Court should have this power. This new court would have, and has, the power to strike down laws made by the democratically-elected Parliament of South Africa. In terms of the final Constitution, other courts may rule on the constitutionality of legislation, but any ruling of constitutional invalidity must be confirmed by the Constitutional Court before it takes effect. The Constitutional Court has various powers which no other court enjoys. It has unique power to influence policy making and political choices.

Because the court has such strong powers, the negotiators followed the world trend of ensuring constitutional judges have fixed terms of appointment. Term limits help to balance the enormous powers of constitutional courts, since tenure beyond a 10–15 year period is seen as giving too much power to judges who may become isolated from society and immune from criticism.

The debate about which system to use has not focused sufficiently on the need to ensure transformation of the bench. Most of the members of the court are white and, of the 11 judges, only two are women. Implementing longer terms of service would entrench the present race and gender composition for the foreseeable future. The need to ensure greater demographic representivity is viewed by many as imperative. It is also a demand entrenched in the Constitution.

The process that has been followed on this matter is problematic. This proposal was only made in the middle of 2001, and insufficient time has been allowed for public debate and comment. It is strange that this matter had not

---

85 See J. Sarkin, 'Problems and challenges facing South Africa's Constitutional Court: An evaluation of its decisions on capital and corporal punishment', 1996 *South African Law Journal* 71; J. Sarkin, 'Abortion and the courts' in S. Liebenberg (ed.), *Towards a final Constitution: a gender perspective* (Capetown, 1995) 217.

yet been referred to the parliamentary committee which investigates possible amendments to the Constitution at the time of writing.

Another problem is removing the issue of the tenure of constitutional judges from the Constitution and placing it into the realm of ordinary legislation, making it susceptible to the whims of Parliamentary majorities. Thus, tenure could easily be amended in the future without the same degree of scrutiny as a constitutional amendment would require. This could reduce judicial independence insofar as tenure could be seen to depend on judges doing the will of the political majority.

Extending the tenure of South African Constitutional Court judges is problematic, especially at this point in our democracy. While it recognised that Constitutional Court judges only receive a generous payment at the conclusion of their term of office while other judges receive a pension, this anomaly can be rectified by dealing with pensions and other benefits without changing their length of service.

CONCLUSION

The courts in many countries have become battle zones for issues that were previously the domain of politics. For this reason, independent and fixed-period constitutional courts have been established. One of the best safeguards of a rights-based democracy is an independent judiciary, intrepid in its willingness to uphold the principle of separation of powers, and acting as the guardian of fundamental human rights and freedoms.

In South Africa, the presence of progressive-minded individuals, women and academics on the Constitutional Court bench has already produced decisions that augur fairly well for the future.[85] However, there is a danger that the court will not be sufficiently robust in its quest to attain legitimacy.

The first Constitutional Court appointees have often been reluctant to strike down post-1994 legislation or executive action taken during the democratic dispensation. The court has also shown that it is reluctant to push the programme of socio-economic change that was envisaged when socio-economic rights were included in the Constitution. It fears that, should it be seen to be critical of the new government and its laws, it will be criticised for being a largely white male institution incapable of supporting the ethos of transformation. The court may therefore continue to favour approving governmental action and legislative enactment at the expense of individual liberty. This has begun to shift in the new millennium.

Tampering with the judicial appointment and tenure procedures affects judicial independence, if only from a societal perception point of view. Changes to the length of tenure are often seen to be rewards by the State to judges who have found in favour of the State and less than robust when examining issues in the realm of government. This can undermine the legitimacy of the courts.

In any case, constitutional amendments should not be undertaken unless they are really necessary. The more frequently the Constitution is amended, the easier it is to amend it again. Tinkering with the Constitution could present real dangers to our young democracy.

Postscript

Parliament amended Section 176 of the Constitution to read: '(1) A Constitutional Court judge **[is appointed]** holds office for a non-renewable term of 12 years, **[but must retire at]** <u>or until he or she attains</u> the age of 70, <u>whichever occurs first, except where an act of parliament extends the term of office of a Constitutional Court judge.</u>'

Bold = deletion
<u>Underline</u> = insertion

Who defends the judges? The false hope of an independent judiciary

ESTELLE FELDMAN

The idea of an independent judiciary based on the separation of powers is unattainable in practice. Yet, it is the basis on which every democracy places its hope for the protection of its citizens against the power of an overweening executive. In addition to an independent judiciary, it is necessary to create other independent institutions at a supra-national and at an intra-national level. Such institutions include the international human rights courts and national ombudsmen. Nevertheless, the maintenance of an independent judiciary, or any other tribunal that offers redress to a wronged citizen, is always at the whim of executive will.

THE JUDICIARY UNDER ATTACK[1]

The catalyst for this paper has been the forced ending of the independence of the judiciary of Zimbabwe at the beginning of the twenty-first century. This is on-going and it has not been well documented in the media. Certainly the responsible press has mentioned some of the threats and some of the actions against judges within the context of their overall coverage of the collapse of democracy in Zimbabwe. Nevertheless, one looked in vain for declarations of outrage by other democratic judiciaries or by leading politicians, or, indeed, a campaign of any continuity by journalists to disseminate and inform the wider public on this gross attack on the fundamental bastion of democracy. It is believed that any public declarations of condemnation by influential individuals or groups outside Zimbabwe at that time would probably have resulted in the death of the Chief Justice. As it was, it has been reported that he was forced to resign under threat of his own government informing him that his safety, the safety of his judges and the safety of his family could no longer be guaranteed.[2]

While the events in Zimbabwe are particularly horrifying, the possibility of threats to the tenure of senior judges who disagree with executive views is

1 The author has had privileged communication on this topic with international senior jurists over a period of years. It is important to acknowledge their courage and tenacity while maintaining the confidence of their trust and candour.   2 A media Internet search using the London *Financial Times* as a search engine of all publications during the period when Chief Justice Gubbay resisted and finally succumbed to the government's insistence on his resignation resulted in approximately a dozen results. Of the handful of major western newspapers represented none of them could be described as dealing with this issue as a major public interest news item.

always present. The Chief Justice of Swaziland is fighting unilateral moves to amend the nature of his contract. A decision to reduce the age of retirement, if upheld, would force him to vacate the bench several years earlier than agreed. The Chief Justice has instituted legal proceedings with the Court of Appeal.

The relationship between the judiciary, the executive and the legislature is always a sensitive one. In Ireland, in 1999, a Circuit Court and a Supreme Court judge were alleged to have compromised the judicial process in the sentence review of a conviction for dangerous driving causing death.[3] The Government obtained their resignations. This obviated the necessity of impeachment proceedings and the possibility of a head-on collision between the judiciary and the legislature. In the rush to condemn, and also to require accountability from, these individuals alleged to have damaged the impartiality of justice, senior politicians, supported by elements in the media, were demanding that conditions in the form of 'spill the beans or get nothing' be attached to the judges' pensions.

I will be returning to the subject presently. Here I need merely note that the present system is unsatisfactory in that it offers only one disciplinary sanction for alleged judicial misconduct – the stark process of impeachment – which clearly will not be appropriate for minor transgressions. If a particular case appears to fall short of warranting impeachment, either because of its relative lack of seriousness or because of problems of proof, politicians may find themselves embroiled in a process of negotiation with the judge. This may not be the best way to support the principle of judicial independence.

INDEPENDENCE OF THE JUDICIARY

It is accepted that a democratic political system is not of itself adequate where citizens want to appeal against decisions made by public officials.[4] An independent, impartial and informed judiciary holds a central place in the realisation of just, honest, open and accountable government.

> Indeed, a judiciary must be independent if it is to perform its constitutional role of standing between the government and the people, reviewing actions taken by the government and public officials to determine whether or not they comply with the standards laid down in the Constitution, and with the laws enacted by the legislature.[5]

3 This is generally known as the Sheedy Affair.   **4** See R. Martin and E. Feldman, *Access to information in developing countries* (Berlin, 1998) at 26. Also an Internet publication: www.transparency. de/documents/work-papers/martin-feldman/index.html   **5** Quotation from an official

Further, only an independent judiciary may be more likely to make decisions that appear to go counter to government interests. *A fortiori*, it is of special significance in relation to international treaties and covenants, especially those dealing with human rights.

A recent publication from the Irish judiciary emphasises the reliance of the people on this independence:

> Judicial independence exists for the benefit of the people. It ensures public confidence in the administration of justice. Without that confidence, the rule of law would be threatened. In particular, the doctrine of the separation of powers, the distribution of the different functions of government between its three arms, executive, legislative and judicial, which lies at the heart of our constitutional structures, would be imperilled if the judiciary could not resolve issues in which the interests of the executive or the legislature were at stake without the threat of dismissal or some other sanction hanging over their hands.[6]

IRELAND

Judicial power

It should be noted that the doctrine of the separation of powers is about balance rather than absolutes and, in a polity where the Constitution is supreme, there must be some mechanism for the interpretation of that Constitution. The Irish Constitution firmly confers this role on the Supreme Court, the Court of Final Appeal.[7] Furthermore, the independence of the judiciary, who take a constitutionally prescribed oath to execute their office without 'fear or favour',[8] is guaranteed by Article 35.2: 'All judges shall be independent in the exercise of their judicial functions and subject only to this Constitution and the law.'

The judiciary, as interpreters of the Constitution, might have the advantage over the other organs of State. The earliest modern authority which defined the judicial power was *Lynham v. Butler (No. 2)*[9] in which Kennedy CJ stated the attitude of the judiciary to defending their power: 'The judicial power of

communiqué of the Commonwealth Law Ministers Meeting, held in Mauritius in 1993, cited in Transparency International *Source Book on National Integrity Systems* (www.transparency.de 1997), Chapter 10: The Judicial System. **6** *Committee on Judicial Conduct and Ethics* Pn. 9440 (Government Stationery Office, Dublin, December 2000) at 3. **7** Búnreacht na hÉireann (The Irish Constitution), Article 34.4. **8** Id., Article 34.5.1. **9** [1933] IR 74.

the State deposited with us and the other constitutional Courts will naturally be the subject of our special watchfulness even to the point of jealousy.'[10] Yet, '[i]t has long been a practice of the judiciary in this State not to act as a judge in a case where they have an interest, or where there are grounds on which a reasonable person might fear that in respect of the issues involved he would not get an independent hearing.'[11]

Nevertheless, where the legal question concerned involves deciding between the respective jurisdictions of the organs of State, the judges will decide. *Murphy v. Dublin Corporation* is one of the leading cases in which the exercise of the executive power of the State and the administration of justice was distinguished:

> The proper exercise of the functions of the three powers of government set up under the Constitution, namely, the legislative, the executive and the judicial, is in the public interest. There may be occasions when the different aspects of the public interest [pull in contrary directions]. If the conflict arises during the exercise of the judicial power then, in my view, it is the judicial power which will decide which public interest shall prevail. This does not mean that the court will always decide that the interest of the litigant shall prevail. It is for the court to decide which is the superior interest in the circumstances of the particular case and to determine the matter accordingly. As the legislative, executive, and judicial powers of government are all exercised under and on behalf of the State, the interest of the State, as such, is always involved. The division of powers does not give paramountcy in all circumstances to any one of the organs exercising the powers of government over the other.[12]

It is clear from *Murphy* that, when there is a conflict with the State as to where the public interest lies, it is the court that will decide.[13] Of course, that assumes that the disputants not only have access to the courts but that the case is justiciable.

Legal protection of individual rights
Post the 1937 Constitution, the Irish superior courts generally find the balance of the public interest in protecting, if not representing, individual rights against

---

10 Id., at 97. 11 *Dublin Well Woman Centre v. Ireland* [1995] 1 ILRM 408 at 421 (*per* Denham J). 12 [1972] IR 215 at 233 (*per* Walsh, J). 13 The substantive issue related to executive privilege over documents and the decision over discovery was held to be an administration of justice. *Murphy* was affirmed in *Ambiorix v. Minister for the Environment (No.1)* [1992] 1 IR 277, [1992] ILRM 209 and endorsed in *Skeffington v. Rooney* [1997] 1 IR 22, [1997] 2 ILRM 56.

the power of the State. The right of the Courts to intervene in both the legislative and executive arenas found expression in a far-reaching manner in *Crotty v. An Taoiseach*. In this case Raymond Crotty, a private citizen, successfully sought an injunction to prevent the government ratifying the Single European Act on the basis that the agreement allegedly infringed the Constitution.

Finlay CJ held that in certain circumstances it is the clear and express right and duty of the High and Supreme Courts to intervene in respect of both the legislative and executive functions:

> With regard to the Executive, the position would appear to be as follows. This Court has on appeal from the High Court a right and duty to interfere with the activities of the Executive in order to protect or secure the constitutional rights of individual litigants where such rights have been or are being invaded by those activities or where activities of the Executive threaten an invasion of such rights.
>
> This right of intervention is expressly vested in the High Court and Supreme Court by the provisions of Article 34.3.1° and Article 34.4.3° of the Constitution and impliedly arises from the form of the judicial oath contained in Article 34.5.1° of the Constitution.[14]

In his analysis of the development of constitutional law under Chief Justice Ó Dálaigh, Professor James Casey, a noted constitutional expert, stated that the Ó Dálaigh court 'impressed upon the public mind the Constitution's potential for the redress of grievances which had somehow contrived to escape the attention of the legislature.'[15] Supreme Court decisions have had significant long-term legislative impact in regard to personal rights including the right to bodily integrity,[16] the right to privacy[17] and the right to personal liberty.[18]

Controlling the executive

A case of particular interest in highlighting the exercise of judicial control over the executive is *Howard v. Commissioners of Public Works.*[19] *Howard* was a planning case involving a consolidated appeal from two distinct High Court judgments each separately relating to the State's intent to build interpretative cen-

---

14 *Crotty v. An Taoiseach* [1987] IR 713 at 772. **15** Casey, 'The development of constitutional law under Chief Justice Ó Dálaigh' (1978) DULJ 3, at 3. **16** *Ryan v. AG* [1965] IR 294. **17** *McGee v. AG* [1974] IR 284. **18** *In re Article 26 and the Offences against the State (Amendment) Bill 1940* [1940] IR 470. **19** *Howard v. Commissioner of Public Works and Byrne v. Commissioners of Public Works* [1994] 1 IR 101. The appeal in *Howard* was in relation to the Mullaghmore interpretative centre.

tres in areas of extraordinary environmental importance and beauty. In the High
Court, in *Byrne v. Commissioners of Public Works*,[20] Lynch J held that the Local
Government (Planning and Development) Act 1963 did not apply to the State,
specifically the Commissioners of Public Works. This appeal was taken by envi-
ronmentalists, whereas in *Howard* the State appealed the decision of Costello J,
who held that the Act did apply to the State. In the Supreme Court, with one
dissentient,[21] the judgment of Costello J that the Commissioners had acted *ultra
vires* was upheld.

Separation of powers

All of this hardly seems consistent with an exercise of the separation of powers
as distinct functions. If in Ireland the legislature can bind the executive, and
the judiciary can intervene in respect of the functions of both the legislature
and the executive, what, then, is there restraining the powers of the State to
prevent the executive or the legislature from controlling the judges so that all
law is administered and interpreted, including Constitutional interpretation,
for the benefit of the Government and the politicians? Is it possible for the
Government to identify those judges who seem to render it support in their
judgments, and favour them over other judges? The answer to these questions
lies in the rule of law and the independence of the judiciary.

Professor David Gwynn Morgan, a prominent constitutional and administrative law authority, in his key text on the separation of powers, has described
the rule of law as a fundamental principle whereby 'the Government is subject
to the law, as enforced through the courts and this ... has never been regarded
as a violation of the separation of powers'.[22]

Disciplining judges

In 1999 the Sheedy Affair highlighted the stark reality that there is no means
of disciplining a judge short of the impeachment process outlined in Article 35
of the Constitution. The Twenty-second Amendment of the Constitution Bill,
2001 introduced as a constitutional remedy, failed to be put to a referendum
through a combination of government ineptitude and inter-party political point
scoring. Consequently, the Irish judiciary remain vulnerable in this regard.

THE MYTH OF CERTAINTY AND CONSTANCY OF LAW

Morgan describes law as follows:

> The word 'law' refers to a fairly detailed code of rules which is the
> antithesis of policy or discretion – so that the same decision can be

---

20 [1994] 1 IR 91. The appeal in *Byrne* was in relation to the Luggala interpretative centre. **21**
Egan, J. **22** D.G. Morgan, *The separation of powers in the Irish Constitution* (Dublin, 1997) at 33.

anticipated whether a rule is applied by Judge A or Judge B. The merit of this is that it means that the laws can establish and underpin rights because (assuming that we are dealing with prospective laws) they make it possible for everyone affected – the owner of a right and those subject to it – to be confident, even without a court judgment, as to both the right's existence and its extent.[23]

Obviously this description does not solely apply to an Irish context. Nevertheless, allowing for the fact that judges sitting on the same bench are presumed to know the law, there can be quite a significant divergence of opinion in applying the law and delivering judgments. This is not only clear from the *Byrne* and *Howard* decisions referred to above, but dissenting judgments are commonplace. Indeed, dissents, which can be indicative of deep philosophical divisions between members of the same bench, provide some of the more pithy and quotable judgments.

In the United States Supreme Court of the late 80s, the members of the court had polarised into two extremes and '[j]udicial actions that might strike a Brennan or a Marshall as the height of judicial statesmanship smacked of judicial tyranny to a Rehnquist or a Scalia'.[24] In a contempt of court appeal, the majority held that a Federal district judge had exceeded his authority in the manner in which he had sanctioned local representatives for their continuing contempt: they had consistently blocked attempts to implement the judge's order in relation to building desegregated housing in the Yonkers district of New York. In a dissent in which he was joined by Justices Marshall, Blackmun, and Stevens, Justice Brennan wrote: 'The Court's decision today creates no new principle of law; indeed, it invokes no principle of any sort.'[25]

The celebrated dissent of Kennedy CJ in the 1930s Irish case of the *State (Ryan) v. Lennon*[26] highlights the dangers to fundamental human rights and individual liberty of a positivist and literal interpretation of a constitution by judges. The question for consideration was a challenge to Amendment 17 to the Free State Constitution. Fitzgibbon J, in a caustic judgment dripping with contempt for the members of the Oireachtas (Parliament) who had passed the amending legislation,[27] held that the effect of this amendment was to deny citizens 'the complicated British and American machinery of an independent judiciary, trial by jury and *habeas corpus*'.[28] He nevertheless affirmed the law and was joined by Murnaghan J, who was equally scathing in his opinion of the new statute: 'The extreme rigour of the Act in question is such that its provisions pass far

23 Id., at 55. **24** E. Lazarus, *Closed chambers: the rise, fall, and future of the modern supreme court* (New York, 1999) at 44. Many thanks to my colleague Alex Schuster for providing this book as source material. **25** 493 U.S. 265 (1990) Quoted in id. at 46. **26** [1935] IR 170. **27** Constitution (Amendment 17) Act, 1931. **28** [1935] IR 170 at 233.

beyond anything having the semblance of legal procedure and the judicial mind is staggered at the very complete departure from legal methods in use in these courts.' [29] Chief Justice Kennedy stood alone in his declaration of unconstitutionality, referred to in *Kelly* as 'the first landmark in the modern Irish history of the view that a natural law of divine origin is above human law, however positively expressed'.[30]

Also addressing personal liberty, in 1942 in the United Kingdom, Lord Atkin famously dissented from the interpretation of the Defence (General) Regulations 1939 adopted by the majority of the Appellate Committee of the House of Lords. Describing the conclusions reached by the other judges as 'fantastic' he said that he had 'listened to arguments which might have been addressed acceptably to the Court of King's Bench in the time of Charles I'. [31] He believed that there was only one authority which might justify the suggested method of construction, Humpty Dumpty in Lewis Carroll's *Alice through the Looking Glass* which he then cited: 'When I use a word ... it means just what I choose it to mean, neither more nor less.'[32] Lord Atkin's dissent is now recognised as stating the law correctly.[33]

SUPRANATIONAL OVERSIGHT

Lord Atkin's judgment is also notable for the following comment: 'I view with apprehension the attitude of judges who on a mere question of construction when face to face with claims involving the liberty of the subject show themselves more executive minded than the executive.'[34] It is for this reason that State Supreme Courts are not always the most reliable in defending the human rights of their citizens.

The concept of human rights is rooted in philosophical developments in Western Europe.[35] This has resulted in international human rights instruments which are products of a European cultural, political, and legal background and which promise inalienable rights to individuals. The earliest of these instruments is the *Universal Declaration of Human Rights,* proclaimed in December 1948, which was reaffirmed by the *International Covenant on Civil and Political Rights* and the *International Covenant on Economic, Social and Cultural Rights* in 1966, already having found endorsement in the *European Convention on Human Rights*, promulgated in 1953. It is not surprising, given the colonial history of the Americas and the political dominance of the United States, that the 1978 *American Convention on*

---

29 Id. at 237.   **30** Kelly, *The Irish Constitution* 3rd ed., eds. Hogan and Whyte (Dublin, 1994) at 673.   **31** *Liversidge v. Anderson* [1942] AC 206, 244. As quoted in D. Pannick, *Judges* (Oxford, 1988) at 20. See id. at 21 for a description of the shunning of Lord Atkin in the immediate aftermath.   **32** Id. at 245.   **33** Lord Atkin's dissent was affirmed first by the Privy Council in *Nakkuda v. Jayartne* (1950) [1951] AC 66 and by the House of Lords in *IRC v. Rossminster* [1980] AC 952.   **34** [1942] AC 206, at 245.   **35** This section is adapted from Martin and Feldman, op. cit.

Human Rights is also expressed in similar form, promising protection for the individual against the State. These Conventions are upheld by international commissions and courts established for this purpose and to which aggrieved individuals may apply for redress.

The 1986 *African Charter on Human and Peoples' Rights* relies upon African documents and traditions, rather than United Nations' declarations and covenants. Individual rights are clearly restricted 'within the law'. The formulation does not in any way establish any limits on the extent to which national legislation may curtail rights, 'which leaves it entirely up to the individual State party to decide how real the freedom of expression may actually be.'[36]

For instance, in the area of access to information, where a State's constitution does not guarantee the right in question or where national legislation is lacking or deficient, the provisions of the African Charter 'do not constitute independently an individual right which can be disputed in the national courts.'[37] Consequently, the phrase 'within the law' means that a State can claim to be acting quite legally even if it legislates for access to information procedures that, for example, include stringent censorship and strict press control.

MARGIN OF APPRECIATION

The doctrine of the margin of appreciation was first explicitly articulated by the European Court of Human Rights (ECHR) in 1976 in a freedom of expression case.[38] According to Mahoney, it is in essence, judicial self-restraint exercised by the ECHR in deference to the Contracting States in their capacity as amenders of the Convention and 'to the national authorities in spheres where in a democratic society there is a legitimate scope for difference of opinion.'[39] The case law since *Handyside* shows that the doctrine has general application to the Convention. '[D]epending upon the nature of the context and the language of the text in issue, the [Court] will show a greater or lesser deference to the decision of the national authorities. It is up to the parties to convince the Court that the circumstances call for one approach rather than the other.'[40]

As an example, the Court's 1996 judgment in *Goodwin v. United Kingdom* states:

> Freedom of expression, as enshrined in Article 10, is subject to a
> number of exceptions which, however, must be narrowly interpreted

---

36 C. Welch and R. Meltzer (eds), *Human rights and development in Africa* (Albany, 1984) at 157. **37** G. Lindholdt, *Questioning the universality of human rights* (London, 1997) at 88. **38** Article 10. *Handyside v. United Kingdom*, 7 Dec. 1976, ECtHR Series A Vol 24. **39** P. Mahoney, 'Judicial activism and judicial self-restraint in the European Court of Human Rights: two sides of the same coin', 11 *Human Rights Journal* 57, 78–88 (1990) at 88. **40** Id., at 80.

and the necessity for any restrictions must be convincingly established.'[41]
In this judgment the ECHR also described the relationship between
its role and that of the individual State. 'The [Convention organs'] task,
in exercising [their] supervisory jurisdiction, is not to take the place of
the competent national authorities but rather to review under Article
10 the decisions they delivered pursuant to their power of appreciation. This does not mean that [their] supervision is limited to ascertaining whether the respondent State exercised its discretion reasonably, carefully and in good faith; what [they have] to do is to look at
the interference complained of in the light of the case.[42]

The Inter-American Convention also allows a margin of appreciation to
the Contracting States. In an advisory opinion on *Enforceability of the Right to
Reply or Correction* the Inter-American Court of Human Rights stated: '[t]he
contents of the law may vary from one State to another, within certain reasonable limits and within the framework of the concepts stated by the Court'.[43]

The protective strength of the Inter-American Commission is evidenced
by the behaviour of the Menem administration in Argentina in relation to
desacato laws.[44] These laws, which exist in several Latin American countries,
criminalise expression which 'offends, insults, or threatens a public functionary
in the performance of his or her official duties.'[45] A complaint was filed with
the Commission by Argentina's foremost investigative journalist, Horacio
Verbitsky, following his conviction with a suspended sentence for comments
on the attitude of a Supreme Court justice towards Menem's successful pack-
ing of the Court. The Commission facilitated a settlement which included the
vacation of the conviction, renunciation of any claim for damages and the
amendment of the Penal Code by the Argentine Congress to delete the offence
of *desacato*. In 1994, the Commission published a report (cited above) finding
desacato laws incompatible with the Convention and not necessary to ensure
public order in a democratic society. Nevertheless, the following year the
Menem administration published a Bill increasing prison terms for libel and
aggravating the crime if the victim is a public official or a public institution.
Verbitsky filed another complaint with the Commission and during the preliminary hearings the Bill was withdrawn.

---

41 *Goodwin v. United Kingdom* (1996) 22 EHRR 12 at para. 60 a).   **42** Id. at para. 60 d). See also
Feldman, 'Open democracy legislation … implementation policies and possibilities', in Jeremy
Sarkin & William Binchy (eds), *Human rights, the citizen and the State: South Africa and Irish approaches*,
220 (Dublin, 2001).   **43** Quoted in V. Krsticevic et al., 'The inter-American system of human
rights protection: freedom of expression, "National Security Doctrines" and the transition to
elected governments', in S. Coliver et al. (eds), *Secrecy and liberty: national security, freedom of expression and access to information* (The Hague, 1999) 161–85 at 178.   **44** This section regarding the
desacato laws is from id. at 179–81.   **45** Id. at 179.

NATIONAL OMBUDSMAN[46] AS REDRESS MECHANISM

Of course, it should not be necessary to have to appeal to international bodies to ensure the exercise of individual rights. Western democracies have established a complex set of systems and procedures 'to allow, and even encourage, the citizen to complain, to place the State in a position of defendant, and to seek redress for grievances'.[47] One such institution is that of Ombudsman now known in South Africa as the Public Protector whose functions, formerly within the remit of the Ombudsman, are 'to look into and try to resolve, among other things, matters of administration, abuse of power and corruption by public authorities'.[48]

The requirement that the office of Ombudsman be independent is well-recognised. In fact, in recognition of the role and performance of the Irish Ombudsman, the Constitutional Review Group recommended a new Article in the Constitution to confirm the establishment of the Office and ensure the independence of its function and operation. It noted that:

> [T]he Ombudsman must be able to operate without being influenced by Government action. It is not enough for him or her to be independent in fact – he or she must also be seen as such by those who use the office. A constitutional guarantee for this independence would reinforce freedom from conflict of interest, from deference to the executive, from influence by special interest groups, and it would support the freedom to assemble facts and reach independent and impartial conclusions.[49]

The recommendation has not been implemented.

Recently, the independence of the Ombudsman has come to greater public notice. Four reports of some significance have been presented to the Oireachtas [Parliament] under the Ombudsman's investigative functions.[50] These investigations arose from individual complaints, generally people who lack the ability to act on an organised basis to lobby successfully for redress. The first report, *Lost Pension Arrears* was published in June 1999. The Ombudsman highlights that all the complainants were pensioners. The Department of Social, Community and Family Affairs, the Government Department concerned, was inactive in efforts to resolve the difficulties during the period 1985 to 1996. Rules were applied rigidly and without equity and, where discretion was available the Ombudsman only discovered it by chance:

46 See Feldman, 'Information law and the ombudsman', in R. Byrne and W. Binchy (eds), *Annual Review of Irish Law 2000* (Dublin, 2001) 273–9.   **47** L. Hurwitz, *The State as defendant: governmental accountability and the redress of individual grievances* (London, 1981) at 23.   **48** The Public Protector is an official, independent of the government, established by the Constitution (1993: Chapter section 10; 1996: Chapter 9).   **49** *Report of the Constitution Review Group* Pn 2632 (Government of Ireland, Dublin, May 1996), Chapter 17.   **50** Ombudsman Act, 1980, section 6(7).

It is noteworthy in the present context that *no High Court action has ever been taken by an aggrieved pensioner who has been refused arrears of contributory pension. Perhaps this inaction is not so much a reflection of weak legal arguments as a reflection of the inability of those concerned to muster the resources to mount a legal challenge*[51] [emphasis added].

These themes, and the wider issues of abuse of secondary legislation and delegated powers also run through the subsequent reports, *Local Authority Housing Loans*, published in July 2000, *Nursing Home Subventions*, published in January 2001 and *Passengers with Disabilities*, published in September 2001.[52] In each of these investigations it is clear that the weakest in society have been inadvertently and, most certainly in the case of the *Nursing Home Subventions*, deliberately, deprived of statutory entitlements involving relatively significant sums of money necessary for their daily living.

THE SINNOTT CASE

It was a matter for politicians and the people as their ultimate masters with, perhaps, the assistance of the media and dedicated campaigners like Mrs. Sinnott to ensure that resources are in fact made available to meet the needs of such people as Mr. Sinnott and other persons with disabilities and disadvantages. (Irish Supreme Court, July 2001.)[53]

Mrs Kathryn Sinnott did go to the High Court. The State forced her into the Supreme Court. She had taken an action on behalf of Jamie, her 23-year old adult autistic son, 'a person of unsound mind', to force the State to acknowledge that not only is he educable but, in so far as possible within a legal system, should be compensated for the years of wanton neglect that the State's failures to vindicate his constitutional right to primary education represented. She looked for a vindication of both Jamie's constitutional rights and her own as his mother. She had engaged in, to quote the Chief Justice: 'unremitting battle to secure proper treatment and educational facilities for her son. [This] eventually became a campaign on behalf of autistic children generally: her commitment to that cause cannot be praised too highly.'[54] Mrs Sinnott won her case resoundingly in the High Court. The State won its appeal.

---

51 *Lost Pension Arrears* (Office of the Ombudsman Dublin June 1999) at 14. All of the reports may be accessed on the Internet at www.irlgov.ie/ombudsman/   **52** This is an investigation, on foot of only three complaints, into the Revenue Commissioners' discretionary scheme of tax relief for private motor vehicles used to transport disabled passengers. It is noteworthy that the Revenue Commissioners accepted the Ombudsman's recommendations in full and are acting upon them. **53** Judgment of Murphy J in *Sinnott v. Minister for Education* [2001] 2 IR 545.   **54** Id. *per* Keane CJ.

As regards the Supreme Court judgment, there has been a public furore. It is not the purpose of this paper to analyse the legal basis of that judgment. Nevertheless, it is fundamental to the hypothesis presented in this paper to state that, much of the outrage lies in a basic misunderstanding in the public mind between what is Law, and what is Justice. Moreover, with regard to the legal community, within days of the judgment two highly respected jurists, my experienced colleagues, demonstrated in the media that their views on the consequential merits of the Supreme Court decision were poles apart. Suffice it to note, notwithstanding sub-editors' zeal, that Gerard Hogan's written contribution was published under the banner: 'Unelected judges cannot remedy some wrongs only a government can put right',[55] whereas William Binchy's comment was headlined: 'Irish judges fail the human rights test'.[56]

REALPOLITIK

The reason why Mrs Sinnott was in court was because over the lifetime of her handicapped son neither the politicians, nor the people as their masters, nor the media nor campaigners such as herself had had any joy in vindicating her handicapped son's education requirements. The relevant government agencies had failed the Sinnotts at every hand's turn. Such is eloquently attested to by the Honourable Mr Justice Barr in the High Court judgment and by the Honourable Supreme Court Justices in theirs. It was not until a public court action brought their plight to daily attention that anything concrete was achieved. It was not until the Supreme Court apparently overruled the High Court judgment that the public became so incensed that woe betide a politician who fails to act appropriately in the immediate future. No doubt, in the not too distant future another issue will occupy the people's vocal energy, and jurists' interest in the Sinnotts will be confined to legal analysis.

What then is the relationship between Kathryn Sinnott, the unnamed aggrieved pensioners and Chief Justices under attack? Each wants redress against the perceived wrongs of the executive. Each is relying for vindication of their rights on the same agencies established and resourced by that executive. Each is as helpless as the other if that executive denies these agencies independent existence. Is this a judicial deficit, a democratic deficit or is it the stark world of realpolitik?

To conclude by borrowing from the Irish poet and Nobel laureate, Seamus Heaney, when he was contrasting the different perspectives of activists and artists:

---

55 Hogan, 'Unelected judges cannot remedy some wrongs only a government can put right', *Irish Times*, 14 July 2001. **56** Binchy, 'Irish judges fail the human rights test', *Sunday Times*, 22 July 2001.

[Jurists] have different priorities from artists, but they too are forced to acknowledge the prevalence of the atrocious while maintaining faith in the possibility of the desired.[57]

57 Heaney, 'Actions speak louder than words in war against racism', *Irish Times*, 27 August 2001.

Some aspects of the role of the Circuit Court in the Irish legal system with particular reference to the role of the Circuit Family Court

ESMOND SMYTH

The modern Circuit Court was established in 1961 by the Courts (Establishment & Constitution) Act of 1961. It is a court of first instance provided for by Article 34.3.4° of the Constitution. Its predecessor (which I shall refer to as the old Circuit Court) had been created by the Courts of Justice Act 1924, which was the Act which established new courts under Articles 64–69 of the Constitution of the then Free State. This Act brought to an end the old courts (including the old County Court) by divesting them of all their jurisdiction, and transferring jurisdiction to the newly established courts of the Free State.

It is occasionally suggested, and in my view wrongly, that the Circuit Court is a successor to the old County Court, whose jurisdiction was restricted by the Civil Bill Act,[1] and the County Officers and Courts Act.[2] In 1932 Gerald Horan, KC, former Master of the High Court, wrote a very helpful guide to Circuit Court practice.[3] In the course of his short, but very definitive, preface to that work, he drew attention to what he described as two outstanding matters which should be kept in mind when considering the status of the Circuit Court. The first, he said, is 'that the Circuit Court is an entirely newly-established Court of Record. It was endowed with defined limited jurisdiction, and has no relation with the extinguished County Court'.[4] As support for this assertion, he drew attention to the case of *Sligo Corporation v. Gilbride and Attorney General*.[5] In the course of dealing with the civil jurisdiction of the Circuit Court, Kennedy CJ said:

> The effect, I think, is that jurisdiction was conferred on the Circuit Court in civil cases generally, subject only to the exclusions specified in Section 56 and the quantitative limitations of Section 48. The Act intended not only to transfer the class of equity cases formerly dealt with in the County Court, but also to confer generally, within the prescribed limits of amount of subject-matter and locality, the jurisdiction in all the classes of equity causes and matters within the special purview of the former Chancery Division.[6]

1 14 & 15 Vict. c.57 (1851). 2 County Officers and Courts (Ireland) Act 1877: 40 & 41 Vict. c.56. 3 *County Court practice* (Dublin, 1932). 4 Ibid., p. v. 5 [1929] IR 351. 6 Ibid. at 361–2.

Fitzgibbon J said in the same case:

> In my opinion the new Courts of local and limited jurisdiction estab-
> lished by the Courts of Justice Act, under the powers conferred by
> Article 64 of the Constitution, are not subject to the restrictions
> imposed by the Civil Bill Act, or the Court Officers and Courts Act
> upon the County Courts whose jurisdiction has been transferred to
> them. The only limitations upon the jurisdiction of the Circuit Court
> are those expressed or implied in the provisions of the Courts of Justice
> Act, and, subject to those limitations, the Circuit Court has within its
> locality all the jurisdiction of the High Court.[7]

As President of the Circuit Court I have more than a passing interest in its
history, and accordingly, when I was preparing a note about the Circuit Court
a few years ago, I asked our late and distinguished Supreme Court judge, Mr
Justice Brian Walsh, if he would be kind enough to do a short note reflecting
his views on the Circuit Court. He responded generously and prepared a short
account of his reflections on the Circuit Court.[8] In the course of it, he discusses
what he describes as the 'vital importance of the Circuit Court in our judicial
system'. He refers to the totally erroneous identification of the Circuit Court
simply as a continuation of some kind of the former County Court, and in that
context he notes the remarks of the former Chief Justice Kennedy and Mr Justice
Fitzgibbon in their judgments quoted above. Mr Justice Walsh adopted these
remarks and went on to say that it had been made quite clear in that case 'that
in no way could the Circuit Court be regarded as a successor to the old County
Court'. Furthermore, in saying that the Circuit Court exercises all the jurisdiction of the High Court subject to certain express exclusions, Mr Justice Walsh
was underlining the remarks of the Judges in *Sligo Corporation v. Gilbride*.

THE CIRCUIT COURT AND THE CONSTITUTION

While the Circuit Court cannot adjudicate on the constitutionality of laws –
that constitutional review function is reserved for the Superior Courts – nevertheless, there is an obligation on the Circuit Court, and the District Court
indeed, to uphold and enforce the Constitution. All judges make the same declaration on their appointment, which is to uphold the Constitution. Walsh J,
in *People(Director of Public Prosecutions) v. Lynch*,[9] emphasised that District and
Circuit Court judges must not overlook their obligation to uphold the
Constitution while discharging their legal functions. The Circuit Court therefore must protect an individual's constitutional rights just as conscientiously as
judges in other courts are obliged to do.[10]

---

7 Ibid. at 367. 8 See Appendix I. 9 [1982] IR 64. 10 See also the remarks of Denham J in

It is a moot point nowadays, whether a declaratory action would lie in the Circuit Court to challenge the constitutionality of a pre-1937 statute. Surely though, if, in the course of proceedings in the Circuit Court, the consistency of a pre-1937 statute was raised, a Circuit Judge would have some function in determining the issue. The reservations of Carroll J, in *The State (Pheasantry Limited) v. Donnelly*,[11] may have in mind a declaratory action in the Circuit Court, rather than an issue as to consistency, which might perchance arise in the course of proceedings.

In his article on the Circuit Court, the late Mr Justice Walsh stated that, in so far as the Circuit Court is concerned, it has full jurisdiction to consider questions of the constitutionality of any law enacted before the coming into force of the Constitution, whether by the former Oireachtas of Saorstát Éireann or the British Parliament, as it has also jurisdiction to adjudicate on the constitutionality of any common law rule or practice. He says that Article 45 of the Constitution, which carries forward all laws in force before the enactment of the Constitution, expressly provides that any law *inconsistent* with the provisions of the Constitution is not carried forward and this is a matter which can be raised in the Circuit Court.

THE INDEPENDENCE OF CIRCUIT JUDGES WITHIN THEIR OWN COURTS

The Circuit Court, and indeed the District Court, is not in any sense subject to direction, control or supervision by the Superior Courts and, within the limits of his or her jurisdiction, a Circuit judge has the sole and exclusive authority to control the proceedings in his or her own court.[12] Gannon J, in the course of his judgment in *Clune*,[13] pointed out that the independence and authority of judges of the inferior courts are secured in their freedom not only from pressures of political or executive nature but also from purported intervention, direction or control by any superior court.

The powers of the President of the Circuit Court

The role of the President of the Circuit Court is to ensure an equitable distribution of the work of the Circuit Court amongst the several judges thereof, and to ensure the prompt dispatch of the business of the Circuit Court in the several circuits thereof.[14] He or she is appointed from amongst the Circuit judges by the President acting on the advice of the government. The President of the Circuit Court is ex-officio an additional judge of the High Court.[15] As such

Coughlan v. Pattwell [1993] 1 IR 31. **11** [1982] ILRM 512. **12** See *Clune v. Director of Public Prosecutions* [1981] ILRM 17. **13** Ibid. **14** See Courts of Justice Act, 1947, s.10(1). **15** See Courts (No. 2) Act, 1997, s.7(3).

he or she takes precedence over all other Circuit judges.[16] While the President is a *primus inter pares,* he or she is also an active manager of the business of the Court. Since the establishment of the new Courts Service, which has taken over the management of the Courts from the Department of Justice, the President sits as a member of the Courts Service Board.

The President of the Circuit Court is also a member of the Board of the Judicial Studies Institute. This Institute came about partly because of the considerable importance which the Presidents of all the courts attach to judicial training. In addition, because of section 19 of the Courts and Court Officers Act 1995 there is a statutory obligation on a person who wishes to be considered for appointment as a judge to undertake in writing to the Judicial Appointments Board, that, if appointed, he or she will take such course or courses of training or education, or both, as may be required by the Chief Justice or the President of the court to which that person is appointed. The Judicial Appointments Advisory Board, of which the President is also a member, recommends persons to the Government as being suitable for appointment as a judge to the various courts.

The President of the Circuit Court works closely with the Presidents of the other courts, that is the Chief Justice, the President of the High Court, and the President of the District Court, in matters which affect the judiciary as a whole, and in relation to the administration of the courts. The President of the Circuit Court, together with the Presidents of the other courts, also sits on a Committee for Judicial Ethics, which has recently reported to the Government.

Some judicial consideration was given to the general powers of the President of the Circuit Court, and, in particular, to the effect of section 10(2)(a)[17] in the case of *State(Hughes) v. Neylon.*[18] In the course of his judgment Finlay P stated:

> The power of the President of the Circuit Court to fix the times in which any particular circuit will sit from time to time after consultation with the judge of that Circuit is an absolute power in the sense that when he has made an Order fixing such venues, then unless and until he amends or varies it not only must the Circuit sit in those venues but it cannot sit anywhere else.[19]

Finlay P, also stated that it seemed clear to him that the powers vested in the President of the Circuit Court by section 10 are not reviewable by the courts provided they are carried out in the bona fide exercise of duty.

Article 36 of the Constitution deals with the organisation of the courts and the number of judges who are to be appointed, and the distribution of their

16 See Courts of Justice Act, 1947, s.9. **17** Courts of Justice Act, 1947. **18** [1982] ILRM 108. **19** Ibid. at 110.

jurisdiction and business. In 1961 there were only eight judges of the Circuit Court; today there are 27 judges plus the President of the Circuit Court. An appendix is attached which traces the legislative increases in the number of Circuit Court Judges since 1961.[20]

Pivotal role for the Circuit Court

I hope that it is not an overstatement to suggest that the Circuit Court has a pivotal role to play in the administration of our four-tiered criminal and civil justice system. It is a national court which exercises its jurisdiction locally through eight regional circuits. These circuits were created by statute, and their boundaries have from time to time been altered by statute. The trial of cases in a local venue was one of the original purposes for which the Circuit Court was established: namely, that it would provide local and cheaper venues for litigants than would otherwise be the case if they had to go to the High Court. Needless to say, it would be easier and more convenient for them to get to the court as well.

To this day, these characteristics of locality, convenience and, hopefully, good value, are essential aspects of the way in which the Circuit Court tries to do its business. Criteria, such as the place of the contract, or where the tort occurred or what the rateable valuation of a particular property might be, are some of the requirements for the exercise by the Circuit Court of its civil jurisdiction. Likewise, the exercise of criminal jurisdiction is usually by the judge of the Circuit where the offence was committed, or where the accused person was arrested or resides. These prerequisites for the exercise of local jurisdiction, however, are not all-embracing. It is clear from the remarks of Mr Justice Walsh in *State (Boyle) v. Neylon*,[21] that the Constitutional provision, in referring to local jurisdiction,

> does not mean that it must be local in the sense of being particularly connected with the place of residence of one party or another ... The details of arranging such matters was left to the Oireachtas and the provisions of the Courts (Supplemental Provisions) Act 1961, and the subsequent legislation appeared to provide both practical and feasible methods for the exercise by the Circuit Court of jurisdiction on a local basis, while at the same time making provision for the avoidance of injustices which might result from a trial being inevitably held in one particular locality.[22]

That case was a constitutional challenge to a provision in the Courts Act 1981 which provided for transfers of criminal trials to the Circuit Criminal Court in Dublin. It was held, *inter alia*, that the fact that there was such provision in

20 See Appendix 2. **21** [1986] IR 551. **22** Ibid. at 557.

the legislation did not alter the essential local exercise of the jurisdiction of the Circuit Court. However, because the provisions in the 1981 Act were regarded as making it too easy for cases to be transferred to the Dublin Circuit, and because it was leading to a backlog of cases waiting for trial from other circuits, a new provision was incorporated in the Courts and Court Officers Act 1995. This provided that a trial could be transferred to the Dublin Circuit Court if the Court was satisfied that 'it would be manifestly unjust not to do so'. The judge's decision to grant or refuse such an application is final and unappealable.[23]

Perhaps this is an opportune time to comment on the absence of such a right of appeal in these situations. May I say that I am not entirely convinced, and I know that a number of my colleagues have the same view, that excluding a right of appeal in these cases is a good idea. It is sometimes the case that local feelings can run high in particularly notorious cases, or there could be other reasons affecting the justice of trying a particular case in a local jurisdiction. Of course, judges are particularly conscious of their obligations to make just decisions, but they are only human and sometimes a decision to try a case on their own circuit in a particular town might be open to question. While it is true that judicial review continues to explore the limits of our jurisdiction, such an application would only be rarely available to a litigant attempting to challenge the decision of a judge made within jurisdiction.

I raise this issue, not least because it is one of the issues relating to the criminal jurisdiction of the courts as a whole, but there are other issues as well for us to consider in the future. In this context, it might be helpful to explain what the jurisdiction, criminal and civil, of the Circuit Court actually is.

THE JURISDICTION OF THE CIRCUIT COURT – CHANGING TRENDS

The framework for the specific jurisdiction of the Circuit Court is to be found in the provisions of the Courts (Supplemental Provisions) Act 1961. This Act broadly carried over the jurisdiction which the Circuit Court was given by the Courts of Justice Act 1924. In so far as its criminal jurisdiction is concerned, the Circuit Court tries virtually all indictable crimes, the only exceptions being offences under sections 2 or 3 of the Treason Act 1939; offences under sections 6, 7 or 8 of the Offences against the State Act 1939; murder, attempted murder, or piracy, including an offence by accessory before or after the fact, and the crimes of rape and attempted rape. The result is the Central Criminal Court spends its time trying murder and rape, and the Circuit Court tries every other indictable crime, (except of course cases which have been referred by the Director of Public Prosecutions to the Special Criminal Court). The Circuit

23 32(1).

Court is also a final court of appeal from summary offences which have been prosecuted in the District Court, and there is a provision for a full appeal and re-hearing of these cases, on facts and law, to the Circuit Court.

The detailed civil jurisdiction of the Circuit Court is set out in the Court (Supplemental Provisions) Act 1961. Presently, the monetary limits of its jurisdiction in tort and contract are £30,000. It is proposed to increase these limits in the future. The Courts Service has estimated that over 70 per cent of all the sole work of the High Court will be transferred to the Circuit Court as a result of this change which could see an additional 21,000 cases on an annual basis appearing in Circuit Court lists. Some idea of how this change will affect the Circuit Court in the future can be gleaned from the fact that, during the year 2000, the Circuit Court alone dealt with over 39,000 civil matters. In the High Court, where cases are inevitably longer and more complex, over 17,000 Orders were granted in 2000 and the District Courts dealt with 79,000 civil matters in 2000 as well. There are undoubtedly swings and roundabouts in this process, not least for the High Court, which should see its judicial resources somewhat freed up by reason of these proposed changes.

However, it is easy to be mesmerised by statistics relating to increased volumes of work. This can conceal some of the real issues which are: how judges do their business and how jurisdiction is distributed amongst them. At the end of the day, all the courts face pressure from increasing volumes of work relating to criminal law, and this is unlikely to change in the future. The fact is that since 1977, when the Circuit Court became the Court of Appeal from the Employment Appeals Tribunal, successive governments have continued to enlarge and broaden the scope of its jurisdiction, so that whenever new rights are created, e.g. divorce and equality legislation, it is usually the Circuit Court which is charged with implementing the statutory provisions. Likewise, there is a noticeable trend for the Circuit Court to absorb, on a concurrent basis, some of what was previously the High Court's exclusive jurisdiction, such as applications for nullity; applications under section 27 of the Planning Acts; applications under the Competition Act, and more recently applications to restore companies to the Register. In addition, and by agreement between the parties, large numbers of Army deafness cases have been remitted from the High Court to the Circuit Court.

What is happening on the civil side is equally happening for the Circuit Court's criminal jurisdiction. New indictable offences go to the Circuit Court. Under the Criminal Justice Act 1999 which created a series of new serious drug related offences, it is provided that these offences are to be tried in the Circuit Court. This, too, is the situation under the Proceeds of Crime Act 1996. It is also worth bearing in mind that certain murder-type offences, such as manslaughter and abortion, are retained in the Circuit Court and some serious rape-type offences such as statutory rape and sexual assault are tried in the Circuit Court as well. It is also notable that the sentencing powers of Circuit judges reflect the gravity of the offences which they have to try. There are a number of offences in respect of which a Circuit judge can impose a life sentence, and, for example, under the provisions of the Planning & Development Acts of 1963 as amended, a Circuit judge can impose fines of up to a million pounds. It is the same under pollution legislation.

What I have referred to above is by way of an example of some of the criminal jurisdiction of the Circuit Court, and it is by no means an exhaustive list.[24] Most of the modern 'white collar' crimes are tried in the Circuit Court and, if there are any charges arising from the various Tribunals of Inquiry, these will be tried in the Circuit Court. Therefore, looking at overall trends in the distribution of criminal jurisdiction by the Oireachtas, what becomes apparent is that while the High Court criminal jurisdiction remains the same, the Circuit Court jurisdiction continues to increase. It is not an exaggeration, therefore, to suggest that a substantial part of the administration of justice from the point of view of indictable crime revolves around the Circuit Court.

Is this view accurate?

Last year, Mr Justice Carney said that it seemed absurd to him, that he could not, as a judge of the High Court, deal with a billion pound fraud – because it came within the jurisdiction of the Circuit Court. He went on to say, and I quote his words: 'People have been murdering and raping each other from time immemorial and these are accordingly very settled crimes. The more difficult areas are in fraud, money-laundering and the developing areas where forum shopping is engaged in by international criminals.' Mr Justice Carney also believes that we should anticipate the impact of substantially new forms of prosecutions in the future, including those arising as a consequence of tribunals and inspectorships, as well as developing European and domestic tribunal law. (Mr Justice Carney enlarges on these views in Chapter 10 of this book.)

Of course, I am sure that Mr Justice Carney is not suggesting for a moment, that Circuit judges have any less expertise in dealing with the serious cases that come within their present jurisdiction. After all, Circuit judges have to have the same qualifications for appointment as are required of High Court judges, and we are all broadly drawn from the same pool of former legal practitioners. However, notwithstanding that, I believe that Mr Justice Carney's point is well made. It received the endorsement of the Chief Justice recently when he stated that there appears to be no rational basis for the distribution of serious crime between the Circuit Court and the Central Criminal Court. He points to the fact, that it has never been explained why, if murder and rape can be tried only in the Central Criminal Court, the same does not apply to kidnapping, manslaughter, robbery with violence, and massive fraud.

The Board of the Courts Service has responded to a suggestion by the Minister for Justice that we take a fresh look at the jurisdictional relationship

24 For further detail see Appendix 3.

between the Central Criminal Court and the Circuit Court, by embarking on a comprehensive review of the present distribution of jurisdiction and business in the courts. This, it seems to me, is the right way to go. After all, it is difficult to see why there should be two separate court systems having jurisdiction to try indictable crime. Alternatively, if separate jurisdictions are to be retained, could not these jurisdictions be operated (at least in so far as certain serious crimes are concerned), on a concurrent rather than an exclusive basis?

If, on the other hand, there is to be a unified criminal jurisdiction for indictable crimes, then its jurisdiction should operate locally as well as nationally, because it is difficult to see the logic nowadays of having all murder and rape trials tried in Dublin, when it would often be more practicable and convenient that they be tried in a local venue. This is provided, of course, that there were not circumstances in any particular case which would make it manifestly unjust for the case to be tried locally.

The Chief Justice has said that in almost all respects the structure of our courts has remained unchanged since 1924. What has changed is the volume and complexity of the work which all the courts have to do; what has changed also are the expectations of the public in respect of the courts, and the degree to which issues of accountability and efficiency are raised on a regular basis. These changing attitudes have implications for the courts system and judges as well. It will not be sufficient in the future merely to draw attention to our developing modern Courts Service with all its new buildings and better technology. In future, all of us, judges and court administrators alike, will have to demonstrate that the pubic is being better served by these changes; that the litigants can get their cases on within a reasonable time of initiating them; that, if a case is specially fixed, it begins on the day fixed for it, and that, if judgment is reserved, its delivery is not too long delayed.

The question of delay is important because the European Convention renders the State liable for delay in civil and criminal matters. We have had our share of delays in the Circuit Court in the past. Indeed, there was a time four or five years ago when litigants had to wait for two years before they could get a civil case on. Now these delays are a fraction of what they used to be. These improvements were mainly brought about by the appointment of more judges in 1995 which had an immediate impact. Better listing systems and a policy of no adjournments except for serious reasons also play a part.

The definition we use for delay is the average waiting time between when a case is ready to go to hearing and the actual date for hearing. When we speak of there being no delay on circuits outside of Dublin, we mean that the case can be listed for the next sessions, i.e. the next court sitting at the venue in question. In Dublin, delays on the civil side are down to three or four weeks, and the delay for a criminal trial is three to four months. One thing is certain, however: whatever changes are to be made in future to our court structures, they will only tinker at the edges of the problem if they are not accompanied by the appointment of significantly more judges. Because the Circuit Court exercises its jurisdiction locally, it brings the law and justice to the local community. I don't think it is unreasonable that the local community should expect from the Circuit Court that it be reasonably expeditious in the despatch of its business, and at a cost to the litigant which is not unfair or excessive. The ideal should be that a citizen is entitled to his day in court – but if it is reasonably possible, he shouldn't be put to the expense of a second day – at least in so far as civil cases are concerned. Of course there are exceptions, but that is the objective which I and my fellow judges strive towards when managing the business of our respective Circuit Courts.

This is not a one sided responsibility though. It has to be accompanied by a willingness on the part of legal practitioners to get to the relevant point of their case quickly, and to be conscious that there are a lot of other cases on the 'runway' behind them. My fear for the future is that, the more the Circuit Court has to absorb some of the existing jurisdiction of the High Court, and the more it becomes customary to distribute new legislative measures and new crimes to the Circuit Court, the more likely it is that the Circuit Court will lose some of the advantages for litigants which it previously had. In so doing, it will become more expensive to do business there and, with longer and more complex cases inevitable, the local citizens' rights of access will be curtailed.

In making these points, I am conscious that the challenges facing the Circuit Court should not be seen in isolation from the challenges which face other courts as well. What I am trying to draw attention to are the dangers of piece-meal changes to the structure and jurisdiction of the courts. What happens when you do that is that you are not just robbing Peter to pay Paul, but you may also be robbing Peter and robbing Paul at the same time! Finally, in so far as this part of the paper is concerned, I have tried to avoid drawing too many conclusions from statistics. Some statistics are unavoidable though – particularly those relating to the mushrooming of compensation litigation over the past 20 years. This is a feature many other jurisdictions share as well.

Perhaps we should lay some of the blame at Lord Atkin's door, for invoking the parable of the Good Samaritan when he enunciated the 'neighbour principle'. This had the effect of expanding the law of negligence beyond all measure, by the repeated assertion that liability for foreseeable damage is the general rule, and that limiting principles deserve close scrutiny before they can be accepted.[25] Lord Macmillan, his colleague in the same famous leading case of *Donoghue v. Stevenson*, doesn't get away entirely 'Scot free' either for reminding the public that the categories of negligence are never closed. I sometimes think that what he really had in mind at the time was that the doors of solicitors' offices are always open! Perhaps in the long run, it would have been better

25 See S. Hedley, 'M'Alister (or Donoghue) (Pauper) v. Stevenson (1932)', in E. O'Dell (ed.), *Leading cases of the twentieth century* (Dublin, 2000), p. 64, at p.71.

if Mrs May Donoghue had asked for a real beer instead of a ginger beer. Then perhaps she'd have forgotten all about it the following day!

FAMILY LAW

I turn now to the sensitive issue of family law. In addition to outlining the jurisdiction of the Circuit Court in this area, I will mention a few of the issues which are currently being addressed in the area of the law.

Jurisdiction of the Circuit Court

Family law proceedings can be initiated in each of the courts vested under Irish Law with originating jurisdiction, i.e. the District Court, Circuit and High Court. In some areas these courts exercise exclusive jurisdiction, in others jurisdiction is concurrent or overlapping. I think it is only fair to say, that in recent years the Circuit Court assumed a central role in family law proceedings. When exercising its jurisdiction to hear and determine such proceedings, it is known as the Circuit Family Court. It is vested with an original jurisdiction concurrent with that of the High Court to hear judicial separation proceedings pursuant to the Judicial Separation and Family Law Reform Act 1989, and also to hear divorce proceedings under the Family Law (Divorce) Act 1996. It also possesses a jurisdiction concurrent to that of the High Court to determine some proceedings under the Family Home Protection Act 1976 and the Family Law Act 1995. Concurrently with the High Court. the Circuit Court may also determine proceedings under the Succession Act 1965, the Partition Acts 1868/1876, and the Family Law Act 1981. It is also vested with jurisdiction to hear and determine suits for nullity of marriage by the Family Law Act 1995. Finally, the Circuit Court has an original unlimited jurisdiction pursuant to the Guardianship of Infants Act 1964; the Family Law (Maintenance of Spouses & Children) Act 1976; the Status of Children Act 1987; and the Domestic Violence Act 1996. The Circuit Court may also hear wardship proceedings. Last year the Circuit Court dealt with over 5,000 family law matters.

Privacy and the media

Article 34(1) of the Irish Constitution states that 'justice shall be administered in Courts established by law ... and save and such special and limited cases as may be prescribed by law shall be administered in public.' Almost all family law proceedings result in disclosure by parties of confidential details of their family life and personal relationships. Thus, in order to prevent unnecessary distress, it is important for the protection of the parties and their families that such proceedings should be heard in private, *in camera*. Consequently, the great majority of family law proceedings come within the 'special and limited' category of cases envisaged in Article 34 (1) from which the public may be excluded.

Under all statutes which contain express provisions for private hearings, the court is obliged to exclude both the general public and the media. In practice only the parties to proceedings and their legal representatives are in most family cases allowed to remain in court during the hearing of family law proceedings. A witness giving evidence, either voluntarily or on subpoena, is usually required to remain outside the court until called to give evidence. On the conclusion of his or her evidence, a witness is usually required to leave the court. However, it is open to the judge hearing a case to determine whether a witness should be excluded from the hearing and, in practice on occasion, upon application by either or both of the parties to the proceedings or on the trial judge's own initiative, the court may determine that it is of help to the court that a witness be present to hear evidence prior to the witness giving his or her own evidence or being cross-examined.

The operation of the *in camera* rule is not without its critics. It is often suggested that because of it family law matters are shrouded in secrecy and mystique. In its *Consultation Paper on Family Courts* the Law Reform Commission spoke of 'the dangers inherent in the absence from the legal process of a salutary check on idiosyncratic or wayward judicial conduct'[26] and referred to the danger of 'false rumours or inadequate assumptions about the conduct of family proceedings'[27] gaining currency due to family law cases being heard behind closed doors. To some extent this is true, and there is now an anecdotal mythology about, which suggests that male or female bias is rampant in the approach of judges to these cases.

I have no doubt that, were the doors of the family law courtrooms to be opened to the media, the public would be reassured that such suggestions are far from the truth. However, for sensible reasons such unrestricted access is not desirable. Is there an alternative? The Law Reform Commission has made recommendations concerning the establishment of a national statistical data base in relation to family law proceedings and for students and researchers to gain access to family court hearings. We are now trying to go some of the way towards this objective. In 2001 a Pilot Scheme commenced in the Dublin area under the supervision of the Courts Service with the appointment of a Family Law Recorder to report on family law cases, principally with a view to giving a note of the Orders which have been made.

The project relies on the consent of the parties which has to be obtained in advance of the date of hearing. The Recorder has the responsibility of ensuring that there is no breach of the right of the individual litigant and that, therefore, only the decision of the judge will be reported. Where additional background material is required for the interpretation of the decision the Recorder will draw up a statement of facts which has to be approved by the judge prior to publication. Needless to say, neither the names of the parties nor their address nor anything which would identify them can be published.

---

26 Law Reform Commission, *Consultation paper on family courts* (1994), para. 7.44.   27 Ibid.

This is a very desirable project but it has run into difficulties because it has been suggested, that, notwithstanding the requirements for the consent of the parties, the existing prohibition prevents any reporting of family law cases. However, it is true to say that the position is not entirely clear. In *RM, Applicant v. DM, Respondent and a Barrister*[28] – a matter involving the barristers' professional conduct tribunal and the Appeals Board – Murphy J held that the law did not imply an absolute embargo on the production of information which derived from, or was introduced in, proceedings protected by section 34 of the Judicial Separation and Family Law Reform Act 1989. Such information could not therefore be the subject matter of investigation in an enquiry by a professional body without the consent of the Court. He distinguished the judgment in *Eastern Health Board v. Fitness to Practice Committee*,[29] in which Barr J obliged the Eastern Health Board to hand over family files to the Medical Council. Murphy J held that the public interest that resolution of family disputes be held in private outweighs the public's right that justice be administered in public.

Barr J found in *Eastern Health Board v. Fitness to Practice Committee* that there was not an absolute embargo on the publication of evidence adduced in the course of *in camera* proceedings, but there was an established practice that the court had discretion to permit others, on such terms as the judge thinks proper, to disseminate information derived from such proceedings where the judge believes that it is in the interest of justice so to do. *Tesco Ireland Limited v. McGrath*,[30] involved a conveyancing request for claims, pleadings and orders made in family law proceedings. Morris P stated that he had no doubt that solicitors for the vendor were not free to furnish such documents as they are covered by the *in camera* rule. The President of the High Court continued as follows: 'I am unable to identify anything in the present case which would indicate to me that it is in the interest of justice or that it is crucial to the public interest that the matrimonial proceedings in this case be made public.'[31]

In the light of the above authorities it may be that the legislature will have to consider the position if some relaxation, however limited, is to be made to the *in camera* rule. From my point of view, I and the other members of the Family Law Committee of the Courts Service continue to have high hopes for the Family Law Recording project. I think it will help to demonstrate that there is a reasonably consistent application of the terms of family law legislation and that, in these difficult family law situations, family law judges are very conscious of their obligation to strike a fair balance between the respective parties and to secure the best interests of children in the cases that come before them.

I turn now to the nature of family law procedures. Sections 33 and 45 of the Judicial Separation and Family Law Reform Act 1989 require that 'family law proceedings' before the District, Circuit and High Courts 'shall be as infor-

28 [2000] 3 IR 373. **29** [1998] 3 IR 399. **30** Unreported High Court, Morris P, 14 June 1999 at 15. **31** Ibid. at 17.

mal as is practicable and consistent with the administration of justice'. Moreover, the Circuit Court, when sitting as the Circuit Family Court to hear and determine family proceedings, is required by section 32 of the 1989 Act 'to sit in a different place or at different times or on different days from those on which the ordinary sittings of the Circuit Court are held'. There is now in Dublin, what effectively amounts to a Family Law Division of the Circuit Court, in that two judges sit throughout the year in a building independent of the Four Courts complex to hear family law matters. The position on Circuits outside Dublin is that special days are fixed for family law where possible, usually on Thursdays, and no other business is done on those days. Neither the judge nor the practitioners wear wigs or gowns. There is still an element of an adversarial approach in family law matters particularly where the 'means' of an applicant or respondent are being tested. However, it has become the practice of judges in these matters to exercise somewhat of an inquisitorial role when determining issues of family conflict. Such a role enables a judge hearing a case to actively seek out the truth by questioning witnesses, or seeking evidence or assistance independent of the litigating parties to facilitate or assist the court in resolving disputes. This sort of approach is particularly helpful in proceedings in which the welfare of a child or any other party to the proceedings is an issue. However, until more resources in the form of psychologists, psychiatrists and social workers are made available to the court, this desirable approach on the part of judges will continue to be restricted. Furthermore, under family law legislation as it presently stands, there is a requirement that the parties be referred to a mediator. I am afraid that this is a 'paper tiger', as there are not remotely enough mediators to satisfy the statutory requirements. This is unfortunate because mediators have a vital role to play in the system – not least in adjusting property matters but in some child related matters as well. Also, their professional expertise can help to diffuse some of the anxiety and uncertainty associated with family law matters.

FAMILY LAW IN CRISIS: INADEQUATE STRUCTURES & MULTIPLE FUNCTIONS

Modernisation of the structures and functions of the Courts System in Ireland was examined in detail by the Working Group on a Courts Commission.[32] The Commission noted a number of unique difficulties associated with Irish family law. One commentator has described the Report as painting 'a graphically depressing picture of the family justice system as an institutional system in crisis'.[33] The Working Group examined three options as possible models for

---

32 The Working Group published six reports from 1996 to 1998. Of greatest relevance is the Sixth Report, entitled *Conclusion* (Pn. 6533), published in November 1998. **33** Martin, 'The Denham

a reform system of family law courts. The three options were: Regional Family Courts; a dedicated Family Courts' structure; and Improvement of the current system.

The Law Reform Commission 1996 report[34] had made earlier recommendations concerning the establishment of Regional Family Courts located in approximately 15 regional centres, and operating as a division of the Circuit Court. These courts would be vested with a unified and comprehensive family law jurisdiction and would deal with all originating substantive family proceedings. It would embrace a wider jurisdiction than that of the present Circuit Court, so as to include proceedings under the Adoption Acts 1952–1998 and also proceedings under the Child Abduction and Enforcement of Custody Orders Act 1991. This is the long-term solution favoured by the Working Group on a Courts Commission. It seems to me to make sense because it does away with two overlapping jurisdictions and because it has the advantages of convenience of locality and possibly cheaper procedures. For this new approach to work it is imperative that it is supported by adequate, in-court counselling and mediation services funded by the State, and because of the way family law orders operate, it might be worth considering whether it should have some method of supervising compliance with, and testing the general effectiveness of, its orders. However, that is a more political question and I will steer clear of it at the moment. Ultimately, it is in the interests of the judiciary, as much as it is in the interest of the public, that whatever model is finally chosen, it should contribute significantly towards a uniform and reasonably consistent application of family law principles and practices, which would lead to the growth of a consistent body of jurisprudence of a cogent and humane nature.

Finally, could I draw your attention to some 'tongue in cheek' advice to District judges which appears in James O'Connor's preface to his great work *The Irish Justice of the Peace*. He advised: 'Be chary of giving reasons for your judgments. If you are not sure of them, give none. A wrong reason destroys respect for a right decision.' Today, although we understand why he said it, may I cast a cold eye on it in the present climate! Today, without reasons, respect for the decision will be harder to justify.

Commission Reports: a critical analysis' [1999] 4 *Ir.J. of Fam. Law*, Part IV, 18 at 19. **34** Law Reform Commission, *Report on family courts* (LRC52 – 1996), Chapter 4.

Extracts from the late Mr Justice Brian Walsh's paper on the Circuit Court

1. I think I may modestly claim to be able to speak with some experience of the operation of all of our Courts. I have spent over thirty years on the Bench all save two of which were spent as a member of the Supreme Court. I was the first Chairman of the Committee on Court Practice and Procedure and I occupied that position from 1962 to 1988. Apart from my general experience on the Bench I had had many years experience as a practitioner particularly in the Circuit Court. During the years of my chairmanship of the Committee on Court Practice and Procedure I had many opportunities to examine closely the operation and the function of the Circuit Court.

2. The vital importance of the Circuit Court in our judicial system was not fully appreciated for many years. It is a regrettable fact that the legal profession as such was the main culprit, being slow to recognise the full implications of the new system of Court jurisdiction established in 1924 and the totally erroneous identification of it simply as a continuation of some kind of the former County Court. One has but to read the Report and the evidence given to the Joint Committee on the Courts of Justice (1930) to understand the ludicrous position taken up by members of the legal profession on the status and importance of the Circuit Court. To some extent this attitude has tended to bedevil the approach to the importance of the Circuit Court ever since.

3. The Circuit Court is one national court exercising its jurisdiction on a local basis. There are certain limitations on its jurisdiction so that it is a court of 'limited jurisdiction' in that sense and, as has been held by a number of Court decisions of the High Court and Supreme Court, is a court of the type envisaged by the Constitution as a 'court of local and limited jurisdiction'. However, the plain fact is that it exercises all the jurisdiction of the High Court subject to certain express exclusions. This was underlined in the decision of the Supreme Court of *Saorstát Eireann* by the late Chief Justice Kennedy and Mr Justice Fitzgibbon in their judgments in the case of *Sligo Corporation v. Gilbride and Attorney General v. Gilbride* 1929 IR 351. It was made quite clear that in no way could the Circuit Court be regarded as a successor to the old County Court.

4. The Committee on Court Practice and Procedure over the years in its various Reports made recommendations which were adopted by the Oireachtas in enacting increases of the civil jurisdiction of the Circuit Court. In matters of equity the jurisdiction of the Court became unlimited and over the years the jurisdiction of the Court in tort and contract went to £30,000. Over the years, as the result of various enactments its jurisdiction in family law matters, and now presumably extending to divorce, adds considerably to the jurisdiction of the Court. What is not often appreciated is that it also has a jurisdiction in constitutional matters. The special provision of the Constitution of

Ireland, which limits to the High Court or the Supreme Court jurisdiction in a case involving the validity of the laws of the Oireachtas having regard to the provisions of the Constitution exclude that particular jurisdiction from every Court save the High Court and the Supreme Court but the limited nature of this must be borne in mind. Firstly, as has already been decided by the Supreme Court, many years ago, the Constitutional provision refers only to Statutes enacted since the coming into force of the Constitution.

Therefore, so far as the Circuit Court is concerned it has full jurisdiction to consider questions of the constitutionality of any law enacted before that date whether by the former Oireachtas of Saorstat Éireann or the British Parliament, as it has also jurisdiction to adjudicate upon the constitutionality of any common law rule or practice. Article 45 of the Constitution which carries forward all laws in force before the enactment of the Constitution expressly provides that any law inconsistent with the provisions of the Constitution is not carried forward and this is a matter which can be raised in the Circuit Court. It is therefore quite true to say that the Circuit Court has all the jurisdiction of the High Court subject only to the specific exceptions made either by the Constitution itself or by Statute. On the criminal side all criminal prosecutions on indictment in the State, save the express exceptions of murder, rape, piracy and treason, are triable only in the Circuit Court subject to whatever exceptions may be made by transferring cases to the High Court, the provisions regarding which are varied from time to time. The Constitution expressly requires that all criminal prosecutions save those which can legitimately be held to be minor offences are triable only by jury (save where, by special provision, they may be referred to Special Criminal Courts) and all of these take place in the Circuit Court, subject to the above exclusions.

5. It is remarkable, if somewhat anomalous, that the number of Circuit Court judges in the State is smaller than the number of High Court judges although in fact the jurisdiction which they exercise throughout the State is, for all practical purposes, the same as the jurisdiction of the High Court, subject to specific exceptions already mentioned. The great merit of the Circuit Court is that it brings to the people where they live a vast jurisdiction – a jurisdiction, which, regrettably often has to be exercised in premises which are thoroughly unsuitable and impose considerable hardship on the Judges concerned and, indeed, on the litigants. The very wide jurisdiction of the Circuit Court is being used increasingly in cases of tort and contract; no doubt so far as tort is concerned somewhat influenced by the unfortunate disappearance of Jury trials in most negligence actions in the High Court. Furthermore, it has been noted that there is an increasing use by parties of the power to agree to the Circuit Court having unlimited jurisdiction. Thus decrees far in excess of £30,000 can be awarded after such agreement of jurisdiction by the parties at far less costs than the same decree would carry in the High Court.

APPENDIX 2

The number of ordinary judges of the Circuit Court shall now by virtue of section 1 of the Courts Act 1996 be not more than 27. The number of judges originally provided for in section 16 of not more than eight was increased by Section 2(1) of the Courts Act 1964 to not more than nine; by section 1(2) of the Courts Act 1977 to not more than 11; by section 30 of the Courts Act 1981 to not more than 12 (with five judges being permanently assigned to the Dublin Circuit at this point). This provision was further amended by Section 2 of the Courts Act 1985 which increased this number to 15 (with six judges being permanently assigned to the Dublin Circuit) and by Section 18 of the Courts Act 1991 which substituted further new paragraphs (a) and (aa) in subsection (1) and a new subsection (2) in Section 2 of the Act of 1977 and had the effect of increasing the number of ordinary judges of the Circuit Court to not more than 17, with eight of these judges being permanently assigned to the Dublin Circuit and two to the Cork Circuit. Section 10 of the Courts and Court Officers Act 1995 increased the number of ordinary judges of the Circuit Court to not more than 24, and Section 36 of that Act substituted further new paragraphs (a) and (aa) in subsection (1) and a new subsection (2) in Section 2 of the Courts Act 1977 and had the effect of increasing the number of judges permanently assigned to the Dublin Circuit to 10 and to the Cork Circuit to three. Note also the terms of Section 2(2) of the Courts Act 1977 as substituted by Section 18 of the Courts Act 1991 and Section 36 of the Courts and Court Officers Act 1995 which makes provision for the assignment of newly appointed judges to particular circuits depending on the existing number of judges assigned to such circuit.

APPENDIX 3

Criminal Law Acts impinging on the Circuit Court jurisdiction since 1990

increased jurisdiction

1.   Larceny Act, 1990.
2.   Firearms and Offensive Weapons Act, 1990.
3.   Criminal Justice (Forensic Evidence) Act, 1990.
4.   Criminal Damage Act, 1991.
5.   Criminal Evidence Act, 1992.
6.   Criminal Justice Act, 1993.
7.   Criminal Law (Sexual Offences) Act, 1993.
8.   Criminal Procedure Act, 1993.
9.   Criminal Justice (Public Order) Act, 1994.
10. Criminal Justice Act, 1994.
11. Criminal Justice (Drug Trafficking) Act, 1996.

12. Sexual Offences (Jurisdiction) Act, 1996.
13. Competition Act, 1996.
14. Proceeds of Crime Act, 1996.
15. Criminal Justice (Miscellaneous Provisions) Act, 1997.
16. Bail Act, 1997.
17. Criminal Law Act, 1997
18. Non Fatal Offences against the Person Act, 1997.
19. Criminal Justice Act, 1999.

Judicial education – how far is it necessary?[1]

BRIAN McCRACKEN

I come from a jurisdiction where there is no tradition of educating judges as such, nor is there any system of training young lawyers to become judges such as exists in many civil law countries in Europe. The purpose of this paper is neither to praise nor condemn judicial education, but hopefully to provoke a few thoughts, and to try to ensure, as any judge should, that both sides of the argument are listened to and taken into account.

Education for judges is very much an 'in' topic. But how necessary is it? Have we carried our zeal for the education of judges to far? Are we going towards a stage where judges will be academics, more interested in the intricacies of the law itself, rather than in the interests of the litigants who appear before them? Lest this be misunderstood, can I immediately say that I am not suggesting that academics cannot make good judges, particularly in courts of final jurisdiction. Indeed, South Africa gives an excellent example of this in that, as I understand it, the Constitutional Court contains a high proportion of academics. Of course, I recognise that judges must keep up to date in their legal knowledge, they must be au fait with all legislation and up-to-date legal precedents. I do accept that occasional conferences or seminars may be very beneficial, particularly so where these involve the views of judges or lawyers from other jurisdictions, but I do challenge the necessity for structured formal education for judges. In my view there is a danger that this will become too formal, too structured and, indeed, an end in itself.

I would emphasise that I am making these remarks in the context of the method of appointment and qualifications for appointment of judges in Ireland which does not really lend itself to any form of instruction for persons who wish to become judges, as a precondition of their appointment. Progress from the Bar, or indeed the Solicitors' profession, to the bench can take place with incredible rapidity. Judges in Ireland are appointed by the President of the Republic on the advice of the government, and then make a declaration before the Supreme Court.

When I was appointed the process could unfold as follows:

Day 1 The prospective judge, whom I will call Mr A, gets a telephone call, probably from the Attorney General, asking whether he would be prepared to act if appointed but very carefully disclaiming any promise of appointment.

---

[1] The views expressed in this paper are personal to the author and do not seek to represent the views of any other member of the Irish Judiciary.

Day 2   At a cabinet meeting the government decides to recommend to the President that she appoint Mr A to be a judge, and normally Mr A would be informed of this decision immediately, probably by the Minister for Justice.

Day 3   Mr A goes to Áras an Uachtaráin, which is both the official residence and offices of the President, and is formally appointed to the position by the President in what is in fact a rather informal ceremony.

Day 4   Mr A, possibly for the first and last time in his life, sits on the Supreme Court bench with the Supreme Court judges and makes a solemn declaration before that court in a form which is set out in the Constitution of Ireland. At some stage during these few days the President of the court to which he is appointed will also have had an informal discussion with him.

Day 5   Mr A sits as a judge in whatever jurisdiction to which he has been appointed and hears his first case.

About six months after my appointment the system changed a little. A Judicial Appointments Board was set up and all judicial vacancies must now be advertised, and applications are submitted to it. The Board then draws up a short list which it submits to the government of persons it recommends for the position, but the Board plays no part in the ultimate decision as to who is appointed, nor is the government bound to appoint one of the persons on the short list. In some ways this in fact speeds up the transition from practitioner to judge, as day 1 of the scenario I have set out above becomes unnecessary. By applying to the Judicial Appointments Board, the practitioner has already signified that he will accept any appointment made.

Thus, the great leap across the fence is made in a few days. There is certainly no time for any form of teaching or training. The new judge is left to his own devices to cope as best he can, finding himself suddenly transported from being one of 'us' as a practitioner, to one of 'them' as a judge. Does this mean that we in Ireland have uneducated judges on the bench? I would submit the answer surely must be 'no', primarily because of the background of the persons who are appointed.

The qualifications for appointment as a judge have become somewhat complicated because of the existence of the European Court of Justice, but basically for a person to be qualified for appointment as a High Court or Supreme Court judge, he or she must have at least 12 years' practice as a barrister or have been a Circuit Court judge for at least 4 years, and to be appointed a Circuit Court or District Court judge the person must have been a practising barrister or solicitor for at least 10 years, and the relevant periods must be those immediately before the appointment. There are certain special provisions for a judge or advocate general of the European Court, but these are exceptional cases. In reality it would be extremely rare to appoint a judge of either the Circuit Court or District Court who has less than 15 years' practice, or a judge of the High Court or Supreme Court who has less than 20 years' practice, and in many cases the experience of the person appointed will be considerably greater. Thus, the person appointed to be a judge will inevitably be an experienced legal practitioner.

Legal practitioners must of necessity be up to date in their knowledge of the law, and surely, if they do not have a good knowledge of the law, they should never be appointed as a judge. Indeed, one of the principal reasons for setting up the Judicial Appointments Board, the majority of members of which are either judges or practitioners, was to ensure that only persons of a sufficient calibre would be appointed. I ask, where, then, is the need for education before appointment, or immediately thereafter?

I would have to concede that in one respect there perhaps is need for education of some kind after appointment in respect of a newly-appointed judge, but this education can come in a practical way. Nowadays there is an ever growing tendency on the part of practitioners to specialise, and, therefore, the persons appointed to the bench will, while having a very considerable amount of experience, perhaps only have that experience in a limited field. Thus, in my own case I came from a background of having practised largely in the field of commercial and company law. It was certainly 10 years before my appointment since I had acted in a straightforward personal injuries action, and I suppose it could be said that I did not know what a whiplash was worth when I was appointed. However, it would be very difficult and rather impractical to tailor courses for newly appointed judges to their individual needs or limit it to individual subjects in which they were not very experienced.

In any event the lack of knowledge of a newly-appointed judge in a particular field can to a considerable degree be cured by the proper placement of that judge during his or her initial few months on the bench. In Ireland we have no formal divisions of courts dealing with different types of cases, as is the case in England and Wales, but we do have a President of each level of courts who determines what work will be done by each judge. In practice, the President will ensure that a newly-appointed judge will initially sit doing work with which he or she is familiar, and that the judge will be introduced gradually, if indeed at all, into more uncharted waters. An example of how this may work in practice may be taken from my own experience. We have a system whereby personal injuries actions in the High Court are heard, not only in Dublin, but in a number of venues outside Dublin, and two High Court judges will sit in each of these venues for two weeks at a time three or four times a year. My first experience as a judge of personal injuries cases came about four months after my appointment when I was asked to sit for two weeks in Waterford with another High Court judge of considerable experience. There were just the two of us hearing the cases, we had lunch and dinner together, and the reality was that if I had any problems with a case before me I could discuss the case with my colleague during lunch or dinner and any advice sought was freely given. Thus, I was introduced by an experienced colleague to the problems of personal injury litigation. In Ireland we have also introduced a further 'learning on the job' innovation. Newly-appointed District Court judges are now required, for a period of some weeks after their appointment, to sit with another District Court judge. I think this is an excellent idea which could well be followed at all levels of our court system, and is of course an excellent form of education. This leads me to a favourite topic of mine namely that judges never see their colleagues sitting in court. I believe that every judge should, for at least one whole day in each law term, have to sit quietly in the back of the court of another judge and learn at first hand how to cope with the day-to-day problems which can arise. This should lead to more consistency in the behaviour and attitude of judges, and perhaps stop bad habits creeping in. If I may take liberties with the biblical phrase, it is frequently easier to see the mote in another judge's eye than to see the beam in one's own eye, and recognition of that mote might well lead to the removal of one's own beam.

The method of learning on the job is in keeping with established traditions of the Bar. In Ireland, as indeed in Scotland, the Bar practises from a central library, which has the great advantage that practitioners get to know each other. We have a tradition at. the Irish Bar that if a young, and indeed sometimes not so young, barrister has a problem he or she is free to approach any other member of the Bar, no matter how senior, and, again traditionally, always addressing such member by his or her first name, seek and be given advice in relation to his or her problems. This is a tradition, I am very glad to say which has carried over to the bench. I can approach any colleague simply by picking up a telephone or going to his chambers, and discuss a problem with him. In addition, High Court judges, all of whom are based most of the time in Dublin, meet every Friday during the law term for lunch, and I understand that our female judges from all levels of courts meet together once a month. On these fairly informal occasions, brains are again picked and many problems solved. I realise that this approach would be much more difficult in a larger jurisdiction, where judges may hardly know each other, but it certainly proves very useful in Ireland. Thus, most judicial education in my jurisdiction arises from the best possible source, namely other judges. By hearing other judges' problems we may have assistance to solve our own. By bringing our own problems to other judges we make them aware of difficulties which may never have arisen with them, or even occurred to them. Thus, the collegiate nature of the bench in fact provides a great deal of ongoing education for our judges, education of the best kind because it arises from the knowledge of others acquired by experience.

If one thinks about it, this has always been a tradition of the legal profession. Solicitors serve lengthy apprenticeships which are at least as important as formal legal education. Budding barristers serve a pupillage or devilling period and also eat dinners at Inns of Court. The purpose of this tradition of eating dinners in times gone by was not for the sake of their digestion or to teach them a liking for good wine, as some would have it, but to be educated, and to learn from those who have most experience in their profession. The King's Inns in Ireland, which plays a large part in the education of law students for the Bar, still tries to adhere to these traditions. In addition to formal lectures, every year students attend a tutorial in each subject they are studying that year which is conducted by a bencher, who will be either a senior barrister or a judge, and in giving these tutorials benchers try to give the students some insight into the more practical aspects of the subject and of practice at the Bar. Also, on one night in every dining term in the King's Inns, a bencher dines at each table with six or seven students, thus continuing the old tradition, at least nominally, of students dining with the most eminent practitioners and judges. While, from my experience, I would have to say the topic of conversation at the tables on such occasions is as likely to be football or politics as it is to be law, nevertheless it gives the students a flavour of what it is like to be a barrister or a judge, and start them on that path of contact between newcomers and senior practitioners which, at least for some of them, will lead hopefully to the same relationship between newly-appointed judges and their experienced colleagues. In this way the tradition of learning from the experience of others continues throughout the entire legal career of even the most senior judge.

This is also in keeping with the traditions and history of judges in common law jurisdictions. One can go back to the middle ages and find judges sitting *in banco*, that is a bench of judges who brought their accumulated knowledge to bear on the particular case. Also judges in the early days, even when giving judgment, frequently openly acknowledged that they had consulted with their colleagues before doing so. So, as I have said, learning on the job goes back a long way.

Of course, this is not to say that there should not be some more formal ongoing learning process for judges. The practice of law is steadily getting more complex, particularly in areas such as family law and administrative law, and, on the practical side the management of cases. In Ireland formal education started as recently as 1995 when under section 19 of the Court and Court Officers Act 1995 it was provided that a person who wishes to be considered for appointment to judicial office shall undertake to the Judicial Appointments Board his or her agreement that, if appointed, he or she will take such course or courses of training or education as may be required by the Chief Justice or the President of the Court to which that person is appointed. Section 48 of that Act then provided: 'The Minister for Justice may, with the consent of the Minister for Finance, provide funds for the training and education of judges.'

Following this, the Judicial Studies Institute was set up by the Chief Justice in mid-1996 to provide for the training and ongoing education of the judiciary. Its first venture in 1996 was to hold a seminar on family law which was attended by judges of all courts. Since then further weekend seminars have been held, although initially on a somewhat ad hoc basis, in some cases for all judges of all courts, and in other cases for judges of courts of a specific level. These have now become formalised, and are held at least on an annual basis. The subject matter of these seminars tends to concentrate, quite rightly in my view, either on the practical aspects of the judicial system or on some recent new developments. As an example, a recent seminar which I attended had sessions dealing with judicial conflicts of interest and how to deal with them and with the problems of DNA testing, in the course of which a fascinating paper was given by an eminent professor of genetics.

These may not seem to be world shattering events, but it must be remembered that the Judicial Studies Institute was a totally new concept when it was formed in mid-1996 and, before educating judges, the Institute had to educate itself on how to operate. Very considerable assistance was obtained from the Judicial Studies Board in England and Wales and from the Judicial Studies Committee in Scotland. I understand that the Scottish model proved particularly helpful as the judiciary is of a comparable size to that in Ireland.

I should mention one further form of judicial education which I think all judges have found to be of enormous assistance, the idea for which I think was suggested by the English Judicial Studies Board originally, although I am aware there are similar procedures in at least some states of the United States. I am referring to what we call 'bench books', that is books of documents and advice which have been prepared usually by judges, for use by judges, frequently while actually sitting on the bench and dealing with practical matters. Two examples will probably suffice. The first of these is what we call the bail pack, the purpose of which is primarily to ensure that the approach to granting bail is consistent, and secondly to bring together in one folder all the relevant Superior Court decisions on bail. It should be said that this is a particularly difficult subject in Ireland, as for constitutional reasons, an accused awaiting trial is *prima facie* entitled as a right to bail, and, if bail is being opposed, it is for the prosecuting authority to show the court that it is likely that the accused will either fail to appear at the trial, may intimidate witnesses, or in certain limited cases is likely to commit an offence while on bail.

The second very useful bench book concerns the hearing of actions before civil juries. These actions are restricted to actions for defamation or assault, and therefore, the number is quite limited. As a result, many judges only occasionally hear such cases. While the bench book is quite small, it is invaluable in that it gives rough precedents of charges to a jury in each of these types of cases, and brings together legislation dealing with juries. I would have to say that in my experience the provisions of these bench books is a far more useful form of education for a judge than a weekend seminar. The bench books are always with you, and may be consulted whenever necessary, while the memory of the seminar may not last. It is a trite, but very true, saying that to be a good lawyer it is not really necessary to know the law, but it is essential to know where to find it. It is invaluable to be able to find the proper law and proper procedures simply by putting one's hand on the correct bench book. I would hope that the future development of our Judicial Studies Institute would lay particular emphasis on practical aids to judges of this nature, and would not in any way lessen the importance of the more informal contacts and exchanges of experience between judges which now take place.

One thing that cannot be learnt from the more traditional and informal contact between judges which I have discussed above is how problems are dealt with in other jurisdictions. I do believe that international conferences and contacts can be of huge value. They can introduce totally new ideas which arise from different prospectives and the differing problems in other jurisdictions, and I think we can learn a lot from how such problems are dealt with under legal systems.

I have been particularly fortunate in the last few years in that I have been privileged to see at first hand how several totally different developing jurisdictions are coping with their problems. I have been here in South Africa for each of the last two years and, while many of the contacts have been of a more academic nature, I have found it particularly interesting to learn how the courts in South Africa deal with customary laws, which is something totally foreign to my jurisdiction, and to understand the concept and the limits of South Africa's Constitutional Court. We had a particularly interesting meeting with members of your Constitutional Court, and I think we in Ireland may have a good deal to learn from this approach to constitutional problems.

Three years ago I also was part of the Dublin University team which visited Tanzania, and we held meetings with members of the Tanzanian High Court over several days. It is, of course, a country with a long judicial tradition, and its courts system is similar to our own. But while that is so, its problems are very different, being those of a third world country with very limited resources and a very large territory. While we in Ireland may complain from time to time of a lack of money being provided by the government for the judicial arm of the State, I think it probably did us all a lot of good to see that courts could function on a small fraction of the funding which we get, and justice could still be done under those circumstances. I have to say I came back with the greatest admiration for the amount of independence of the judiciary which existed there, even in the those difficult circumstances.

Finally, some four years ago I had the fortune to a be member of a delegation of Irish judges which spent 10 days in China as guests of the Chinese judiciary. The emergence of a judicial system as we know it is something which has really only occurred in that country in the last 15 or 20 years. Indeed, 25 years ago there were less than a thousand lawyers in the whole of China. While the primary purpose of our visit was to advise and assist the Chinese judiciary, it has to be said that we all learned a lot from the visit. Particularly interesting and instructive was their approach to family law, where there was a huge emphasis on mediation, but mediation in which the judge played an active part.

Quite apart from having a court to sit in, there was a room available where the judge would meet the parties, either individually or together, and act as an negotiator or mediator, and it was only as a last resort that the judge actually sat on the bench. There is probably a great deal we can learn from this approach.

Judicial education certainly has its place. Contact with other jurisdictions, such as those which I have experienced, provide a form of education in the wider sense, and are of great importance, not purely for the factual matters which one learns but to enable one to have a much wider, and hopefully more thoughtful, view as to the administration of justice. My definition of 'education' would be a very broad one encompassing attitudes to law and litigation and the conduct of the courts as well as to law simpliciter. Such education should be in practical matters rather than in pure law. Law can be found in textbooks and reports, and judges should not need to be taught to keep up to date. However, it is very important that there should be education of judges that leads to consistency in the approach of judges to practical matters, such as how to deal with an awkward personal litigant, or how far one should insist that a case is conducted strictly within the confines of the pleadings. In criminal cases, consistency is even more important, consistency in sentencing, consistency in addressing juries, consistency at times in controlling some of the more extreme excesses of counsel.

I certainly believe in judicial education in its broad sense, but I think it can often be achieved more successfully through consultation and co-operation between judges than through formal judicial education. My arguments, therefore, are not against judicial education as such, but only that its emphasis should be on education in all its aspects, and, in particular. education in the broad sense to which I have just referred.

To sum up, therefore, my basic thesis in relation to new judges is quite simple. If a person knows enough law to be appointed a judge, there is no need for a training course in law. If the person does not know enough law, they should not be appointed. A newly-appointed judge has enough difficulties to face which are not connected with the law, such as to how conduct a court. What a new judge needs to be taught can only be learnt on the bench and from colleagues. In relation to judges already on the bench, I think it should be assumed that such a judge will keep up-to-date in the law, although education may well be necessary in relation to technical matters such as, for example, DNA testing or advances in computer software. This does not mean that there may not be some lazy judges, but if a judge is inherently lazy, he or she is unlikely to improve his or her knowledge by sitting through a number of lectures at a weekend seminar.

Finally, and in many ways most importantly of all, there are certain aspects of the work of a judge which cannot be taught. These are not connected with knowledge of the law, but of human nature. Among the essential attributes of a good judge are patience, politeness and a consideration for others, be they lawyers or litigants. These things cannot be taught, although they can perhaps be learnt by experience. It is of course important for a judge to know the law, or at least to know where to find it, but it is perhaps more important that litigants, who after all in one sense we are here to serve, should at least leave the court room, winner or loser, acquitted or going to prison, with a feeling that justice has been done. A judge who can achieve this is an educated judge.

Resolving conflict: arbitration v. litigation with some past and present references to Ireland

RODERICK MURPHY

The dominant feature of resolution is understanding. Problems susceptible to mathematical analysis can be resolved by an understanding of the relevant quantities. In this way engineers will attempt to resolve problems by reducing them to measurements. In a similar way the analysis of conflict requires a mutual understanding both of substance and of procedure so that the parties in conflict – and their advisors – can resolve the various elements of conflict.

Conflict resolution essentially requires some mutual understanding. This is so whether the resolution derives from the parties themselves, from facilitators acting as mediators or conciliators, by arbitration or by litigation. The extent to which this is a self-evident truth depends on one's experience in conflict resolution. As a university lecturer, one has a more idealistic view of what ought to be; as advisor or consultant, one appreciates practical limitations of one's client's position; and as a barrister, attempting to settle disputes between parties, one relies even more on the mutual understanding and co-operation between colleagues to achieve justice. An arbitrator or judge has to draw on each of these perspectives.

RESOLUTION OF CONFLICT BY ARBITRATION

Arbitration is an alternative to litigation in resolving disputes in an internationally enforceable way. The attitude of courts towards arbitrators' awards and their enforcement through the New York Convention gives validity to this method of conflict resolution which is, in fact, potentially of wider enforceability than orders of national courts. The ethos of arbitration is expressed in the French phrase *l'espirit de l'arbitrage*. That is in the spirit rather than in the letter of the law which enables the arbitrator achieve justice. Awards, being confidential, are binding only on the parties. There is, accordingly, no necessary concern regarding precedent.

In this regard the seminal wisdom of Fali Nariman, one of the vice-presidents of the International Court of Arbitration in Paris, in the 10th Annual Goff Lecture,[1] is inspiring. Who but a lawyer of his eminence would take as his theme St Paul's second epistle to the Corinthians in which the apostle proclaims that God 'hath made us able ministers of the new testament; not of the letter but of the spirit: for the letter killeth but the spirit giveth life'?

---

1 (2000) 16, *Arbitration International*, 3, 261.

Arbitration, particularly in the area of commercial disputes, can be fast, flexible, informal, private, confidential and relatively inexpensive in addition to being final. This continues to be so in commodity arbitrations – the so called 'look – sniff' resolutions regarding quality and price. Arbitration is, of course, the preferred method of resolution in construction and investment disputes. However, increasingly, it has become over burdened with litigation challenges. It then, to that extent, begins to lose its attributes.

The strength of arbitration lies in party autonomy: the parties decide not alone on the arbitrator or tribunal but on the law governing substance and procedure. Indeed, the International Court of Arbitration has upheld the parties' right to choose a *lex mercantoria* rather than any particular national law. Where the parties do choose institutional arbitration, whether the London Court of International Arbitration, the American Arbitration Association or the International Court of Arbitration of the International Chambers of Commerce, the parties, at a cost, can ensure that certain steps are taken in the process, including scrutiny of the award before it becomes final. A system whereby the parties can challenge the arbitrator, ensure that terms of reference net the issues and have an examination of the draft award encourages the process of final resolution and of prompt enforcement.

The practice of arbitration has become enriched in two ways. First, arbitrators come from various professional backgrounds. Architects, engineers and other technologists can develop an insight into international commercial law through exposure to arbitration references on a systems basis rather than a comparative law basis. Lawyers, in turn, benefit from this insight. The second element forces all arbitrators – and counsel – to be open to other legal systems. Dr Robert Briner, Chairman, ICC International Court of Arbitration, referred to a construction case between an undisclosed African country and a continental contractor in which the Chairman of the Arbitral Tribunal was a judge of the English Court of Appeal and his co-abritrator an English engineer. English counsel estimated a minimum of four weeks for examination and cross examination of witnesses. However, the mixed tribunal was able to reduce the hearing schedule to 12 days and was also able successfully to nudge the parties to settle the entire case before the hearing commenced.[2]

LITIGATION

It is sometimes said that arbitrators have greater power than High Court judges insofar as the parties have conferred that power on them. The nature of plenary hearings in common law has often meant that, apart from pleadings, there

---

2 Briner, 'Domestic arbitration: practice in continental Europe and its lessons for arbitration in England', (1997) 13 *Arbitration International* 2 at 158.

are no advance written submissions available to the trial judge. Indeed, even where a full book of papers is available the trial judge may not have had an opportunity of perusing those papers until the opening of the case. In contrast, the civil law position of filing of submissions resembles what arbitrators term a documents only reference. The European Court of Justice, while maintaining the civil law requirement to file written submissions, allows a limited amount of oral hearing.

Irish and English courts today require expert witness statements to be exchanged before the hearing in personal injury cases. To this extent there has commenced a convergence of practice between common law and civil law procedures. This is particularly evident in commercial cases where the courts are empowered to supervise the management of such cases. However, this is far from an attempt to require terms of reference of issues or to have critical path analysis of the timing and costing of the discrete elements of litigation. Perhaps we need to learn more from other professionals with regard to problem identification and problem-solving techniques.

COMPENSATION FOR COMPULSORY PURCHASE OF LAND AND OTHER PROPERTY ARBITRATION

Land rights had been a contentious issue in nineteenth-century Ireland. The landlord and tenant legislation gave increasing rights to tenants since 1860. It was, however, the establishment of the Land Commission in 1895 which provided machinery for acquisition of land for the benefit of congestees. The Asquith and Balfour Acts at the beginning of the twentieth century provided for payment to landowners and for annuities to be discharged by transferees. By virtue of successive Land Clause Acts community agencies – and, indeed, commercial undertakings perceived as meeting community needs – were empowered to acquire property compulsorily. Compensation was and still is determined, in default of agreement, by statutory arbitration having regard to open market valuation.

The Acquisition of Land (Assessment of Compensation) Act 1919, which is one of the Land Clauses Acts, provides for assessment by the official arbitrator (now the property arbitrator) having regard not only to the value of the land to be purchased or taken but also to the damage, if any, sustained by the owner of the lands by reason of the severing of the lands taken from the other lands of the owner or otherwise injuriously affecting such other lands by the exercise of the statutory powers. That process has well served the development of railways and roads and more recently, by virtue of the Housing Act 1960, has allowed local authorities to acquire land for housing and other purposes.

Today chartered surveyers and property economists act as arbitrators in disputes concerning property valuations and rent reviews which, a generation ago, had been the preserve of the Circuit Court.

IRELAND AND INTERNATIONAL ARBITRATION

Ireland has adopted the model law of the United Nations Commission on International Trade Law as the core of its International Commercial Law Act of 1998. The Irish Bar has made a significant investment in providing an international centre for dispute resolution in the centre of Dublin adjacent to the courts. University College Dublin provides post-graduate diplomas in domestic and international arbitration. The multi-disciplinary background of candidates is, itself, a significant element in developing analysis of problems and resolution of differences. The international division of the American Arbitration Association has its European headquarters in Dublin. The first international conference of the Chartered Institute of Arbitrators held outside London took place in Dublin under the chairmanship of Dr Noel Bunni in 2000. Meanwhile a vibrant Irish Branch of the Chartered Institute of Arbitrators with over 500 members ensures a continued professional forum for arbitrators of differing backgrounds. This augurs well for the further development of *l'espirit d'arbitrage*!

2   THE CRIMINAL LAW PROCESS

The right to bail: some comparative aspects

KEVIN O'HIGGINS

At least a reasonable overview of the law relating to bail in Ireland can be found in the judgment of the Supreme Court in the case of *People (AG) v. O'Callaghan*,[1] taken together with the provisions of the Bail Act, 1997, introduced following the 16th Amendment to the Constitution in 1996.

To put the topic in context it is worth noting that according to information emanating from the Council of Europe Prison Information Bulletin for equivalent periods in 1988, 1990 and 1991 the percentage of persons remanded in custody in Ireland is very low.If a group were to come together to devise a regime for the granting or refusal of bail, I think it likely that there would be consensus – or near consensus – not only on at least some of the criteria that would apply, but also on the factors to be taken into account in evaluating these criteria. If that be so, one would expect to see widespread similarities in at least some of the features of the law relating to bail across different regimes. Many of the grounds for refusing bail would be as applicable in Caherciveen as in Cape Town. It is for example highly probable that most bail regimes would make provision for the refusal of bail in circumstances where there was a likelihood that a person charged with a crime would abscond. Of course there are likely to be variations in the degree of apprehension of absconding required to deny bail from one jurisdiction to another, but the principle is the same.

Likewise it is likely that considerations involving the protection of the trial or the criminal justice process would be common concerns of bail regimes across a wide range of different jurisdictions. Our conscientious group would, no doubt, agree that the potential interference with witnesses and the destruction or concealment of evidence are factors to be taken into account when deciding on bail in an individual case. The level of apprehension of such interference with the integrity of the criminal law process necessary to refuse bail is of course likely to vary from one jurisdiction to another.

Not only are certain criteria for the refusal of bail likely to be relatively non-contentious; the indicators by which the risk may be evaluated are also likely to have similarities in different jurisdictions. For instance, the severity of the likely penal sanction for the offence seems a fairly obvious factor to take into account in assessing the likelihood of not standing trial.

In the light of the foregoing it seems to me that the law on bail in Ireland as articulated by the Supreme Court in *O'Callaghan* would be unlikely to cause

---

1 [1966] IR 501.

any surprise to the group devising a bail regime. The grounds on which the court may exercise its discretion to refuse bail as set out in *O'Callaghan* are concerned with the applicant evading justice and the following matters were held to be relevant in that regard:

1. The nature of the accusation or the serious nature of the charge. South African legislation provides that, in considering the likelihood of an attempt to evade trial, the Court may take into account 'the nature and the gravity of the offence'.

2. The nature and cogency of the evidence. This fairly obvious factor is contained in South African legislation: section 60 (6) (g) of the Bail Act refers to 'the strength of the State case and the incentive to flee'.

3. The likely sentence to be imposed on conviction. This *O'Callaghan* criterion is expressed in statutory form in South African legislation as 'the nature and gravity of the likely penalty'.

4. The reasonable probability of disposal of illegally held property was held to be a ground for refusal of bail in the context of apprehension of the destruction or concealment of evidence. This matter also is dealt with specifically in section 60(4)(c) of the South African Bail Act which provides for the refusal of bail 'where there is a likelihood that the accused, if he or she were released on bail, will attempt to influence or intimidate witnesses, or to conceal or destroy evidence'.

5. Likewise the reasonable possibility of the interference with prospective witnesses and jurors mentioned in *O'Callaghan* has echoes in South African legislation in section 60(4)(c) of the Bail Act.

6. The failure to answer bail on a previous occasion – a factor which the courts can take into consideration according to the decision in *O'Callaghan* – comes under the umbrella of 'any other factor' under section 60(6)(j) of the South African Bail Act.

7. The fact that the accused has been caught red handed is under *O'Callaghan* a factor to be taken into account in a bail application. However, if the presumption of innocence is to be respected it can scarcely be regarded as more than an illustration of the 'strength of the State case' factor already mentioned.

8. The objection of the prosecuting authorities is not a ground for refusing bail but is something to which the courts may have regard, not *in vacuo,* but only if supported by sufficient evidence to enable the court to draw conclusions as to the probability of the applicant evading justice if granted bail. In practical terms I am not sure how meaningful is this particular stipulation.

9. The substance and reliability of those offering to go bail is a matter for the court to assess.

10. The probability of an early trial is not a ground for refusing bail. However, the fact that there might be a delay in obtaining a trial is considered a factor that might cause a court to exercise its discretion in favour of granting bail in cases where it might not otherwise do so.

In the course of his judgment in *O'Callaghan*, Walsh J, having briefly reviewed the history of the jurisdiction to grant bail, emphasised that the object of bail was to secure attendance at trial. He said (at pp 513–14):

> It follows therefore that the object of fixing terms of bail is to make it reasonably assured that the applicant will surrender at his trial ... for the purposes of the High Court, – while there is no case in which bail may not be granted and (subject to the exception under the Irish Habeas Corpus Act, already referred to) no case in which bail is available as of right, the guides to a decision on the fundamental test are the same in all cases ... though the emphasis may vary depending on the seriousness of the offence and other matters. These guides have existed from the earliest times. According to Bracton regard was to be had to (1) the importance of the charge (2) the character (meaning the condition) of the person and (3) the gravity of the evidence against him. In Hawkins, *Pleas of the Crown* (7th ed. vol. 3, Ch. 15, s.4) the guides are stated to be (1) the ability to give bail (2) the quality of the prisoner (3) the nature of the offence.'

Unfortunately Walsh J did not explain what Hawkins meant by the quality of the prisoner – an interesting concept.

The judgment continues: 'Over the course of the years and as a result of many judicial decisions the guides have remained fundamentally the same'. Walsh J considered the evasion of justice to be the criterion on which bail might be refused. Apart from the matters enumerated in *O'Callaghan*, in practice our courts take other matters into account – the ties of the applicant to the country by way of family, property or business interests, matters which are provided for in South African legislation on a statutory basis; and it is a matter of routine to require the surrender of a passport as a term of setting bail.

So far so good. On the basis of the matters mentioned so far can we just leave it at that – congratulating the Irish judiciary and the South African legislature on their wisdom and dismissing our group, thanking them for their consensus? I think not, because it is beyond matters already discussed that the scope for divergence in bail laws really exists. In that regard it is to be noted that in *O'Callaghan* the Supreme Court dismissed the notion of the likelihood of the commission of further crime when on bail as a factor to be taken into account in the most trenchant terms.

Ó Dálaigh CJ was of the view that such detention (at pp 508–9):

transcends the respect for the requirement that a man shall be considered innocent until he is found guilty, and seeks to punish him in respect of offences neither completed nor attempted. I say 'punish' for deprivation of liberty must be considered punishment unless it can be required to ensure that an accused person will stand his trial when called upon.

Walsh J was equally forceful in his view, describing the concept of refusing bail because of the likelihood of the commission of other crimes as: 'a form of preventative justice that has no place in our legal system and ... quite alien to the true purposes of bail.' His view (at pp 516–17) was that:

> in this country it would be quite contrary to the concept of personal liberty enshrined in the Constitution that any person should be punished in respect of any matter upon which he has not been convicted, or that in any circumstances he should be deprived of his liberty upon only the belief that he will commit offences if left at liberty, save in the most extraordinary circumstances carefully spelled out by the Oireachtas and then only to secure the preservation of public peace and order or the public safety and the preservation of the State in a time of national emergency or some situation akin to that.

He considered that any imprisonment before conviction has 'a substantial punitive content'.

The Law Reform Commission's Report, *An Examination of the Law of Bail* (LRC50–1995) points out (p. 169) that the United States Supreme Court took a directly opposite point of view concluding that pre-trial preventative detention was not punitive. Interestingly, the Report also notes an article in the 1967 *Irish Jurist* ('Preventive Justice' (1967) in *Ir Jur (ns)* 233) in which Ronan Keane, later to become Chief Justice of Ireland, wrote as follows (at p. 238):

> Ó Dalaigh CJ and Walsh J conceded that a person could be legitimately refused bail on the grounds that he might tamper with the State's witnesses or with jurors. What is the situation of the same person if he is subsequently acquitted? He has suffered imprisonment, not for the offence with which he was charged, for of that he is innocent, and not for the offence of interfering with the course of justice, which he never had the opportunity of committing. It is impossible to resist the conclusion that his imprisonment is not in the nature of punishment at all; it is in fact a measure of preventive justice, designed to ensure that the future offence of interfering with the course of justice is not committed by the individual concerned.

He concluded (at p. 239) by stating:

There may very well be good reasons for the general principle enunciated by the court (in Ó Dálaigh CJ's words) 'the single question in
all bail applications is, is the applicant likely to stand his trial'. But it is
respectfully submitted that the argument based on preventive justice
which was used in support of this principle does not appear either logical or convincing. If a person charged with a criminal offence is alleged
to have committed other offences while on bail on a previous charge,
the Court in refusing him bail is manifestly not punishing for an offence
which he has not committed. It is exercising the jurisdiction which it
possesses to grant or refuse bail in such a manner as to ensure the prevention of crime; and it is no more inflicting punishment on an accused
person than it does so in making a binding over order against a person
who is innocent of any offence.

Whatever the rights and wrongs as to whether the function of bail is to
secure attendance at trial, or whether pre-trial detention to prevent crime while
on bail is punitive or not, the matter has been rendered of academic interest
only in Ireland by the passing of the 16th Amendment to the Constitution and
the introduction of the Bail Act 1997.

It is worth noting that pre-trial detention is specifically authorised by Article
5(1)(c) of the European Convention on Human Rights where it is reasonably
necessary to prevent the accused committing offences.

The 1996 referendum

Article 40.4.7° of the Constitution, introduced by the Sixteenth Amendment
to the Constitution, states that: 'Provision may be made by law for the refusal
of bail by a court to a person charged with a serious offence where it is reasonably considered necessary to prevent the commission of a serious offence
by that person.'

The Bail Act, 1997

Following this referendum, the Bail Act, 1997 was enacted. It came into force
in May 2000. The Act has two main purposes. The first is to give effect to the
Constitutional amendment. It defines the offences which are considered 'serious' and outlines the matters which a court may take into account in determining whether to grant bail under this regime. These are:

(i)   the nature and degree of seriousness of the offence with which the accused
      is charged and the likely sentence on conviction;

(ii) the nature and degree of seriousness of the offence apprehended and the
      likely sentence on conviction;

(iii) the nature and strength of the evidence against the accused;

(iv) any conviction of the accused in relation to an offence committed while he or she was on bail;

(v) any previous conviction of the accused, including a conviction under appeal;

(vi) any other offence in respect of which the accused is charged and is awaiting trial.

Additionally, where the court has taken one of these factors into account, it may have regard to the fact that the accused is addicted to drugs with the meaning of the Misuse of Drugs Act, 1977. The court may hear submissions on these matters from either the accused or the prosecution. In reaching its decision, it does not have to be satisfied that any *specific* offence is likely to be committed by the accused.

The Act provides that a refusal of bail under the new regime may be reviewed if the trial has not commenced within four months of the initial refusal. It also introduces reporting restrictions in order to ensure that evidence of a person's previous criminal record shall not prejudice his or her right to a fair trial. The Act introduced other changes in the bail regime which need not be dealt with in the present context. A short article by two practitioners on the operation of the Bail Act, 1997 contains the following observations:

> Since the Act came into force experience in the courts has shown that if they wish to object to bail using Section 2, Garda witnesses need to be very specific in detailing the basis for their belief that the accused is likely to offend while on bail ... Indeed, the Section 2 ground for refusal has been used on very few occasions in the High Court and where it has been used successfully the Garda witnesses have based their objections on multiple factors, including substance addiction, previous convictions which are all of a similar nature, and which conform to a chronological sequence, as well as on the strength and nature of the evidence against the accused on the relevant charge on which he or she is seeking bail.

That statement tallies with my own impression. It is I believe very rare to see a bail application, at least in the High Court, resisted solely on Section 2 grounds. I think it is probably rarer still to see it succeed.

In an article in the *Bar Review*, May 1998 – 'Bail – a privilege or a right?' volume 7, p. 318 –Micheál O'Higgins points out that the broad wording of section 2 has been criticised by opponents of the Act. Section 2(1)(f) in particular has been criticised because it obliges the court to take into account any other offence in respect of which an accused person is charged and awaiting trial. On first flush it is difficult to see how the fact that someone is charged with an offence in respect of which the presumption of innocence exists can be of assistance in assessing whether a person should be granted bail on an entirely separate offence in respect of which the same presumption applies.

The author refers to the judgment of Finlay CJ in *Ryan v. D.P.P.*[2] in which he anticipated some of the practical difficulties with such a provision as well as questioning it on other grounds. The former Chief Justice said (at p. 407):

> An intention to commit a crime, even of the most serious type, is not in our criminal law a crime itself unless it is furthered by overt acts of preparation or converted by an agreement with another into a conspiracy. The courts cannot create offences or crimes, though the Oireachtas may. Are they, however, to be permitted to detain a person because he is suspected of an intention which even if proved in a full criminal trial could not lead to his punishment? If such a power did exist in the courts, why should its exercise be confined to cases where the suspect is an applicant for bail? Why should the courts' prevention of the apprehended harm cease in the event of the determination without a sentence of imprisonment of the original charge, which charge may in its character and seriousness bear no resemblance at all to the feared offence? How can such an intention be proved and by what standard of proof must it be established? Could there be any grounds on which an accused person suspected of such an intention would be afforded less comprehensive notice of the evidence to be offered against him on the grounds of such suspicion and less opportunity to prepare and be represented to contest such allegations than he is afforded in relation to the presenting of a criminal charge against him?
>
> Would every application for bail accordingly in which this ground was advanced as a substantial ground of opposition, take on the nature and necessary requisites of a criminal trial? These queries not only indicate practical problems but more importantly highlight the nature of the jurisdiction which it is sought to invoke without legislation.

Some of the questions of the former Chief Justice still remain to be answered. I am not aware that any standard practice has grown up concerning the nature of the notice and the basis of the evidence to be offered in support of that ground. Even in this more contentious ground there are similar provisions in the legislation in Ireland and in South Africa. It is, however, the position that South African law has additional grounds for consideration in deciding the question of bail, including the likelihood of the accused endangering public safety, the likelihood that the accused if released on bail will undermine or

2 [1989] IR 399.

jeopardise the objectives or the proper functioning of the criminal justice system including the bail system and also the likelihood, in exceptional circumstances, that the release of the accused will disturb the public order or undermine the public peace or security. Some of these have been the subject matter of recent scrutiny by the South African courts.[3] The relevance of scandalising public feeling is recognised in some European jurisdictions as a ground for refusing bail. For example, the Netherlands has a provision whereby a detention on remand may be imposed if the offence has seriously shocked the community, where the offence carries a penalty of life imprisonment or at least twelve years. In Spain, detention may be considered necessary because of 'the social alarm caused by the offence or the frequency with which similar offences are committed' and in certain circumstances in Denmark detention on remand may be used to protect the public sense of justice if the *prima facie* evidence is very strong.

This very brief survey demonstrates, I hope, that, while there are many legal principles in common relating to bail laws throughout many countries, there is, nonetheless, the possibility for particular countries to come to distinctive solutions. The Irish experience may, therefore, be of interest for lawyers in other countries, including South Africa.

---

3 *S. v. Dlamini* [2000] 2 LRC 239.

The role of the judge and jury in criminal cases

YVONNE MURPHY

Article 38 of the Irish Constitution makes provision for trial of offences in due course of law. Leaving aside, for the moment, Article 38.3, Article 38.4 and Article 38.6, which relate to Special Courts and Military Tribunals, the Article provides as follows:

1. No person shall be tried on any criminal charge save in due course of law.
2. Minor offences may be tried by Courts of Summary Jurisdiction [...]
5. Save in the case of the Trial of Offences under Section 2, Section 3 or Section 4 of this Article no person shall be tried on any criminal charge without a jury.

The reference to 'due course of law' in the first of these Articles has been held to be equivalent to 'due process of law' as used in the Fifth Amendment to the United States Constitution. It refers to the whole body of rights now considered essential in a criminal trial and 'requires a fair and just balance between the exercise of individual freedoms and the requirements of an ordered society'.[1]

Trial by jury for non-minor offences was certainly part of the common law heritage Ireland incorporated into the Constitution of the Irish Free State in 1922, and re-stated in 1937. It might, therefore, be regarded as an incident of a trial in due course of law but was in any event made the subject of the special provision quoted above. This specific safeguarding of trial by jury was stated by former Chief Justice, Mr Justice Ó Dálaigh, to be a 'safeguard ... against an improbable but not to be overlooked future: it is for this reason the Constitution enshrines it.'[2] In the same case Kingsmill Moore J observed that:

> trial by jury had for centuries been regarded popularly as a most important safeguard for the individual, a protection alike against the zeal of an enthusiastic executive or the rigidity of an ultra conservative judiciary. Especially was this so in the history of Ireland. It seems to me reasonably clear that the [Free State] Constitution meant to preserve and extend this right.

1 *In re the Criminal Law Jurisdiction Bill 1975* [1977] IR 129.   2 *Melling v. Ó Mathghamhna* [1962] IR1.

While the last quotation states correctly the popular attitude towards jury trial in Great Britain, the historic Irish experience of the institution was rather more nuanced. Jury trial had been a feature of Irish law since the common law was first introduced in the twelfth century, but for a large part of the long history of Ireland as a colony, and later as an integral part of the United Kingdom, the actual conduct of trials, whether by jury or otherwise, had not commanded public endorsement. In *DPP v. O'Shea*[3] Mr Justice Henchy sketched his historical impression in the following words:

> The Irish race memory of politically appointed and executive oriented judges, of the suspension of jury trials in times of popular revolt, of the substitution therefor of summary trial or detention without trial, of cat and mouse releases from such detention, of packed juries and sometimes corrupt judges and prosecutors, had long implanted in the consciousness of the people, and therefore in the minds of their political representatives, the conviction that the best way of preventing an individual from suffering a wrong conviction for an offence was to allow him … to be tried for that offence by a fair, impartial and representative jury, sitting in a Court presided over by an impartial and independent Judge appointed under the Constitution, who would see that all the requirements for a fair and proper jury trial would be observed.

This affection for jury trial as an institution, combined with the consciousness that the composition of juries, and the conduct of trials, require minute supervision, is a feature of the modem Irish jurisprudence of the subject.

Nature and purpose of jury trial

In *O'Callaghan v. The Attorney General*[4] Mr Justice Blaney having surveyed various authorities said: 'There appears to emerge a fairly clear consensus that the essence of trial by jury is that the decision as to the guilt or innocence of the accused is made by a group of his fellow citizens and not by a judge or a number of judges'. The value thus expressed seems to me to lie at the heart of trial by jury. While the trial is conducted, as Mr Justice Walsh put it in *De Burca v. The Attorney General*,[5] 'in the presence, and under the authority, of a presiding judge having power to instruct the jury as to the law and to advise them as to the facts', nevertheless 'the jury should be free to consider their verdict alone and without the intervention or presence of the judge or any other person … I think it also imports an element of secrecy.'

The decision as to guilt or innocence, therefore, is to be that of a lay body 'broadly representative of the community so that its verdict will be stamped with the fairness and acceptability of a genuinely defused community decision'.[6]

---

3 [1992] IR 384.   4 [1992] 1 IR 538.   5 [1976] IR 38, at 67.   6 Ibid. at 75, *per* Henchy J.

The role of the judge

In *DPP v. Davis*,[7] the Supreme Court found that a direction by a judge that the jury return a verdict of guilty of murder was inappropriate. Although the judge could 'express an opinion that a particular verdict of guilty would be reasonable or proper on the evidence' his rights, 'must of necessity fall short of the right to direct a verdict of guilty'. Chief Justice Finlay held that the authorities 'lead inevitably to the conclusion that the Constitutional right to trial with a jury contained in Article 38.5 … has as a fundamental and absolutely essential characteristic the right of the jury to deliver a verdict'.

Jury trial in practice

In my view, on the basis of current experience in presiding at jury trials, the values underlying these dicta are given real substance on a daily basis to a quite remarkable degree. The seriousness with which jurors take their duties constantly impresses me as does their assiduity and grasp of the facts of a case, as evidenced in their questions. One can often see quite palpably the heightened sense of responsibility and seriousness as a jury comes to realise that the verdict is indeed, in substance as well as in theory, theirs: that the court is not going to dictate or even suggest what the result should be. And, from the point of view of the participants in a case, I think there is an independent value in the detailed exposition to an impartial lay body of the principles of law to be applied.

Is a trial by jury different in texture and in nature to a trial before a judge or judges? I believe that not infrequently it is. Many trials involve a factual background of which a professional judge may have little or little recent experience: a housing estate in the grip of some excitement, a nightclub in the small hours, feelings of debauchery or passion, the nocturnal behaviour of a group of young people. Chief Justice Ó Dálaigh, in *Melling*, felt that a jury could bring to these and other matters what he called 'the commoner touch'; it may also be a surer touch. Again, in the not uncommon case which is a swearing match between Gardaí and the defendant and his witnesses if any, I have never felt a jury to be less competent than myself as estimators of the plausabilities of each version and have sometimes felt the reverse. It is indisputable that many accused persons feel, rightly or wrongly, that in a case of the last sort they are more likely to get a fully impartial verdict from a jury simply because they see the police and the judiciary as two groups with constant interaction. For this reason alone the jury fulfils an important function.

Jury or non-jury trial

The provision for the trial of minor offences by courts of summary jurisdiction, i.e. the District Court, applies to the trial of numerically the great majority of

7 [1993] ILRM 407.

offences from parking tickets upwards. It is a feature of our courts system that summary trial is very broadly used and has an unusually high maximum jurisdiction, up to two years in certain instances where there are two or more offences. It is also noteworthy that a trend in recent years was meant to confer the right of election for trial on indictment on the prosecution only, which I think may be a retrograde step in certain cases. It is also noteworthy that prosecutions on indictment for offences of assault on Gardaí have virtually ceased, the prosecution preferring to use alternative charges which can be disposed of summarily. However, in general, there is little doubt that the vast majority of offences prosecuted in the District Court are minor offences suitable for summary disposal.

Article 38.3 and 4 provide respectively for special courts and for military tribunals. It has to be borne in mind that, almost since independence, Ireland has had a (generally) low level of paramilitary activity directed either at de-stabilisation of the State or attacks in the United Kingdom. Part 5 of the Offences against the State Act, 1939 provides for a Special Criminal Court, by enacting, in Section 35(1):

> If and whenever and so often as the Government is satisfied that the ordinary courts are inadequate to secure the effective administration of justice and the preservation of public peace and order and that it is therefore necessary that this part of the Act shall come into force, the Government may make and publish a proclamation declaring that the Government is satisfied as aforesaid, and ordering that this part of the Act shall come into force.

Once this is done, it is competent to establish a Special Criminal Court. There is provision in the Act as to the membership of the special court; it may consist of either judges, lawyers of a certain seniority or army officers of a certain rank. In fact, since 1986 all members of the Special Criminal Court have been serving judges.

There is no doubt, historically, that the Special Criminal Court was occasioned by political emergencies. In *People (DPP) v. Quilligan (No. 1)*[8] Mr Justice Walsh said:

> It is common knowledge, and indeed, was discussed in the debates in the Oireachtas leading to the enactment of the 1939 Act that what was envisaged were cases or situations of a political nature where juries could be open to intimidation or threats of various types. However, a similar situation could well arise in types of cases far removed from what one could call 'political type' offence. There could well be a grave situation in dealing with ordinary gangsterism or well financed ... drugs dealing or other situations where it might be believed or established

---

8 [1986] IR 495, at 509–10.

that juries were for some corrupt reason, or by virtue of threats or illegal interference, being prevented from doing justice.

In fairly recent times there have been a number of cases which are not
political in the ordinary sense of the term but which have none the less been
sent for trial by the Special Criminal Court. The power to do this is now vested
in the Director of Public Prosecutions and is exercised by him by certifying:
'that the ordinary courts are, in his opinion, inadequate to secure the effective
administration of justice and the preservation of public peace and order in relation to the trial of such persons on such charge'. In a number of decisions the
superior courts have held that this power is unreviewable.[9]

If this decision is, indeed, unreviewable, then it is one of a very small
number of administrative decisions which have this characteristic. In recent
times, in *Kavanagh*[10] the United Nations Committee who implement the
International Covenant on Civil and Political Rights has indicated its unhap-
piness with the unreviewable nature of this decision. This, in turn, casts an onus
on Ireland to respond within a specified period indicating what the State proposes to do on the foot of the committee's findings. It may be, therefore, that
some change may be anticipated in this area.

Eligibility for jury service is now governed by the Juries Act of 1976. Prior
to that the jurors were selected from persons having a certain property qualification, a practice that in effect limited jury service to men as they were they
main property owners in the country. In *de Burca v. The Attorney General*[11] the
property qualification and the exclusion in practice of women was held to be
unconstitutional by the Supreme Court and that gave rise to the enactment of
the Juries Act 1976. Under that Act every citizen aged 18 and upwards and
under the age of 70 years who is entered in the Parliamentary Register of
Electors in a particular jury district is qualified. Persons are liable to serve, unless
at the time they are called they are ineligible or disqualified. Persons who would
be deemed ineligible would be the President of Ireland, people concerned with
the administration of justice, i.e. a practising barrister, a practising solicitor,
members of the police force, and welfare officers, members of the Defence
Forces and persons who are illiterate or deaf or mental patients. In addition,
people can be disqualified from jury service if for example, they have been convicted of an offence attracting a certain type of prison sentence. There is also
a process whereby others such as medical practitioners who cannot be spared
from certain jobs may be excused from jury service.

Persons selected for jury service are notified by written summons and are
required to attend at the court for the period specified in the summons. The

9 See *O'Reilly v. DPP* [1984] ILRM 224; *Foley v. DPP*, High Court, unreported 25 September 1989. **10** Communication No. 819/1998: Ireland 26/04/2001. CCPR/C/71/D/ 819/1. **11** [1976] IR 38(SC).

number summoned will depend on the number of trials there are to be heard. Dublin is the capital of Ireland and has a population of approximately 1.2 million people. Those required for jury service are usually summoned for a period of two weeks. Several hundred people will be summoned for the start of the two-week period. At any one time there could be seven criminal jury trials proceeding in the Dublin Metropolitan area. The jury summons which a person receives sets out in clear and unambiguous terms the rules relating to eligibility, disqualification or potential excusal from jury service. A person who does not fall into any of those categories and who fails to attend when summoned can be prosecuted. Similarly if a person makes a false declaration in relation to his or her eligibility to serve he or she too can be prosecuted.

Empanelling the jury
The first interaction between the judge and potential jurors arises when the jury is about to be empanelled; prior to that any potential juror is dealing with staff from the Courts Service. A ballot is held in open court in front of a judge to select a particular jury for a particular case. The judge has a duty to warn jurors that they should not serve if they ineligible or disqualified or if they have any connection with any of the parties associated with the case or if they know any of the witnesses or the defendant in the case.

Both the prosecution and the defence have a right to object to a particular jury member. Two forms of objection can be taken. A peremptory challenge means that no cause has to be shown as to why either side does not want a particular juror serving on the jury. Both the prosecution and the defence have seven challenges of this sort. Once their respective peremptory challenges have been exhausted, they can then challenge further members of the jury provided they can show cause. In practice this is rarely done although both the prosecution and the defence usually use up the peremptory challenges. Each jury person is sworn or if they have an objection to taking an oath they are required to affirm. When the jury of 12 people have been selected then the trial is in a position to proceed.

Functions of the judge and jury
The business of the trial is divided between the judge and jury. The judge presides over the trial to see that it is fairly conducted and to decide questions of law which may arise. The role of the jury is to decide all questions of fact that may arise between the prosecution and the defence: it is the jury and nobody else who will find the defendant guilty or not guilty. Mr Justice Henchy of the Supreme Court in *People v. O'Shea*,[12] expressed what he envisaged the constitutional right to a trial with a jury to be:

12 [1982] IR 384, at 431.

[A] trial before a judge and jury, at which the judge will preside, ensures that all conditions necessary for a fair and proper trial of that nature are complied with, decide all matters esteemed to be matters of law, and direct the jury as to the legal principles and rules they are to observe and apply; and in which the jury, constituted in a manner calculated to ensure the achievement of the proper exercise of their function, would under the governance of the judge, be the arbiters of all disputed issues of fact and, in particular, the issue of guilt or innocence.

When the jury is empanelled and the trial is ready to start the accused is given into their charge and the charges to which the accused has pleaded not guilty are read over. At this stage they will have elected a foreman and will have been equipped with writing materials and assigned a jury room.

The trial

Many issues that arise in the course of a criminal trial are issues of law which do not involve the jury. Issues such as the validity of a search warrant, an arrest warrant, legality of detention and the admissibility of statements are debated in the absence of a jury. The continuance of any criminal trial will often depend on the success or otherwise of such applications in the absence of the jury.

This sort of application has increased in importance in recent times, with an increased tendency for prosecutions to depend wholly or partly on alleged oral or written confessions. Until very recently it was generally believed by criminal lawyers that, if a confession was allowed to go to the jury, they were likely to accept it. But I have noticed an increased scepticism on the part of juries toward alleged oral confessions, especially if they are very brief and general in terms. This may be attributable to certain notorious cases of apparently forced confessions in Ireland and in Britain. Statutes and regulations have considerably tightened up the treatment of persons in custody. Provision has been made for the electronic recording of interviews. But this has, so far, been little used and it remains to be seen how juries will react to it.

Aside from these matters there are many issues of a legal and practical nature that arise in the course of a criminal jury trial where the judge is required to direct the jury in a particular way. This obligation arises not only from statute but as a result of a substantial body of case law which has built up over the years, and it is on some of these areas that I now intend to concentrate.

Visual identification

Miscarriages of justice have occurred where witnesses have mistakenly identified the accused as the perpetrator of the crime. The case of Adolph Beck has been well documented.[13] The leading Irish case in this area is *People v. Casey*

---

13 See Williams, *The proof of guilt* (3rd ed. 1963).

(no. 2).[14] The Court directed that trial judges were required to give a mandatory warning to juries in cases where the prosecution was relying substantially or wholly on the visual identification of the accused as the person who perpetrated the crime. Mr Justice Kingsmill Moore said:

> [W]e are of the opinion that juries as a whole may not be aware of the dangers involved in visual identification, nor of the considerable number of cases in which such identification has been proved to be erroneous; and also that they may be inclined to attribute too much probative value to the test of an identification parade. In our opinion it is desirable that in all cases where the verdict depends substantially on the correctness of an identification, their attention should be called in general terms to the fact that in a number of instances such identification has proved erroneous, to the possibilities of mistake in the case before them and to the necessity of caution. Nor do we think that such warnings should be confined to cases where the identification is that of only one witness. Experience has shown that mistakes can occur where two or more witnesses have made positive identifications. We consider juries in cases where the correctness of an identification is challenged should be directed on the following lines, namely, that if their verdict as to the guilt of the prisoner is to depend wholly or substantially on the correctness of such identification, they should bear in mind that there have been a number of instances where responsible witnesses, whose honesty was not in question and whose opportunities for observation had been adequate, made positive identifications on a parade or otherwise which identifications were subsequently proved erroneous; and accordingly that they should be specially cautious before accepting such evidence of identification as correct; but that if after careful examination of such evidence in the light of all the circumstances and with due regard to all other evidence in the case they feel satisfied beyond a reasonable doubt of the correctness of the identification they are at liberty to act on it.[15]

The direction

Such direction as laid down by the Supreme Court in *Casey* has to be adapted to the particular circumstances of each case. Aspects which may be useful to draw to the jury's attention include the time which the witnesses had to see the features of the person identified, the distance the witness was away from the person identified, the lighting that was available, the state of mind of the witness if it was affected by fear, whether the person was moving or stationary, among other things. Many of these factors were stressed by Lord Widgery CJ in the English case *R v. Turnbull*.[16]

---

14 [1963] IR 33.   **15** Ibid. at 39.   **16** [1977] QB 224.

Corroboration

A person may be convicted on the evidence of a single witness. It is useful to note that this is an area where there has been a good deal of development both from the statutory point of view and also from the case law. Corroboration is defined as some evidence independent of the complainant's evidence which confirms in some material particular that the offence was committed and that the accused committed it. In such cases juries must be warned that although they may convict on uncorroborated evidence it is dangerous to do so in the absence of corroboration in certain cases. For instance, special warnings are required in relation to the uncorroborated evidence of an accomplice or of an accomplice's spouse. In *Attorney General v. Lenihan*[17] Kennedy CJ observed that 'a person implicated either as principal or as accessory in the crime under investigation is an "accomplice" within the rule though the degree and gravity of such complicity may vary, and inasmuch as the extent of the effect of such complicity upon the credit of the witness or the weight of his uncorroborated testimony will vary accordingly, so should the degree and gravity of the warning be measured.' The wife of an accomplice is defined as per the judgment of Murnaghan J in the Court of Criminal Appeal decision of *Attorney General v. Durnan.*[18]

Section 10 of the Criminal Procedure Act, 1993 says that, where at a trial of a person on indictment evidence is given of a confession made by that person, and that evidence is not corroborated, the judge shall advise the jury to have due regard to the absence of corroboration. It is not necessary for a judge to use any particular form of words under this section. Two relatively recent pieces of legislation reduced the necessity for a trial judge to give a mandatory warning but introduced the concept of doing so at his or her discretion having regard to the evidence adduced. Section 7(1) of the Criminal Law (Rape) Amendment Act, 1990 provides:

> Subject to any enactment relating to the corroboration of evidence in criminal proceedings, where at the trial on indictment of a person charged with an offence of a sexual nature evidence is given by the person in relation to whom the offence was alleged to have been committed and, by reason only of the nature of the charge, there would, but for this section, be a requirement that the jury be given a warning about the danger of convicting the person on the uncorroborated evidence of that other person, it shall be for the judge to decide in his discretion, having regard to all the evidence given, whether the jury should be given a warning; and accordingly any rule of law or practice by virtue by which there is such a requirement as aforesaid is hereby abolished.

However, Charleton, McDermot & Bolger point out in their text, *Criminal Law* (1999), para 8.156, that the Court of Criminal Appeal has held in *People*

17 [1929] IR 19 at 23. 18 [1934] IR 308. 19 [1993] 2 IR at 186.

(DPP) v. Reid[19] that despite the enactment of section 7 there will be cases at which the trial judge will consider it desirable to warn the jury as to the dangers of convicting on the uncorroborated evidence of complainant. The same principle applies to the unsworn evidence of a child. This is covered by section 28 of the Criminal Evidence Act, 1992 which abolished section 30 of the Children Act of 1908.

In addition to highlighting these two areas, corroboration and visual identification, the judge must abide by the fundamental principles which govern any deliberations by a jury, by indicating in clear and unambiguous terms that:

(a) the defendant is presumed innocent until proven guilty to their satisfaction and that the onus of proof rests on the prosecution at all times.

(b) it is for the prosecution to prove the defendant guilty, not for him to establish his evidence; and

(c) the prosecution's task is to prove the defendant's guilt beyond reasonable doubt and not to any lower standard and the jury must be satisfied that there is no reasonable doubt of the defendant's guilt before it can convict.

While juries are invited to participate in the proceedings and to query any of the witnesses or have points clarified, it is useful to note that in some cases the jury members will want to question the defendant, particularly if he gives evidence. There is an onus on the trial judge to point out to the jury that there is no requirement on the defendant to give evidence in a criminal trial. No inference should be drawn from the fact that he has not given evidence and the fact that he has refused to answer questions in the police station during a period of legitimate detention should not be a source of comment by the judge.[20]

Jury bias
The issue of jury bias was considered by the Court of Criminal Appeal in *Director of Public Prosecutions v. Nicholas Tobin*.[21] In this case the appellant was convicted of 11 counts of rape and indecent assault and sentenced to concurrent sentences of imprisonment. A query arose on a certificate from the trial judge after he refused to discharge the jury when the foreman had informed him that one juror during the jury's deliberations related a personal experience of sexual abuse. The foreman felt they could deal with the matter objectively but that they were concerned as a body, and felt the matter should be reported to the court. The court was reassured that the ability of the relevant juror to decide the case impartially was not affected. On that assurance the trial judge allowed the matter to go to the jury and the conviction resulted. Reversing the conviction, Mr Justice Fennelly said that the appropriate test to be applied

20 See *People (DPP) v. Finnerty* [1999] 4 IR 364. 21 [2001] 3 IR 469.

to a challenge of jury bias is whether a reasonable person in the circumstances would have a reasonable apprehension that the defendant would not receive a fair trial. The application of this objective test depends on the facts of each case and it must be assessed according to the standard of a reasonable and fair-minded observer who knows the relevant facts. Where the actual facts were meagre and were simply that the appellant was on trial for a serious offence which must have been sufficiently similar to the juror's experience to cause him or her to relate his or her personal experiences of sexual abuse during the jury's deliberations, a reasonable and fair-minded observer would consider that there was a danger in the sense of a possibility that the juror might have been unconsciously influenced by his or her personal experience. However, Mr Justice Fennelly added that the court did not discount the possibility that a judge might sufficiently counteract dangers of this nature by a considered and carefully worded special direction such as would render it unnecessary to discharge the jury.

Duration of deliberation by jury and overnight stays
It is accepted that in the interests of justice juries should not be expected to deliberate in serious criminal cases without a break for a long period of time and they should not deliberate particularly late into the night. In the criminal courts the jury sit from approximately 10.30 a.m. until 1.00 p.m. and from 2.00 p.m. until 4.00 p.m. Clearly if they are considering their verdict they will be allowed to take until about 7.30 p.m. in the evening to consider that verdict but after that period they will be put up in a hotel and advised that they should use the time to relax, and should not discuss the case until they resume their deliberations the following morning.

Majority verdicts
Since the Criminal Justice Act, 1984 which came into effect on 1 March 1985 Irish juries can now give majority verdicts. Section 25(3) provides that such a verdict will not be accepted by a court unless the jury have had such a time for deliberation as the nature and complexity of the case requires provided such time shall be not less than two hours. The Court of Criminal Appeal subsequently added ten minutes onto this. Depending on the nature and complexity of the case a judge may, after a period of two hours and ten minutes has elapsed, tell a jury that they are entitled to bring in a majority verdict. In this case a majority verdict means the jury must decide 11:1 or 10:2, either that the defendant is guilty or not guilty. Section 25(4) of that Act provides that if the jury are returning a not guilty verdict it should not indicate whether the verdict was unanimous or by a majority

Number of jurors
The Juries Act 1976 provides that, if a person is ill or unable to attend having commenced deliberation on a case, a trial may reach conclusion provided the number has not been reduced to less than 10 members.

A recent study from Glasgow University concluded that the number of twelve jurors might not be the most effective form and that the number should be reduced to 6 or 7. This was based on the fact that groups of 12 people are more likely to disagree. No such study has been done in Ireland but an analysis of the trials of the Circuit Court over the past year reveals a very low level of disagreement.

This paper is a brief overview of some of the areas where the judge and jury impact in criminal trials. In Britain there is constant debate about the effectiveness of criminal jury trials but it would be fair to say that the thinking in Ireland is that they should continue and it is recognised that they provide a major contribution to the criminal justice system in this country.

The case for a national court for indictable crime

PAUL CARNEY

For many years I have commented on certain anomalies in the distribution of criminal business in the courts of Ireland. Delays in the listing of cases in the Central Criminal Court have now prompted the Minister for Justice, Equality and Law Reform to have the jurisdiction of the courts examined with a view to tackling the delay problem. Others are known to be now interested in a more fundamental examination of jurisdiction.

I understand that the Circuit Criminal Court in Dublin can give a trial date within weeks. In the Central Criminal Court it takes about a year to get a trial. If the case has to be adjourned it takes a further year to get it back on the rails. While there is a 'no adjournment' rule, that cannot be absolute. Essential witnesses get heart attacks, accused persons periodically self-mutilate to postpone their trials and victims have to sit their Leaving Certificate and so forth.

As the judge having charge of the list in the Central Criminal Court I regularly receive letters from the families of victims and the relatives of persons allegedly murdered. There is great distress occasioned by the year's delay in families seeking closure. The alleged attacker is likely to be on bail and frequently lives near the alleged victim involving daily contact. What causes particular distress is when the case is adjourned by either the prosecution or defence occasioning a further year's delay without notice to or consultation with the victims or relatives of a deceased. I am constantly struck by the frequency with which defence counsel come into court on the eve of a trial seeking an adjournment where it is obvious that there is another side by way of victims or relatives whose interests have in no fashion been taken account of. Such applications are refused.

It should be remembered that the year's delay in the Central exists in spite of a high level of pleas of guilty. For some years there has been in existence a special discount in sentence for those who deliver their plea at the earliest opportunity, leaving their trial date available for the disposal of another accused. This system has to date ensured a high level of pleas of guilty and early sentencing of those who plead. It has also meant that all of the cases listed for trial are 'fighters', the pleas having been shaken out of the tree at an early stage.

If these pleas were one day to cease to be forthcoming the effect would be to either double the delays or double the number of High Court judges devoted exclusively to crime. A majority (or as near as makes no difference) of those who contest their guilt in rape cases secure acquittals. Interest groups should note that these acquittals come from on average evenly sexually mixed juries. I can generally profile those cases in which there will be an acquittal but that is a matter to be dealt with in another paper. It may be that those done 'bang to rights' have pleaded, leaving as fighters those cases with a fight in them. Nevertheless, it should be appreciated that the present balance could be adversely altered at any time by an appreciation of the rate at which sexually balanced juries are acquitting or by a harsher sentencing regime. Many will find the concept unpalatable but the reality is that while resources are limited the administration of criminal justice depends in part on the co-operation of the rapist and child molester.

Until 1981 the Central Criminal Court, being the criminal division of the High Court, had exclusive jurisdiction in relation to:

1   Treason.
2   Piracy.
3   Genocide.
4   Murder.
5   Certain offences under the Offences against the State Act.

All other indictable crime was returned for trial to the Circuit Criminal Court but each side, both prosecution and defence, had the right of transfer to the Central. The prosecution could, thereby, transfer to the High Court a serious fraud or a case giving rise to public concern.

The transfer system was misused by accused persons for the purpose of delaying their trials. In my time at the Junior Criminal Bar the tactics frequently directed by petty criminals were:

1   Elect for trial by judge and jury.
2   Call for 'open depositions'. The term 'open depositions' had no legal standing but was invariably used by the defendant calling the shots.
3   When the trial date was reached in the Circuit Court transfer to the Central. The Judges rarely insisted on the seven days' notice which was required for a transfer as of right. The effect of this was that a trial for the theft of a chocolate bar not infrequently went all the way up the High Court.

To deal with the problem the executive over-reacted. It completely abolished the right to transfer, leaving the Central Criminal Court with jurisdiction to try only the five matters set out above in which it had always hitherto enjoyed an exclusive jurisdiction. At a later stage as a result of Rape Crisis Centre lobbying an exclusive jurisdiction was added in rape and aggravated sexual assault.

There has never in the history of the State been a prosecution for treason, piracy or genocide. There has been one prosecution in the Central under the Offences against the State Act. This was in respect of alleged intimidation of a clerk in the Chief State Solicitor's office over a bail motion and resulted in an acquittal. The reality is that the Central has jurisdiction to try only cases of murder and rape.

People have regrettably been murdering and raping each other for centuries so that they are very settled crimes. There is, no doubt, an emotional need in the body politic that they be tried by the highest rank of first instance judge but no such requirement is justified by their complexity. As a judge of the High Court, while I *must* try a case which might have come into being because a young man didn't have the good manners and sense to see a girl home after some inappropriate sex, I *cannot* try a billion pound fraud, not because it is above my jurisdiction, but because it is beneath it. That case must be tried in the Circuit Court and depending on the place of arrest perhaps in a remote part of the country. I am sure there are inexhaustible categories of cases which would merit the attention of the High Court but cannot at present have it. I would suggest as prime candidates serious fraud, international money laundering, drugs dealing and importation, internet crime, perjury, bribery and corruption, and crimes committed in the context of holding government or other high office.

Exclusive jurisdiction in rape was conferred on the Central as a badge of the heinousness of the crime. The position in the hierarchy of the crimes just listed seems to me to be giving them a certificate that they are not too bad at all, at all.

Though it has the power to do so the Central Criminal Court has never sat outside Dublin. The exclusive jurisdiction in rape is now putting an excessive burden on the jurors of Dublin. There are now up to six juries being sworn every Monday, most of them for rape trials. It is no easy matter empanelling a jury. Prosecution and defence exercise their challenges to the full, many jurors are available only for limited periods of time and many volunteer that they couldn't give an impartial verdict in a sex case. As a result of regularly coming close to running out of jurors it has now been found necessary to summon 500 jurors every Monday. This is, of course, additional to the requirements of the Dublin Circuit Criminal Court and the civil side of the High Court.

Another feature of the present regime is that due principally to the increasing length of contested cases to severed indictments and to separate trials I have repeatedly to tell the parties on Mondays that I have no judge available for them. This will result in a year's delay. It is my understanding that at the same time there may be judges in the Dublin Circuit Criminal Court who have no trials to take up and are free. There are, of course, Chinese walls between our jurisdictions and I cannot avail of their services.

WHERE LIES THE SOLUTION?

The most simplistic solution and one which would have wide support would be to send rape back to the Circuit Court. The first effect of this would be to disperse rape around the country back to local courts. The unique overview of sexual crime as it is available to the judge in charge of the Central Criminal Court list would be lost. This would result in a serious diminution of the understanding of what is happening in Ireland today. Such a diminution is already happening by reason of the policies in the media to cut back in their reporting of this area. Anyone who thinks the courts are merely mopping up the sexual crime of decades ago is seriously deluded.

More seriously, merely to offload rape would not deal with the problem of appropriate cases being denied access to the High Court. Nor would it be a solution to say that fraud, money laundering or other specified crimes should be transferred to the Central. Whether a crime should be tried at the highest level or at a lesser one should depend not merely on the textbook description of the crime but on its totality including the manner of its commission, its value, the effect on its victim and the antecedents of the accused.

What needs to be considered is the establishment of a permanent national court for indictable crime whose judges would be drawn from the ranks of both the High Court and the Circuit Court. Any such consideration must start with a look at the Crown Court in England and Wales. This was created in 1971 to replace courts of assize and quarter sessions. It is a unified national criminal court in continuous session and, while the trappings of the Old Bailey are retained, no doubt in the interests of the tourist trade, the English Central Criminal Court is by statutory definition the Crown Court when it is sitting within the city of London.

That the Crown Court model is unsuitable for total adoption in Ireland can be simply illustrated by stating that the judges range from lay magistrates at one end of the scale to the lord mayor and aldermen of the City of London at the other. For the most part they are High Court judges, Circuit judges and recorders. Another aspect of its composition can be rejected straight away as unsuited to Ireland. Circuit judges may try murder, rape and child sexual abuse cases if they are individually approved for that purpose by the presiding judge and the Lord Chief Justice. This is known colloquially as the Circuit judge having his 'murder ticket' or 'rape ticket', as the case maybe. I do not believe that it would be in line with our constitutional scheme of things for one judge to be licensed to hear a case which could not be heard by a judge of co-ordinate jurisdiction for want of that licence. This is not to say that cases could not be directed towards experienced judges in a more subtle or less structured fashion.

Crimes in England and Wales are assigned to five classes:

In class one are all capital cases, treason, murder, genocide and Official Secrets Act offences.

In class two are manslaughter, infanticide, child destruction, abortion, rape, sexual intercourse or incest with a girl under 13, sedition, Geneva Convention offences, mutiny and piracy. It is interesting to note that piracy appears to rate a slightly lower position in the hierarchy in England than here.

In class three are all other offences triable only on indictment.

In class four are wounding or causing grievous bodily harm with intent, robbery or assault with intent to rob and conspiracy.

Class five comprises all offences which are triable either summarily or on indictment.

Cases in class one must be tried by a High Court Judge. A murder may be released by the presiding Judge to a Circuit Court Judge who has his murder ticket. Cases in class two must be tried by a High Court Judge unless a particular case is released by the presiding Judge to a Circuit Judge. A case of rape or serious sexual assault of a child in any class may be released only to a Circuit Judge or recorder who has his rape ticket. Class three cases may be tried by a High Court Judge or in accordance with general or particular directions given by the presiding Judge before a Circuit Court Judge or a recorder. Cases in class four may be tried before a High Court Judge, a Circuit Judge or a Recorder but shall not be listed before a High Court Judge without his consent or that of the presiding Judge.

Presiding judges may issue directions as to when it is appropriate to reserve a case to a High Court Judge and as to the allocation of work between Circuit Judges and Recorders. In such directions specific provision shall be made for cases in the following categories:

(a) cases where death or serious risk to life or the infliction of grave injury are involved, including motoring cases arising from reckless driving and/or excess alcohol;

(b) cases where loaded firearms are alleged to have been used;

(c) cases of arson or criminal damage with intent to endanger life;

(d) cases of defrauding government departments or local authorities or public bodies of amounts in excess of £25,000;

(e) offences under the Forgery and Counterfeiting Act 1981 where the amount of money or the value of goods exceeds £ 10,000;

(f) offences involving violence to a police officer which result in the officer being unfit for duty for more than 28 days;

(g) any offence involving loss to any person or body of a sum in excess of £100,000;

(h) cases where there is a risk of substantial political or racial feeling being excited by the offence or the trial;

(i)   cases which have given rise to widespread concern;

(j)   cases of robbery or assault with intent to rob where gross violence was
      used, or serious injury was caused, or where the accused was armed with
      a dangerous weapon for the purpose of the robbery, or where the theft
      was intended to be from a bank, a building society or a post office;

(k)   cases involving the manufacture or distribution of substantial quantities of
      drugs;

(l)   cases the trial of which is likely to last more than 10 days;

(m) cases involving the trial of more than five defendants;

(n)   cases in which the accused holds a senior public office, or is a member
      of a profession or other person carrying a special duty or responsibility
      to the public, including a police officer when acting as such;

(o)   Case where a difficult issue of law is likely to be involved, or a prosecu-
      tion for the offence is rare or novel.

As I indicated already, the Crown Court model is not suited to total adoption in this jurisdiction but deserves to be looked at. It seems to me that there
is a need for greater flexibility in relation to the trial of indictable crime particularly of the more serious kind and of cases which give rise to public concern. This could perhaps best be met by enacting a new jurisdiction in which
judges of various levels would sit in the one unified Criminal Court and have
cases assigned for hearing at their respective levels by recognised and established
criteria. Policy considerations in relation to such a change are, of course, a
matter for the executive and the Oireachtas and the detail is a matter for parliamentary counsel to draft.

   I would make two observations from my experience of having charge of
the list in the Central Criminal Court as follows:

1   It is essential that there should be a permanent presiding judge and deputy
    presiding judge for the purpose of consistency and discipline in relation to
    the administration of the list. I still remember how the list was decimated
    for a full year ahead during my absence for two weeks hearing personal
    injuries cases in the country.
2   Judges assigned to sit in the Court must do so for a reasonable period –
    preferably for a year at a time but certainly not less than for a full term. At
    present judges come to sit in the Central for shorter periods and it is hap-
    pening on a weekly basis that a case is called as going on, having an expected
    duration of two to three weeks but the only judge free is moving on to some
    other duty in a week's time. In such a situation the case has to be adjourned
    and the further year's delay comes yet again into play.

Legal aid in South Africa: a new direction – towards justice for all

MOHOMED NAVSA

The Legal Aid Act 22 of 1969 was not enacted to enable the vulnerable and exploited sections of South Africa's population, which were and are still over-whelmingly made up of its black citizens, to resist and challenge exploitation and oppression. It was part of the effort to give apartheid a respectable face. Prior to 1990 the Legal Aid Board provided legal assistance mainly in civil matters including divorce cases and personal injury claims. From 1989 to 2000 State-funded legal aid provided assistance in criminal cases to such extent that it became the main focus of the Board's work. In the early 1990s this was at least in part due to pronouncements by courts about the necessity for legal representation in criminal matters.[1] From the beginning of the new constitutional order the Board was bound to meet the constitutional guarantees of legal representation in criminal cases.

A few years before the advent of democracy, because of an increasing rights awareness flowing from what is described later, efforts were made by the Board to co-operate with university legal aid clinics, to establish its own clinics and to extend by other means the scope of State-funded legal aid. These efforts must be seen against the fact that the Board had limited resources and was compelled by circumstances and the law to devote most of its efforts to providing legal representation in criminal cases.

The 1980s saw the proliferation of privately funded public interest law firms such as the Legal Resources Centre, Lawyers for Human Rights, The Centre for Applied Legal Studies and the Black Lawyers' Legal Education Centre. Community advice offices mushroomed in townships throughout South Africa and lawyers provided back-up services to assist victims of apartheid to launch such legal challenges to State lawlessness as was possible within the narrow space that the prevailing legal order provided. Test case or impact litigation was carefully planned and instituted to achieve maximum benefits for the most number of people. Two of the most successful cases which resulted in 'benefits' for hundreds of thousands of people were *Rikhoto v. East Rand Administration Board* 1983 (4) SA 278(W) and *Komani NO v. Bantu Affairs Administration Board, Peninsula area* 1980 (4) SA 448(AD). These cases successfully challenged the

---

1 *S v. Radebe, S v. Mbonani*, 1988 (1) SA 191 (T); *S v. Khanyile and Another*, 1988 (3) SA 795 (N); *S v. Rudman and Another; S v. Mthwana*, 1992 (1) SA 343 (A).

State's attempts to restrict the influx of black people into what was regarded as 'white' South African urban areas. Whilst black people continued to be antagonistic to the legal order they began to increasingly recognise that the law and legal processes could be used to ease some of their burden and to challenge in a limited manner the government's apartheid policies.

The trade union movement not only increased political awareness but also ensured that their members used such legal mechanisms as were at their disposal. Against the background of the advent of the new Constitutional order and a justiciable bill of rights, which contains, *inter alia,* guarantees of representation in criminal cases and in related appeals, it had to be anticipated that a demand for legal aid would increase. Then there were the following additional factors: the establishment of the Truth and Reconciliation Commission for which the State was bound to provide legal representation. It chose to do so through the Board. The State also made funding available for litigation in land related matters and the Board was required to act as its agent for this purpose. The following table of statistics shows the exponential growth in demand for legal aid from 1989 to 1999 and then a downturn for the period 1999–2000:

Year	New cases
1989/1990	24,281
1990/1991	35,513
1991/1992	57,692
1992/1993	67,103
1993/1994	79,501
1994/1995	85,231
1995/1996	113,774
1996/1997	163,749
1997/1998	198,762
1998/1999	211,992
1999/2000	149,763

These statistics must be seen against the fact that rural areas were largely under-served and that the Board had in the past not responded to the needs of the indigent in a structured and strategic manner. There was thus a rural mass whose access to justice problems were largely ignored. The Board was not in the forefront of challenges to unlawful administrative action by State institutions. Given that there was no drive to ascertain what the true needs of the indigent were and that vulnerable groups such as women and children were not considered to be a priority and that NGOs and communities had not been engaged to ascertain the burning problems of the indigent, one could safely conclude that there was a large unmet need. Another complicating factor was that the bureaucracy charged with the issuing of new instructions on behalf of the Board (made up mostly by employees of the Department of Justice) was not doing enough to ensure that only the indigent received State-funded legal assistance. So, although the statistics shown above were inflated because of this fact, it was mostly understated in respect of the total needs of the country. As spelt out above it was predictable that the demand for legal aid would balloon with resultant cost implications. Sadly the Board's forward planning was non-existent. Its systems were geared to funding legal assistance within a narrow compass. With an almost tenfold increase in demand for legal assistance between 1989 and 1999 logistical and resource problems were bound to arise. The Board had antiquated administration and management systems. It had a largely untrained and de-motivated staff with limited management expertise. It had flawed and unreconciled historical and accounting data. As if these factors were not bad enough the Board persuaded the first Minister of Justice under the new democratic Government that in order for it to maintain the confidence and co-operation of the legal profession it had to increase fees substantially. At that stage the Board rendered legal aid mainly through employing private practitioners – i.e through the judicare system. This increase in fees to levels that would have made a developed country think twice was an error in judgement for which the country has paid and continues to pay a heavy price. Add to all of these factors that a small but not insignificant percentage of unscrupulous lawyers were submitting fraudulent accounts and it becomes clear that the Board was heading towards a catastrophe.

At the beginning of 1998 the cracks in the system were widening and were apparent to all. The Auditor-General in a report on the Board's activities and financial statements for the 1996/1997 financial year (at that stage the Board was at least 18 months behind in its financial accounting) condemned the lack of financial controls and the abysmal state of the Board's accounting systems. There was a backlog in the payment of tens of thousands of practitioners' accounts. The Board continued to incur new debt by issuing new instructions. All of this led to the position where the Board's actual and contingent liability was threatening to spiral out of control. Because of its inadequate record- keeping its contingent liability could not be estimated with any degree of confidence. The Board could not accurately calculate its actual liability. During 1997 the Board after being pressured by the Justice Portfolio committee resolved to move away from the judicare system towards a system of salaried lawyers.

Another development took place during the first half of 1998. Government arranged a meeting between the Board, interested agencies, representatives of the legal profession, universities and NGOs active in providing legal services to the poor. At this consultative forum it was decided that the Board would move away from providing legal services to the poor through the judicare system. It would, in future, provide representation to accused persons through a public defender system which would employ salaried public defenders. It was decided that the Board would be innovative in providing legal services in civil cases. Government was also intent on transforming the Board and making it more representative. By this time the legal profession was beginning to threaten a walk-out because of the Board's failure to pay its members' accounts. A new Board was installed in October 1998. It was faced with a chaotic situation. Shortly after it took office it discovered that matters were worse than at first appeared. During the first quarter of 1999 it conducted its own investigations and discovered that six out of ten files could not be traced by simply referring to the existing file control system. It found tens of thousands of documents unattached to files. It discovered a number of duplicate payments. The Board was being sued a number of times per day. Government had delayed in the approval of new posts at the Board's head office resulting in skilled tasks being outsourced to consultants not all of whom delivered value for money. There was very little effective control being exercised over these consultants. The Board's relationships with its offices and employees located away from its head office in Pretoria were tenuous. At one stage during 1999 estimates of the Board's actual and contingent liability included an estimation of debt upwards of R500 million. This has to be seen against the fact that at that stage the Board's annual grant was in the region of R200 million. In the interim the Board continued to issue instructions as its debt was escalating. Practitioners were granted increased fees in cases considered complex (on top of an already generous fee, particularly if regard be had to the country's limited resources) with the result that a small number of cases was using up a disproportionate part of legal aid funding. In the past some cases were too readily classified complex. The Board was bankrupt. If it had been a trading corporation it would have been guilty of reckless trading. The Board had to continue operating to ensure that the Constitutional guarantees of legal representation in criminal cases were met. It had to appease the legal profession. During 1999 because of a substantial reduction of fees a number of legal practitioners removed themselves from the Board's rotation list. The Board had to engage Government to provide additional funding and at the same time provide a business plan that would lead the way out of the morass and provide a sustainable legal aid system.

The Board's mission is set out in section 3 of the Act:

> *3. Objects and general powers of board.* – The objects of the board shall be to render or make available legal aid to indigent persons and to provide legal representation at State expense as contemplated in the Constitution …

It has not changed in substance from its original form. The real change was that the Board now comprised a membership with a hands-on approach, driven by a passion to ensure that the guarantees of equality to justice before the law and access to courts set out in sections 9 and 34 of the Constitution did not prove illusory if you were poor. It had to be innovative and find ways in which to stretch the legal aid rand.

Fortunately Government was forthcoming with additional funding and a commitment to ensuring the Board's survival. The Ministries of Finance and Justice were very helpful in providing logistical and technical support. The Auditor-General provided guidance. The Board which is a non–executive Board became actively involved in running the Board through its chairperson and sub-committees, whilst it set in motion processes that would enable it to engage competent and committed managers at salaries beyond civil service scales. It resorted to measures which saw an already hostile profession become even more antagonistic. It had to drastically reduce fees. The Board halted legal assistance in personal injury claims explaining that it was funding mostly hopeless, though not exclusively, hopeless cases. Deserving cases could be funded on a contingency basis. Increased fees were restricted to exceptional cases. The maximum fee was itself drastically reduced. Management systems were introduced to ensure accurate record keeping. Software for a reliable accounting system was introduced to ensure that the backlog in the payment of outstanding accounts was reduced and that the auditor-general's requirements were met. The Board was candid in reporting on its position to parliament. It is after all an institution that serves the people and nothing less that full accountability, transparency and integrity would do.

The Board engaged treasury, accepting that there were many demands on the public purse. It met with the Director-General of the Department of Finance to clarify its business plan and undertook to embark on a determined move away from judicare to ensure cost savings. It requested additional funds to establish justice centres which it envisaged as a one-stop centre where the poor could go for legal assistance in criminal as well as in civil cases. The Board contemplated the limited use of para-legals to provided assistance in defined areas such as maintenance claims. It was willing to consider funding organisations involved in the provision of legal services to the poor. It envisaged that it could use the infrastructure of such organisations and would insist only that the cost per case to the Board was less than that provided through judicare. The relationship between the Board and these organisations would be regulated by co-operation agreements. The Board would identify new areas which it identified in consultation with communities as priority areas of operation. It would also identify geographical areas of need and would move with such speed as circumstances would allow to address this need. The Ministries of Justice and Finance were extremely supportive and approved these plans and provided the funding.

By the beginning of 2001 the backlog in the payment of accounts was almost completely eliminated. A top management team took up its appointment at the beginning of February 2001. The Board's business plans were revised and amended and refined. There was an emphasis on skills development. Justice centres were established and a further roll-out plan approved.

Funding is available for impact litigation and in this regard the Board has already assisted in representing families of victims of the Ellis Park soccer tragedy. The Board is financially more sound than it has been in years. It plans to be in a position at the end of the 2001 financial year to meet its contingent liability from existing funds – in other words complete solvency. It presently has no cash flow problem.

The Board has begun to win back the confidence of the legal profession. It recently increased fees modestly and will probably be in a position to increase fees further during the next financial year. It has however made its position clear: that whilst it values its relationship with the profession and sees a continuing but limited role for judicare it will not return to the past scale of fees that made legal aid unsustainable. The Board insists that it exists for the poor and not to provide a living for practitioners.

Most importantly justice centres have been established and preliminary statistics show conclusively that the justice centre model is cheaper per case by hundreds of rand running into savings of tens of millions of rand. Clinics that were run under the aegis of the Board have been upgraded to justice centres and relationships between them and the Board's head-office continue to strengthen. There are 26 justice centres. Further justice centres are to be established: Kroonstad, Lichtenburg, Louis Trichardt, Lusikisiki and Upington. The Board has resolved to give a rural thrust to the establishment of justice centres and this is beginning to materialise. The roll-out plan addresses under-resourced rural areas. The Board has charged its justice centres with ensuring that it focuses on providing assistance to vulnerable groups who have hitherto not had its assistance.

The Board has also resolved to ensure that a legal aid lawyer will be assigned to each of 43 Regional Courts which deal with a high volume of criminal cases. A number of other Regional Courts are serviced by justice centres. The remainder will be serviced through the judicare system.

The Board is working on establishing a telephone service to ensure that people have access to its services from the time of arrest.

The Board is far from perfect. It still has a long way to travel in its quest to ensure justice for all. However, it is on the move. It is gaining momentum and will establish itself in the pysche of the nation. The business of building a nation and democratic institutions is very much with us. For as long as the poor and the deprived are on the outside looking in, democracy is imperilled and the Constitution is in danger of being reduced to a worthless document. The Legal Aid Board is an important democratic institution. It must strive to ensure that the reality is not that justice is only for the wealthy. The rule of law demands that the Board succeed. I have no doubt that the Board will succeed and it will show that it can provide legal assistance to the poor in a creative and cost effective manner. It is on the road and gaining steam in its endeavours to make justice for all a reality.

Problems of legitimacy and respect for human rights in the globalisation of penal norms: Confiscation in South Africa as a case in point

NEIL BOISTER

International treaty law is used as a mechanism for globalising penal norms of substance and process. Member States of the international community have become enthusiastic users of treaty law to suppress forms of deviant behaviour perceived to be the common concerns of States. This enthusiasm has resulted in the globalisation of extremely invasive procedures which, in the wrong hands, could prove dangerous to innocent individuals. It raises concerns about the respect for the human rights of those subject to these processes. This is particularly the case in jurisdictions where norms and procedures have not developed organically as part of domestic criminal law, but have been applied through treaty obligations from the top down under the tutelage of law enforcement agencies from metropolitan States and the United Nations' criminal justice machinery. South Africa has become an enthusiastic recipient of extreme foreign and international legal solutions to its crime control problem. The purpose of this paper is to explore, with reference to South Africa's adoption of new and radical confiscation procedures, two conflicting interests in the development of this transnational criminal law – effective law enforcement and the protection of human rights.

'TWO CARS, A TRUCK AND A TRAILER?' CORRUPTION AND CONFISCATION IN THE SOUTH AFRICAN NARCOTICS BUREAU (SANAB)

I am going to begin this paper with reference to a specific case because it crystallises the problem. In the early 1990s I interviewed the newly-appointed head of the local Narcotics Bureau in Durban, Major Pieter Meyer. I was greeted by an urbane, obviously intelligent man, who seemed to have a firm grasp on the reins of his organisation. I recall pressing him on how he dealt with corruption in his organisation. He explained in detail how he rotated members in order to avoid them becoming too familiar with their 'clients'. In 1999, I returned to South Africa, still interested in drug control, but this time in the operation at a practical level of the confiscation provisions enacted in South African law since it became party to various international conventions. At the time there was a case which received widespread local media coverage, one of the first major cases using the new confiscation procedure of the new Prevention of Organised Crime Act 121 of 1998. The case had to do with the illicit proceeds of the now Senior Superintendent Meyer's involvement in various alleged crimes, many of which involved defeating the administration of justice in respect of drug trafficking by other individuals.[1] The two cars, truck and trailer in his garage were the alleged to be the proceeds of these crimes. The reports revealed that the State was having problems, as were the courts, with retrospective application of the new procedure. I was struck, however, by the unbridled enthusiasm of the South African authorities for the use of confiscation laws in fighting the crime wave engulfing the country. I was particularly struck by the fact that one of the first cases of their use was an attempt to confiscate the possessions of the head of the organised crime unit of the police service in Durban, a person who one assumes would play a key role in the use of these very same provisions against others. These are extraordinary legal procedures, and domestic alarm at their adoption and use should not ignore the process of their development. In particular, concerns have been raised about: a) the questionable legitimacy of their development in international law; and b) their imposition by international law without consideration for their human rights impact. Before exploring these problems of legitimacy and control, it is worth charting the development of confiscation laws in South Africa.

THE GLOBALISATION OF ASSET CONFISCATION: FROM THE UNITED STATES VIA INTERNATIONAL LAW TO SOUTH AFRICA

Stage one: domestic development in developed States

Global action aimed at confiscating the profits of crime is one of the most significant achievements in transnational law enforcement co-operation of the last 15 years. It has its origins in the domestic practice of the United States, which in 1970 saw the enactment of both criminal and civil forfeiture provisions in the Racketeering Influenced and Corrupt Organisations (RICO) statute,[2] Continuing Criminal Enterprises (CCE) Statute[3] and Money Laundering Control Act (MLCA),[4] although due to procedural defects the forfeiture provisions of RICO and CCE were not used until the passage of the Comprehen-

---

1 See *National Director of Public Prosecutions v. Meyer* [1999] 4 ALL SA 263 (D) at 268–9 for the full schedule of his alleged activities.   2 Title XI of the Organized Crime Control Act (18 USC ss.1961–1968).   3 Part of the Controlled Substances Act (21 USC ss.848 ff).   4 Sections 1956 and 1957 of Subtitle H of the Anti-Drug Abuse Act of 1986, incorporated as part of chapter 53 of Title 31.

sive Crime Control Act of 1984. The distinction between criminal confiscation or *in personam* proceedings and civil forfeiture or *in rem* proceedings as fleshed out in US law is now well known. In the former procedure, jurisdiction flows from a convicted person, and the confiscation order is limited to assets owned or possessed by that person at the time of conviction. From the point of view of the State, the advantages of the latter procedure are notorious. There is no necessity to establish the criminal guilt of the owner or holder of the property. The State proceeds against the thing itself. Allegations of specific facts are made to support a reasonable belief that the property has been linked to a criminal offence. The evidence need only establish this connection on the basis of the civil standard of proof which means the action can succeed even when criminal prosecution fails. The forfeiture order relates back to the time of illegal use which makes it enforceable against all third parties, guilty or innocent, who subsequently obtain rights over the property regardless of their involvement in or knowledge of the underlying criminal conduct. Both procedures are predicated on an initial seizing or freezing of the assets.

Stage two: transnational transfer via international law
A problem for US law enforcement agencies was that many of the assets they sought to confiscate were held in foreign jurisdictions, where confiscation provisions were outdated and civil forfeiture unknown. This transnational dimension of crime is the engine of international legal co-operation. By the mid-1980s, some States had begun to follow the American lead, enacting legislation designed to secure the confiscation of assets derived from drug trafficking but not linked to a specific offence. Thus the United Kingdom's Drugs Trafficking Offences Act, 1986, in a 'value confiscation' variation of criminal confiscation on the theme of civil forfeiture, allowed a court to order the defendant, after conviction, to pay an amount equal in value to the court's assessment of the value of his proceeds from drug trafficking at any time, and not just in connection with the offence for which he has just been convicted. It also allowed the courts to register, upon application by a designated country, a confiscation order made in another State. But the problem was that most other States did not have anything resembling such legislation and calls were made for steps to be taken to bring the international position into line with the more advanced domestic jurisdictions.

International lobbying through the UN for an advanced crime control convention resulted in the conclusion of the 1988 United Nations Convention Against Illicit Traffic in Narcotic Drugs and Psychotropic Substances (hereinafter the 1988 Convention).[5] Article 5 of the 1988 Convention was designed to attack the patrimonial benefits that accrue from the international drug traffic wherever they may be held. It was specifically aimed at enabling the greatest number of States to use confiscation against traffickers, and removing impediments to the

5 UN Doc. E/CONF.82.15.

recognition of confiscation orders of other States by ensuring that every State has such a mechanism in place. Article 5(1) obliges a State party to take domestic measures to provide for the domestic use of criminal confiscation or civil forfeiture where 'appropriate'.[6] It contemplates a value confiscation system as well as the confiscation of assets determined to be the proceeds of a particular crime for which the owner or holder was convicted. Article 5(4) provides for identical measures on the application of another State party, by either submitting the confiscation request of the other State to its own authorities, or by recognising the confiscation order made by the requesting party's authorities. Article 5(3) removes bank secrecy to prevent it being used to shield illicit assets from confiscation. Subsequent international provisions like article 13 of the Council of Europe's Convention on Laundering, Search, Seizure and Confiscation of the Proceeds of Crime[7] have developed along the same lines, although refinements have been made. Domestic law enforcement agencies in developed States such as the United States' Drug Enforcement Agency (DEA) have played a key role in the development and global application of these international laws, and they have been assisted by international organs like the G9's Financial Action Task Force (FATF) and the UN's Office for Drug Control and Crime Prevention (UN ODCCP), which have been tasked with fostering the uniform global application of seizure and confiscation provisions to a broad range of offences. Asset confiscation provisions are now commonplace in multilateral crime control treaties, the latest being the 2000 United Nations Convention against Transnational Organised Crime (hereinafter the TOC Convention),[8] which contains extensive provisions in this regard in article 12.

Stage three: domestic adoption and application by a developing state
South Africa has always been a good international citizen as far as non-political international crimes are concerned, and it was quick to implement the confiscation provisions of the 1988 Convention through the Drugs and Drug Trafficking Act 140 of 1992. The International Co-operation in Criminal Matters Act 75 of 1996 dealt with issues of international co-operation and the application of foreign confiscation orders,[9] and the Proceeds of Crime Act 76

---

6 Article 1(f) provides that confiscation includes forfeiture, so although the Convention does not specify that States parties should adopt civil forfeiture, it clearly anticipates that doing so will meet their obligations in terms of article 5. **7** *ETS* 141. **8** In terms of General Assembly Resolution 53/111 of 9 December 1998, the General Assembly established an Ad Hoc Committee open to all States for the purpose of elaborating such a convention and three draft protocols – on illegal transport and trafficking in migrants, on illicit manufacturing trafficking in firearms and ammunition, and on trafficking in women and children. The process of development of the Convention and the first two Protocols was completed by the signing of the Convention between 14 and 20 December 2000. The Convention is annexed to UN GA Doc. A/55/383. **9** Section 19 provides for requests to foreign States for assistance in confiscation, while sections 20–26 provide for the registration of foreign confiscation and restraint orders. Section 1 of the Act provides that confis-

of 1996 focused on 'all crime' laundering and confiscation specifically. The latter statute was repealed and the confiscation provisions of the Drugs Act substituted by the Prevention of Organised Crime Act 121 of 1998 (as amended), which has now become the key piece of legislation in asset confiscation, replacing the relevant provisions in the earlier statutes and anticipating to a very large extent the obligations of the TOC Convention.

The foreign influence on the provenance of these provisions is patent. Shaw notes that these legislative 'initiatives were taken largely as a result of foreign pressure, particularly from the United States and Great Britain'.[10] Their enactment was, however, also driven by international obligation. In an affidavit in the *Director of Public Prosecutions v. Bathgate*,[11] Willem Hofmeyr MP, then a member of the Justice Portfolio Committee in the National Assembly, noted the importance of the obligations flowing from the 1988 Convention in the formulation of national legislation. In a sense the treaties provide the obligatory framework, while the foreign legislation provides the model for the detail of the provisions.

Although confiscation provisions were not foreign to South African law prior to the enactment of the Prevention of Organised Crime Act,[12] what was novel was the employment of civil procedures in asset confiscation.[13]

Chapter 5 of the Act provides for criminal confiscation orders sounding in money, and is based closely on the value-confiscation system used in the UK and other Commonwealth countries.[14] It allows any benefit of an offence to be confiscated in a civil action after the accused has been convicted, in addition to any punishment imposed. The State obtains a judgment against the accused for the value which he or she has benefited from the crime or other criminal activities, or the amount that may be realised at the time, whichever is the lowest.[15] The judgment can be executed against any of the assets of the accused, without the necessity of establishing that the particular asset is tainted by crime. To assist the State, however, presumptions assume that everything the criminal owns and all his or her income and expenditure over the last seven years are the proceeds of crime.[16] While the Act provides that the effect of a

cation orders include forfeiture orders made under the Prevention of Organised Crime Act (see below), thus making it possible to both make and receive requests for assistance in civil forfeiture as well as criminal confiscation. **10** M. Shaw, *Organised crime in post-apartheid South Africa*, Institute for Security Studies Occasional Paper no. 28, January 1998, p. 9 referring to the South African Police Services, Crime Information Management Centre, *The incidence of serious crime: January to March 1997*, Quarterly Report 2/97, 13 June 1997, pp. 23–44. **11** 2000 (1) SACR 105 (CPD) at 111ff. **12** This had always been possible in terms of section 35(1) of the Criminal Procedure Act 51 of 1977. **13** C. Goredema, 'Legislation in South Africa, Swaziland and Zimbabwe to combat organised crime', in C. Goredema (ed.), *Organised crime in southern Africa: assessing legislation*, ISS Monograph Series, No. 56, June 2001 (Institute for Security Studies, Pretoria), pp.25–60 at p.45. **14** W. Hofmeyr, 'Taking the profit out of crime', South African Institute of Race Relations, *Fast Facts*, No. 11/November 2000, p.4 www.sairr.org/za/members/pub/ff/200011/crime/profit.htm. **15** Section 18. **16** Section 22.

confiscation order is that of a civil judgment,[17] section 18 provides explicitly that a confiscation order can only be obtained once a person has been convicted, which clarifies its nature as a criminal confiscation procedure.[18] Chapter 5 also provides for a restraint order as an interim measure to secure the availability of the property for confiscation.[19]

Chapter 6 of the Act provides for civil forfeiture, an innovation in South African law based on US, Australian and Irish legislation.[20] It was adopted because it is considered an effective weapon against organised crime.[21] The procedure allows the State to confiscate the proceeds of crime through a civil action[22] against tainted property without the necessity of first obtaining a criminal conviction against the owner of the property. It is a two stage process. On *ex parte* application by the National Director of Public Prosecutions, the High Court can first make simultaneously a 'preservation of property order', which has the effect of prohibiting any person from dealing in any manner with property subject to such an order,[23] and a seizure order. All those known to have an interest in the property must be informed that a preservation order has been made (a notice must also be published in the Government Gazette). Interested persons have 14 days to give notice of intention to oppose the application of a forfeiture order or to apply for the exclusion of their property from the order.[24] This provision serves to protect innocent third parties but only if they can establish both the lawfulness of their interest in the property and that they neither knew nor had good reason to know that it was such a criminal instrumentality or the proceeds of crime.[25] To vest the property in the State,[26] the High Court may upon application grant a forfeiture order with regard to the property subject to the preservation order, if it is satisfied on a balance of probabilities that the property is either an 'instrumentality' of a scheduled crime, or more significantly, to be 'the proceeds of unlawful activities'.[27] Proceeds can be direct profits, or property representing the proceeds.

Money obtained through both procedures is deposited in a Criminal Assets Recovery Account,[28] to be used to compensate the victims of crime and to financially assist law enforcement agencies in combating not only organised crime but crime generally.

---

17 Section 23. **18** This is in spite of the fact that section 13 provides that the proceedings for application are civil and civil rules of evidence apply. **19** Section 25–29. **20** See Hofmeyr note 14 at 4. Chapter 6 appears to be modelled on the Criminal Assets Recovery Act 1990 (NSW). **21** The Minister of Justice in a press statement of 7 May 1998 announced that, after careful consideration, South Africa would follow the US model of civil forfeiture in RICO. See M Cowling, 'Fighting organised crime: comment on the Prevention of Organised Crime Bill 1998' (1998) 11 *SACJ* 350 at 364. **22** Section 37 specifically labels the proceedings 'civil'. **23** Part 2 of Chapter 6. Sections 38–47. Section 38(1) authorises the National Director of Public Prosecutions to make such an application, and section 38(2) provides that the court may grant it if there are reasonable grounds for the belief that the property is an instrumentality of an offence or the proceeds of an unlawful activity. **24** Section 39. **25** Section 52. **26** Section 56. **27** Section 50. **28** Chapter 7 establishes the account.

In the awkward context of seemingly incompatible concerns with establishing a due process-oriented criminal justice system driven by the new constitutional order while resorting to drastic crime control measures to control a massive crime wave,[29] these new powers have been put rapidly into operation, with the establishment by the National Directorate of Public Prosecutions of an Asset Forfeiture Unit (AFU) in order to ensure their effective use.[30] Its first director, the same Advocate Willem Hofmeyr who played a formative role in the development of these new procedures,[31] anticipated resistance to their use when he noted that

> many overseas experts warned that [the AFU] should expect much litigation from rich and powerful criminals who are desperate to hang on to their ill-gotten gains and who could afford to employ the best legal brains in the country to try to find any possible weakness or lack of clarity in the law. In addition, they warned that some judges would be reluctant to employ the law, which they see as too drastic.[32]

The Act soon fell under the judicial spotlight, with three reversals for the AFU on the point that the Act applied retrospectively to property used or derived illegally prior to enactment.[33] The Act was amended to make it clearly retrospective[34] and the story since then has been one of apparent success for the

---

29 See Cowling note 21, for an evaluation of the Act in bill form against the two values of constitutionality and crime control. Cowling notes that the General Council of the Bar expressed reservations about its inroads into the right of ownership (at 367). **30** The AFU's establishment owes much to the US experience with forfeiture specialists being attached to US attorneys' offices in order to improve the implementation of a process which pursues property rather than the normal law enforcement concern, criminals. See M Schonteich, 'The Asset Forfeiture Unit: Performance and priorities', *Nedbank ISS Crime Index* 3 (2000), 25. **31** The current head is Ouma Rabaji – *Financial Mail*, 25 May 2001. **32** See note 14 at 1. **33** *The National Director of Public Prosecutions v. Carolus* 1999 (2) SACR 27 (C); *National Director of Public Prosecutions v. Meyer* [1999] 4 All SA 263 (D), and *National Director of Public Prosecutions v. Basson* (TPD case 2248/1999, unreported). M. Cowling, 'Some Developments in the Prevention of Organised Crime Act: Comment on *National Director of Public Prosecutions v. Carolus*' (1999) 12 *SACJ* 379, argues at 383 that the Act did not operate retrospectively, but that it simply interfered with existing 'rights'. Nevertheless, the Supreme Court of Appeal in *Carolus v. The National Director of Public Prosecutions* (2000) 1 SA 1127 (SCA) confirmed that neither chapter 5 nor 6 operated retrospectively, but the matter was resolved by legislative amendment. **34** The Prevention of Organised Crime Act was amended by the Prevention of Organised Crime Amendment Act 24 of 1999, and again by the Prevention of Organised Crime Amendment Act 38 of 1999. The Act uses the phrase 'proceeds of unlawful activity' and defines it in section 1, as amended by section 1(c) of the second Amendment Act, as 'any conduct which constitutes a crime or which contravenes any law whether such conduct occurred before or after the commencement of this Act and whether such conduct occurred in the Republic or elsewhere'. The definition of 'proceeds of unlawful activity' was amended to mean 'any property or any service, advantage, benefit, or reward which was derived, received or retained, directly or indirectly, in the Republic or elsewhere at any time before or after the

AFU. Hofmeyr claims that the judiciary has become less wary of the Act.[35] The AFU expanded from seven professional staff trying mostly test cases in 1999 to nearly 30 staff members making a full-scale attack on the profits of crime in 2000, in order in Hofmeyr's terms 'to start making as impact on the major crime figures in South Africa'.[36] In doing so, the AFU works closely with elite police units like the Organised Crime Branch and the National Directorate of Public Prosecution's Directorate of Special Operations (the 'Scorpions'),[37] targeting the criminals and crime syndicates on the Scorpions' most wanted list.[38] Confiscation statistics indicate that the AFU is delivering on the promise of lucrative returns for the initial investment.[39] Its current priority is to integrate its work with that of law enforcement agencies working at all levels.[40] The plan is to institutionalise forfeiture as a crime suppression method in South Africa, following the model provided by the United States.[41] Hofmeyr provides a classic valediction of the procedure:

> All international experience indicates that asset forfeiture is a vital part of the fight against crime. Not only does it help to ensure that crime does not pay, but it also has the advantage that the seized assets are used to fight crime. … The lesson from overseas is certainly that forfeiture is a vital part of any strategy to deal more effectively with crime, especially organised crime. In the US, more that R5bn is paid into the asset forfeiture fund every year. While other countries lag behind, the European Union (EU) has now set up a special inspectorate to evaluate each member State to ensure that they have effective forfeiture laws, and are implementing them properly.[42]

The lesson from abroad is that forfeiture is essential to stop crime from paying and to make crime pay in its own suppression. US 'drug war' rhetoric is patent in the claim by the Institute for Security Studies that the AFU is considered 'a

---

commencement of this Act, in connection with or as a result of any unlawful activity carried on by any person, and includes any property representing property so derived'.   **35** See note 14 at 2. **36** See note 14 at 2.   **37** See E. Schonteich, 'Deadly poison for criminals: The Scorpions take on form' (2000) 4 *Nedbank ISS Crime Index* 5–8.   **38** F Haffejee, 'Forfeiture becoming part of the attack on crime', *Financial Mail*, 13 April 2001.   **39** 58 Seizures have been made, 51 are in force, with a success rate of 87.9% and an asset value of R210 million, of which 64.5% will be returned to victims. 32 forfeitures have been begun, 16 are in force, with a total asset value of R25,8 million, of which 29.9% will be returned to victims. Only R1.1 million has been paid to victims and R145 700 into the Fund. *Financial Mail*, 13 April 2001.   **40** *Financial Mail*, 25 May 2001.   **41** F. Haffejee, 'Forfeiture becoming part of the attack on crime', *Financial Mail*, 13 April 2001.   **42** See note 14 at 2. He makes reference to the prosecutors in the US speaking of the impact of forfeiture on the mafia, and how it is more of a deterrent than incarceration. He provides all the classic justifications: the use of forfeiture to reach the upper echelons of criminal organisations, to eliminate infrastructure and to remove funding from criminal organisations.

major component of the State's war against organised crime'.[43] But war has hidden costs and dangerous weapons are dangerous to friend and foe alike.

THE DANGERS OF ASSET CONFISCATION[44]

Hofmeyr concedes in his discussion of civil forfeiture that there are proportionality problems and that in his words 'one would not take a million-rand mansion because a few dagga [cannabis] plants were found in the back yard'.[45] The South African courts have already confronted problems such as the degree of involvement of a thing with a crime before it can be validly forfeited, and the problem of discriminating licit from tainted assets.[46] Unfortunately, potential and actual dangers abound as a result of the global asset confiscation scheme.

Most of these dangers flow from the fact that legislation construes the criminal confiscation and civil forfeiture processes as one akin to a civil reparation for damages, and blurs or denies its penal nature. This is most obvious with the civil forfeiture, but value confiscation systems ape civil forfeiture and shift the onus of proof on to the convicted criminal to prove that the property she owns is not the proceeds of her crimes, thus crossing the line between penal and civil processes. The abandonment of a direct link to an offence and the shift in the onus may be a knockout blow to many defendants. The reasons for avoiding links with criminal guilt are simple: doing so is in the interests of States taking more effective action against crime and thus protecting the basic rights of citizens subject to crime.[47] Van der Walt expands on these reasons.[48] Criminal confiscation functions ostensibly to remove contraband from society, because its possession is illegal. It prevents criminals enjoying the benefits of crime and compensates society for the harm they have done. Nevertheless, the contraband confiscated is somewhat contradictorily seldom destroyed; who would destroy money? But using it for good purposes implies dependency on crime. Civil forfeiture does not have a regulatory purpose of this kind; its purpose is

---

43 M. Schonteich, 'The Asset Forfeiture Unit: performance and priorities' (2000) 3 *Nedbank ISS Crime Index* 24.   **44** There is a wealth of literature in this regard but see generally on the impact of these types of laws in the US and UK respectively: R. Banoun and R.G. White, 'US money laundering and forfeiture laws and their impact on innocent third parties' in D. Atkins (ed.), *The alleged transnational criminal* (The Hague, 1995), pp. 219–51; E. Bell, 'The ECHR and the proceeds of crime legislation' [2000] *Criminal Law Review* 783–800. In the South African context see J.L. Pretorius and H.A. Strydom, 'The constitutionality of civil forfeiture' (1998) 13 *SA Public Law* 385; C. De Koker and J.L. Pretorius, 'Confiscation orders in terms of the Proceeds of Crime Act: some constitutional perspectives' (1998) 38 *Tydskrif vir Suid-Afrikaanse Reg* 39, 277, 467 (in three parts).   **45** See note 14 at 4.   **46** See *National Director of Public Prosecutions v. Carolus* 1999 (2) SA 27(C) at 39 (per Blignaut J).   **47** See Cowling note 21 at 356.   **48** See A.J. van der Walt, 'Civil forfeiture of instrumentalities and proceeds of crime and the constitutional property clause' in (2000) 16 *SAJHR* 1 at 6–7.

acquisitive, to vest ownership of the property in the State for the public benefit. However, it assumes that society is the victim and that society will have
the money restored to it, whereas this is not always the case.

These procedures are most vulnerable to criticism as a result of their negative effects on human rights. The main problem with criminal confiscation
orders[49] is that they may function as an additional punishment which may be
excessive and unfair as they are not factored into the tariff applied on sentence.
It is not enough to argue that the criminal does not deserve the property, and
cannot get legal title and thus cannot be punished by removing the property
from him, when the amount confiscated is completely disproportionate from
the crime. Shifting the onus of proof may also violate the right against self-
incrimination. As far as property rights are concerned, while the loss of the
rights of those involved in the crime are not unjust or unreasonable, it may
unfairly affect third party creditors, lessors, lessees, lenders and co-owners.

Civil forfeiture poses a great danger to the property rights of lenders, co-
owners, mortgagees and creditors ignorant or unable to control the use of
tainted property, and there are no guarantees of protection. Van der Walt
explores the question of when it is reasonable and justifiable to allow the public
interest in crime fighting to use civil forfeiture to trump constitutionally-pro-
tected rights to property.[50] He rejects the orthodox explanation for the extraordinary nature of civil forfeiture, the 'personification' or 'guilty property' fiction, which justifies the forfeiture of the property because the property is guilty
of the crime itself and poses a danger to society, noting that pragmatic considerations served to justify this extraordinary procedure in its modern revival,
and this remains true today where it is justified as necessary for the suppression
of crime.[51] The US Supreme Court has played a central role in the debate in
justifying the human rights impact of forfeiture. The court has swung from a
pro-government position that civil forfeiture is not penal and rejecting the
innocent owner defence,[52] to a more anti-government stance recognising the
procedure as penal and being more open to the innocent owner defence,[53] and
then back[54] to a pro-government stance linked to denial of the penal nature of
the procedure and characterised by reference to piracy and prohibition and a
reversion to the guilty property fiction as the justification of forfeiture.[55] The
European Court of Human Rights has also been executive-minded in this
regard, although Van der Walt notes that in his dissenting judgment in *Air
Canada v. United Kingdom*.[56] Martens J was clearly aware of the inclination of
governments to penalise without appearing to do so. He noted that 'the recent

---

49 See Van der Walt note 48 at 4.   **50** See note 48 at 6.   **51** See note 48 at 7–8.   **52** *Calero-Toledo
v. Pearson Yacht Leasing Company* 416 US 663 (1974).   **53** *United States v. Halper* 490 US 435 (1989);
Austin v. United States 509 US 602 (1993).   **54** *Bennis v. Michigan* 116 S Ct 994 (1996).   **55** M.M.
Jochner, 'The US Supreme Court turns back the clock on civil forfeiture in Bennis' (1997) 85
Illinois Bar Journal 314 n3 commenting on the *United States v. Ursery* 116 S Ct 2135 (1996). See
Van der Walt note 48 at 17 n78.   **56** [1995] 20 EHRR 150.

wave of legislation for depriving criminals of the proceeds of their crimes makes it all the more necessary to firmly maintain this principle: we know from experience that Governments in their struggle with international crime do not always heed the limits set by the Convention. It is the Court's task to ensure that these limits are observed'.[57] Van der Walt recommends that the label civil should neither prevent a court from deciding that the procedure is in fact penal nor exclude constitutional protections for those with rights in the property, declaring unfair forfeitures unconstitutional without compensation.[58]

There appears to be a growing concern that this attention to fairness is not being paid in jurisdictions where the process is heavily used.[59] Complaints have been heard in States where forfeiture is common that people lose their cars and homes without due process and that it has been used to target suspected criminals against whom evidence is thin but suspicions are high. A key problem is the used of confiscated assets to partly fund law enforcement, and this has been identified particularly in the US as being open to abuse with law enforcement agencies pursuing confiscation targets to keep funding high. These agencies have a fiscal interest law in the profits of crime – $1.6 billion worth of private property is seized in the US every year and State and local police collected $218 million in confiscated shared assets in 1992. Effectively this taxes a small number of individuals, many of them innocent, in order to provide adequate crime control. Finally, there is the danger that the facilitation of occasional seizures of the proceeds of crime will not affect the profit incentive of criminals. There is little evidence that the enactment and enforcement of forfeiture laws has in any way curbed the activities at which they are aimed.[60]

These concerns are amplified in a developing country like South Africa. South African legislators have shown some concern about the threats that forfeiture laws offer to the innocent by making legislative provision for potentially affected persons to receive proper notice, for the appointment of a *curator bonis* in respect of property subject to a restraining order, and for the protection of the interests of *bona fide* third parties in property. However, as Cowling points out it is difficult to decide whether there should be more protection or whether greater protection will undermine the effectiveness of the forfeiture procedures.[61] One issue that has not been directly addressed is that, while these procedures are designed to protect the innocent, they may deliberately be used against them. Questions have been raised about alleged corruption in Sanab, the police generally,[62] amongst Department of Justice officials and in the Department of Correctional Services.[63] South Africa is in the

---

57 Para. 5. Cited by Van der Walt note 48 at 31. **58** See note 48 at 43. **59** See E. Blumenson and E. Nilson, 'Policing for profit: the drug war's hidden economic agenda' (1998) 65 *University of Chicago Law Review* 35–114. **60** See note 59. **61** See Cowling note 21 at 367. **62** See U Ho, 'Police, courts fail to curb drug epidemic', *Mail and Guardian*, 31 August 2001–6 September 2001, where various commentators raised questions about law enforcement integrity in the face of financial inducements from the illicit drug trade. **63** Shaw, see note 10 at 6.

process of drafting a new Prevention of Corruption Act, but this too will be reliant on the law enforcement agencies being able to police themselves.[64] From a more legally ambiguous but politically realistic point of view, confiscation threatens many who as a hedge against political and economic instability may be involved by necessity in 'grey economies' and are not in a position to question the derivation of property. Moreover, legal challenge to a seizure or confiscation order may well be out of the financial reach of many. The attraction of financing law enforcement by forfeiture is also much greater when so many other pressing demands are being made on the tax purse. The lure of the forfeiture of such large amounts to the South African law enforcement community is obvious, with frequent reference being made by its advocates to the contribution forfeiture makes to the State purse in the United States.[65] The purpose of the Asset Recovery Fund was to house monies where there was no identifiable victim, but one wonders how much will be used to fund drug rehabilitation, rape crisis and trauma centres, and how much will be ploughed back into the AFU's work.[66] There is also the issue of whose activities forfeiture is aimed at suppressing. Media references to 'big time criminals'[67] being subject to forfeiture does not allay the suspicion that it is open season on all tainted property, and this is confirmed by the linking of criminal confiscation to a broad range of offences in schedule 1 of the Act.[68] The former director of the AFU, Willem Hofmeyr, has stated that the intention of the State is to make forfeiture part of general prosecution in all criminal cases involving sums over R200 000 that are close to conviction, and that it would be necessary to amend the Prevention of Corruption Act in order to make it simpler in smaller cases.[69]

The legal development of confiscation and forfeiture is constantly in danger of becoming isolated from its purpose. These procedures can be fair and socially useful – in the prosecution of serious criminality – but they can also be unfair to innocent people and can be subject to abuse in the name of crime control. The courts are aware of the extreme caution necessary when applying these procedures,[70] and this caution is justified when one also takes into account the

64 The new bill provides for a Prevention of Corruption Commission with a strategic role but no direct investigative powers. *Mail and Guardian*, 7–13 September 2001.   65 M. Schonteich, 'The Asset Forfeiture Unit: Performance and priorities'(2000) 3 *Nedbank ISS Crime Index* 24.   66 The options set out by former AFU director Willem Hofmeyr. F Haffejee, 'Forfeiture becoming part of the attack on crime', *Financial Mail*, 13 April 2001.   67 F. Haffejee, 'Forfeiture becoming part of the attack on crime', *Financial Mail*, 13 April 2001.   68 In *National Director of Public Prosecutions v. Mcasa and another* 2000 (1) SACR 263 (TkH), it was contended by the respondent that the Preamble of the Act made it clear that the Act was intended to suppress money laundering, organised crime, criminal gang activities and racketeering, and not other forms of criminality, but the court per Madlanga AJP and Kruger AJ rejected its confinement to these specific types of offences, noting that the specific sections of chapter 5 refereed to 'an offence', 'any other offence' and 'any criminal activity' (at 280).   69 F. Haffejee, 'Forfeiture becoming part of the attack on crime', *Financial Mail*, 13 April 2001.   70 See, for example, *National Director of Public Prosecutions v. Mcasa and another* 2000 (1) SACR 263 (TkH) at 275f, where the court noted that

further problems of the questionable legitimacy of the development of these norms in international law and the general disregard for human rights in this process of development.

THE QUESTIONABLE LEGITIMACY OF THE DEVELOPMENT OF GLOBAL PENAL NORMS

A liberal interpretation of the right of individuals to participate in government[71] supports the argument that individuals have a right under international law to participate in the law-making process,[72] and even though this claim is weakened due to lack of support in State practice, there is no doubt that individuals have an interest in participation in the making of laws that apply to them. That interest extends to the penal provisions that flow from the suppression conventions. Closer examination reveals, however that that interest is largely ignored in the development of these conventions, which casts doubt on their legitimacy.

Sheptycki[73] warns us generally about the democratic deficit in the development of the suppression conventions. He notes that the assumption in a democratic society is that the elected control policy, and thus that they produce legal responses to crime in the shape of the suppression conventions. He highlights, however, the important role of the 'transnational law enforcement enterprise' – the complex global network of transnational law enforcement agencies – in the development of these treaties and the resulting domestic law. He gives as a significant example of this role the 'legalisation' of the use of controlled delivery of illicit drugs in Europe. Controlled delivery was contrary to the general principles of civilian legal systems, which adhere to the legal duty on law enforcement and judicial authorities once they become aware of an illegal shipment to intercept it and arrest and prosecute suspects. Non-prosecution of suspects in a controlled delivery operation had the potential to

the 'constitutional tension' of the chapter 5 procedure called for the exercise of extreme caution in considering whether the requisite reasonable grounds for a restraint order existed.   **71** Recognised in article 21 of the Universal Declaration of Human Rights (UDHR), UN GA Res. 217A (III), GAOR, 3rd Session, Part I, Resolutions, p. 71; and article 25 of the International Covenant for Civil and Political Rights (ICCPR), 999 UNTS 171.   **72** In a general comment on article 25 the Human Rights Committee has stated: '5. The conduct of public affairs, referred to in paragraph (a), is a broad concept which relates to the exercise of political power, in particular the exercise of legislative, executive and administrative powers. It covers all aspects of public administration, and the formulation and implementation of policy at international, national, regional and local levels. The allocation of powers and the means by which individual citizens exercise the right to participate in the conduct of public affairs protected by article 25 should be established by the constitution and other laws.' See 'The right to participate in public affairs, voting rights and the right of equal access to public service (Art. 25)': 12/07/96. CCPR General comment 25.   **73** J. Sheptycki, 'Law enforcement, justice and democracy in the transnational arena: Reflections on the war on drugs' (1996) 24 *International Journal of the Sociology of Law* 61–75.

result in the prosecuting authorities breaching the law themselves. Nevertheless, the value of controlled delivery as an investigative tool was advocated first by foreign and then by local law enforcement officers who persuaded prosecutors and judicial officers likewise, and finally it was sanctioned by international treaty law.[74] Sheptycki's point is that law enforcement agents have been establishing legal standards rather than applying standards established by elected law-makers. Sheptycki's work rests on the insights of Nadelmann who maps how international treaty law is used for the construction of what he terms 'global prohibition regimes'. He argues that individuals and organisations within States develop a cosmopolitan international morality, and use treaty law to globalise these norms. He identifies key 'transnational moral entrepreneurs' who propagate these ideas first domestically and then internationally. He argues, for example, in respect of the global drug prohibition regime that the de facto subjects of the policy of global drug prohibition, the citizens of the States parties to the drug suppression conventions appear to have had little to do with its adoption or application.[75] Anti-drug crusaders in key States use the influence of these States to introduce drug prohibition in treaty law. Importantly, because the international war on drugs is directed at individual transgressors within foreign States and not at those States themselves, it does not threaten powerful constituencies or vested interests in the States who receive these new laws,[76] and they willingly join in the moral condemnation of drugs, sign the drug suppression conventions and enact the necessary legislation.[77] The conjuring of the new folk-devil of organised crime is likely to have much the same impact, with local elites queuing to sign up to the TOC Convention.[78] In general, the *de jure* nature of international society – a democracy of states rather than individuals within states – makes it easy for the generation of global crime control treaties implementing contentious policies with little participation of citizens subject to the norms that these treaties generate.

Sheptycki alerts us to the fact that law enforcement agencies act as transnational moral entrepreneurs, engaged in the sale of both the moral condemnation and criminalisation of certain practices such as organised crime as well as the extraordinary legal mechanisms like civil forfeiture needed to suppress these practices effectively. While the law enforcement agencies of influential States like the United States clearly play this role, it is submitted that the UN's crime control agencies are also key transnational moral entrepreneurs. They are intergovernmental organisations that not only perform their designated role of

---

74 Article 11 of the 1988 Convention.   **75** See E Nadelmann, 'Global prohibition regimes: The evolution of norms in international society' (1990) 44 *International Organisation* 479 at 481.   **76** See Nadelmann note 75 at 510.   **77** See Nadelmann note 75 at 511.   **78** For example, 11 of the 14 member States of the Southern African Development Community (SADC) members have signed – C. Goredema, 'Acknowledgements' in C. Goredema (ed.), *Organised crime in Southern Africa: assessing Legislation*, ISS Monograph Series, No. 56, June 2001 (Institute for Security Studies, Pretoria), p. 3.

administering the policy developed in functional crime control committees of the UN Economic and Social Council where States are represented, but which also develop transnational criminal justice policy because they initiate much of the work of these committees and develop suppression conventions. A recent example of this is the critical role played by Pino Aarlacchi, director of the UN ODCCP, in the development of the TOC Convention.[79]

As with many others, South Africans are on the receiving end of 'transnational' norms suppressing practices like organised crime and legal mechanisms like civil forfeiture that make this moral suppression most effective, and they have very little say in the development of these norms or mechanisms. The argument that suppression of immoral behaviour requires extraordinary legal measures is crucial. In the general jurisprudence of confiscation and forfeiture, the intimate relationship of civil forfeiture with morality is striking. The US Supreme Court has struck a strong moral note in defence of this procedure by linking forfeiture to the mythical fiction of the guilty-property, by ignoring the pragmatic purposes of the procedure, by ignoring its penal nature, and by justifying all violation of rights on a moral basis. The globalisation of the procedure of civil forfeiture appears to have taken on something of the air of a transnational moral crusade, justified by the badness of the things to be confiscated. Yet the mythical notions of guilty property conceals the real public policy origins and justifications of the procedure, and make it possible to avoid the political debate in the adoption of these procedures. It is important to recall in this context the reasons given for South Africa's adoption of these procedures. In *Director of Public Prosecutions v. Bathgate*,[80] Willem Hofmeyr MP stated by way of an affidavit before the court that '[m]easures such as restraint and confiscation were both equitable and morally justified'. In the same case, after providing a page of Latin maxims on the subject of immorality and wrongfulness of filthy lucre and the moral justification of restraint and confiscation,[81] Van Zyl J held:

> The reasons for the promulgation of the Proceeds Act, as set forth in Hofmeyr's affidavit ... are, in my view, compelling and persuasive. He quite correctly refers to the international legal sources relating to similar legislation elsewhere in the world. This Court is obliged in terms of s39(1)(b) of the Constitution to take cognisance of such sources, including international conventions, whether or not they are party thereto. In this regard the Vienna Convention of 1988 appears to have played a singularly important role in the international fight against drug dealing. It has been supplemented by other international instruments and has provided

---

79 See F. Gregory, 'Private criminality as a matter of international concern' in J. Sheptycki (ed.), *Issues in transnational policing* (London, 2000), p.100 at p.116ff. **80** 2000 (1) SACR 105 (CPD) at 111ff. **81** At 130a–e.

the model for national legislation in a number of countries plagued by the deleterious effects of such abominable crimes. I agree with Hofmeyr that this country is indeed obliged to follow and apply the international precedents set in this regard. Full and unequivocal co-operation in this sphere is not merely recommendable; it is essential and compelling.[82]

The link to morality makes it possible to defer attention from the lack of consultation of those people to whom these laws are going to apply. South African Law Commission projects[83] and parliamentary debate do not change the fact that, once international obligations of this type are undertaken by the executive, it is almost inevitable that they will become national law. International treaty law is used to impose morality/policy developed elsewhere by individuals who are not accountable in a process that is opaque to most ordinary people. In theory the process is 'democratised' by the consultation of various states and the democratic participation of state representatives in diplomatic conference that establishes the treaty. In democratic states like South Africa, the treaty ratification process and transformation of international obligation into domestic legislation also provide avenues for formal input into the establishment of these laws through legislative review of executive decision. The problem is that the existence of an international legal obligation has a powerful influence on domestic lawmakers. The suppression conventions rest on a global order engineered by bureaucrats. Elected representatives struggle to control this process. The executive both legislates and if the matter comes before court it provides a guide to interpretation of these extraordinary legal measures by referring the court to the practice of other influential states and reminding the court of South Africa's international obligations.

Greater difficulties arise when one considers that the treaty development process takes no account of the fact that many states are non-democratic and assume obligations without their citizens having even had a nominal say in the matter.[84] Nadelmann points out that the prohibition regimes are easily subscribed to by the elites of states with strong external sovereignty, although these laws are often poorly implemented because these same states often have a weak

---

82 At 129f–130a. **83** The South African Law Commission Project 98, *International cooperation in criminal matters* (1995), concluded that asset confiscation would pass the constitutionality test by meeting the requirements of the limitation clause (pp.118–120). **84** Oscar Schachter wrote that when it comes to government being based on democratic principles: 'Many, probably most, States do not meet the standard; they are nonetheless recognized as having legitimate governments' in J. Charney, D. Anton and M. O'Connell (eds.), *Politics, values and functions: international law in the 21st century: essays in honor of Louis Henkin* (The Hague, 1997) p. 24. Thomas Franck claimed in 1994 that around 130 States were 'legally committed' to democracy, but conceded that a few may only be democratic in form – *Fairness in international law and institutions* (Oxford, 1995) pp 85–6. Glennon has it that of the 185 UN member States, 50 could be described as undemocratic – M Glennon, 'Sovereignty and Community After Haiti: Rethinking the Collective Use of Force' (1995) 89 *AJIL* 71.

internal sovereignty.[85] The issue is pertinent for states in the Southern African Development Community (SADC). Goredema notes that some of the practical problems in harmonising and implementing legislation flowing from the TOC Convention may '[s]tem from the troubled contexts in which changes will be expected to take place. Fragile political and economic systems plague SADC'.[86] This fragility is an invitation equally to criminality and heavy-handed legal responses, and legal legitimacy is a significant problem in such contexts.[87] Goredema concludes pessimistically on the prospects for legislative transformation of the TOC Convention by SADC members:

> Some legislative changes will need to be complemented by political reforms to be acceptable to civil society and the judiciary alike. There are disturbing signs of a retreat to autocracy in certain parts of SADC, which does not augur well for positive political reform. If the trends in Zambia, Zimbabwe, Swaziland, Lesotho, Mozambique and Angola continue, there is little hope that the expansion of State powers envisaged by the Convention will be accepted by civil society in these countries.[88]

In South Africa the situation is more complex, but it too suffers from the problems of a weak internal sovereignty. The danger in South Africa is that apparently legitimate process like civil forfeiture will be undermined through misuse by the State.

These doubts about the legitimacy of the globalisation of penal norms place an onus on those who manage the application of these norms to protect the individual human rights and interests of the persons caught up by them. I am not suggesting that South African law enforcement agencies are usurping the legislature in the same way that drug enforcement agencies did in Europe with controlled delivery.[89] But they are the beneficiaries of laws developed by sister agencies in developed States and by the UN's transnational criminal justice administrative machinery,[90] and there is cause to be cautious in the application of these new laws because of issues about their legitimacy.

---

85 See Nadelmann note 75 at 486 citing RH Jackson, 'Quasi-States, dual regimes, and neo-classical theory: International jurisprudence and the Third World' in (1987) 41 *International Organization* 533–49. **86** C. Goredema (ed.), *Organised crime in southern Africa: Assessing legislation*, ISS Monograph Series, No. 56, June 2001 (Institute for Security Studies, Pretoria), p. 4. **87** See C. Goredema, 'Harmonising legislation against organised crime in SADC countries' in C Goredema (ed.), *Organised crime in Southern Africa* at p.190 who notes misgivings about the extension of law enforcement powers in SADC States where such powers are already being abused for political ends. J Banda, 'Institutional responses to organised crime in Malawi', in the same volume at p. 61 at p. 71 examines the misuse of a since repealed overtly political Forfeiture Act in Malawi. **88** See Goredema note 86 at 198. **89** By all accounts they are fighting to keep their heads above water. See, for example, U Ho, 'Police, courts fail to curb drug epidemic', *Mail and Guardian*, 31 August–6 September 2001, who notes that up to 45% of drug cases are being tossed out of court, and that cases are being withdrawn by the police, not by prosecutors. Quantities of illicit drugs seized show a dramatic increase in the last two years. **90** See, for example, the UN ODCCP's participation in the implementation of the TOC

THE ABSENCE OF HUMAN RIGHTS PROTECTIONS IN THE
SUPPRESSION CONVENTIONS

A problem related to legitimacy is the dearth of explicit human rights protections available in the suppression conventions. While States have become more mindful about the human rights impact of the provisions of the suppression conventions[91] in response to the development of the 'Soering' approach to the application of human rights norms in international criminal legal co-operation,[92] the authors of the suppression conventions have deliberately created highly invasive instruments and they rely mainly on domestic constitutional protections. They rely to a much smaller extent on international human rights protections to limit the impact of these procedures on human rights. If we consider confiscation, for instance, specific provision is made by article 5(8) of the 1988 Convention for the protection of the human rights of *bona fide* third parties with respect to the confiscation procedure provided for in article 5, and identical provision is made in the TOC Convention in article 12(8). However, these provisions do not define these 'rights' or '*bona fide*' and characteristically leaves this to the Parties to do so in their domestic law, with all the attendant difficulties discussed above. The general approach is apparent from the UN's own assessment of the impact of the 1988 Convention's confiscation provisions. The UN's Official *Commentary on the United Nations Convention Against Illicit Traffic in Narcotic Drugs and Psychotropic Substances, 1988* (hereinafter the *1988 Commentary*) recognises: 'The system of confiscation constitutes a serious interference with the rights of individuals and with their economic interests. It is deliberately draconian in character'.[93] The *1988 Commentary* continues in respect of confiscation: 'For this reason, particular care must be taken to ensure compliance with relevant constitutional protections and applicable international human rights norms.'[94] Unfortunately, left to themselves, States will take highly invasive measures in the 'spirit' of the convention and transnational law enforcement co-operation. The negative effect that development of these measures by the transnational law enforcement enterprise can have on human rights is easily illustrated. When the 1988 and TOC Conventions were drawn up, no specific requirement of non-retrospective application of any of their provisions including confiscation or forfeiture was included in these conventions. States parties were left to choose. As we have seen, at first the South African law was also silent on the matter and the Supreme Court of Appeal applied the interpretative presumption against retrospectivity. However, the legislature, following foreign examples, was quick to step in and clarify that these measures operated retrospectively. Even when constitutional protections apply,

---

Convention in SADC through regional forums – C. Goredema, 'Acknowledgements', as note 78 above. **91** Evidence of this is the increased reference to procedural rights in the TOC Convention by comparison to their almost complete absence in the 1988 Convention. **92** *Soering Case* ECHR Series A, vol. 161 (1989). **93** (New York, 1998) UN Doc. E/CN.7/590; UN Publication Sales No. E.98.XI.5, p. 144. **94** 1988 Commentary at 144.

they may be rendered useless in the hands of an executive-minded judiciary. International human rights instruments have not been heavily used in restricting the application of draconian measures called for by the suppression conventions.[95] While international human rights and the suppression conventions have evolved side by side within the United Nations, the latter have not been subject to scrutiny for compliance with international human rights standards.[96] The conventions are under the technical supervision of specialist agencies like the UN ODCCP, which has played an important role in their elaboration. Yet the UN must also guarantee respect for the Universal Declaration of Human Rights. As Kingham and Wallon point out, the UN is both judge and party here.[97] There appears to be few links between the human rights and crime control arms of the UN,[98] and the suppression conventions do not provide the platform for such a link. It appears that the ODCCP is willing to pursue crime control regardless of the human rights records of individual governments and national agencies involved in this process.[99] The UN Intergovernmental Expert Group on Extradition counters this type of criticism by stating that compliance with the conventions cannot result in human rights breaches and that observance of human rights makes the conventions more effective.[1] It is apparent, however, that the development of these conventions has been driven by the exigencies of effective law enforcement and has to a large extent avoided dealing with consequential human rights infringement.

CONCLUSION: PROTECTING POLITICAL INTERESTS AND HUMAN RIGHTS IN THE GLOBALISATION OF PENAL PROVISIONS

Bassiouni noted in 1990 that all recommendations for improvement of the indirect control system of international criminal law, the system where States implement international penal obligations created by treaty 'must be applied in confor-

---

95 A good example is the criminalisation of the simple possession of drugs. Because the drug conventions are ambiguous about such criminalisation, the UN drug control organs have called for the application of presumptions in domestic legislation that possession of more than a specified small amount of an illicit drug is intended for distribution – see the The *Commentary on the Single Convention on Narcotic Drugs, 1961* (New York, 1973) UN Publication Sales No. E.73.XI (hereinafter the *1961 Commentary*) at p.113. In the *Salabiaku* Case ECHR Series A vol. 141–A (1988), the European Court held famously that a possession-based presumption that the accused was smuggling in article 392(1) of the French Customs Code was compatible with the presumption of innocence in article 6(2) of the European Convention on Human Rights.   **96** See N. Gilmore, 'Drug use and human rights: privacy, vulnerability, disability, and human rights infringements' (1996) 12 *Journal of Contemporary Health Law and Policy* 355 at 401.   **97** R.A. Kingham and A. Wallon, 'The role of the European citizen's associations in strategies and policies to combat drugs' in G Estievenart (ed.), *Policies and strategies to combat drugs in Europe* (Dordrecht, 1995) p. 311 at p. 316.   **98** See generally ND White, 'The World Court, the WHO and the UN system' in N.M. Blokker and H.G. Scheremers (eds), *Proliferation of international organizations* (The Hague, 2001), pp. 85–109.   **99** See, for example, the willingness of the UN Drug Control Program (UNDCP) to do business with the Taliban in Afghanistan despite its egregious human rights record – K. Fish, 'The United Nations and the Taliban: An unholy alliance in the name of drug control' (1998) 35 *Drug Policy Letter* 15–16.

mity with international, regional and national human rights norms and standards'.[2] Despite these warnings, it appears that law enforcement agencies from different States, co-operating within a transnational law enforcement enterprise, develop and apply extraordinary legal measures without much concern for democratic consultation about these measures or consideration of their human rights impact. The suppression conventions are an important vehicle for this developmental process, serving as the central legal framework around which direct agency to agency contact and the use of developed States legislation as model legislation by developing States perform significant developmental roles. The 'transnational hook' – the theoretical proposition that extraordinary legal measures are necessary to fight crimes with a cross-border element – is the key rationale of the globalisation of these penal norms. Yet it is probably true that most of these norms will not be applied to situations that actually involve transnational elements. They are most likely to be applied to purely domestic offences. Thus, for example, confiscation in South Africa is not so much a weapon against transnational organised crime as a weapon against all domestic South African crime. The suppression conventions, ostensibly driven by the need to fight transnational crime, globalise special norms of general application. Whether social defence in the common interest requires extraordinary legal measures to be applied in this way is a matter about which there must be informed public debate. Moreover, a proper balance should be maintained between the effectiveness of special law enforcement measures and the protection of individual rights. Experience with confiscation suggests that the crucial buffer between ordinary citizens and the transnational law enforcement enterprise is not likely to be the executive – given its need to show influential States in the international community that they are willing to do their bit against transnational crime – or the legislator – given its enthusiasm for these laws as a solution to seemingly intractable domestic crime problems. This burden falls upon the national judiciary, armed with the Constitution.[3] Just as the judiciary has played a formative role in the early development of international criminal legal co-operation,[4] so must it play a restraining role as this area of legal co-operation matures. The judiciary cannot democratise the treaty-making process, but it can defend rights affected by these international obligations conscious of the legitimacy problems within that process.[5]

---

1 1996 Report cited by D. Stafford, 'Combating transnational crime: The role of the Commonwealth' in W.C. Gilmore and P.J. Cullen (eds), *Crimes sans frontieres: International and European approaches: Hume Papers on Public Policy*, vol. 6, nos 1 and 2 (Edinburgh, 1998), p. 41 at p. 48. **2** M.C. Bassiouni, 'Policy considerations on inter-State cooperation in criminal matters' in A. Eser and O. Lagodny (eds), *Principles and procedures for a new transnational criminal law* (Max Planck Institute, Freiburg im Breisgau, 1992), p.807 at p.823. **3** See Cowling note 21 at 373. **4** See M. Kremnetzer, 'The world community as an international legislator in competition with national legislators', in Eser and Lagodny (eds), p. 337 at p. 340. **5** The record of the South African judiciary in this regard thus far is mixed. A poor example is the *Prince* debacle in CPD where the High Court made much of the obligation to criminalise simple possession of illicit drugs in terms of the drugs conventions while it appeared to take no cognisance of the fact that these conventions specifically provide for constitutional limitation of the obligation to criminalise. *Prince v. President of the Law Society, Cape of Good Hope and others*, 1998 (8) BCLR 976 (C). See generally 984–5.

The Scottish and South African courts' response to the notion of undue delay in criminal cases

ESTHER STEYN

> Time present and time past
> Are both perhaps present in time future,
> And time future contained in time past.
> If all time is eternally present
> All time is unredeemable.[1]

I INTRODUCTION

If we consider the rules governing civil or criminal matters, then it is evident that time fulfils an important function in most legal systems all over the world. Much depends, for example, on the lapse of time between the issuing and serving of a legal document; or bringing a matter to trial before the prescription period of the offence; or disposing of a matter without it being unduly delayed. Despite varying practices that regulate these processes that are all concerned with a period of time, we find that time is neither specified nor defined as a standardised unit in most criminal justice systems. Nevertheless, courts are expected to determine whether a criminal matter has been unduly or unreasonably delayed without being given a yardstick by which to do it. In some cases it is crucial to determine the starting point from which the time period should be calculated: whether it begins when an accused person is charged, or whether one should start counting from the first day that he appears in court. It is therefore essential to analyse these questions in order to consider the approaches adopted by the courts in South Africa and Scotland in deciding whether a matter has been unduly or unreasonably delayed, in circumstances where time is not standardised.

Why should we look specifically at the systems of these two countries? The answer is simple: both Scotland and South Africa recently adopted human rights

* The financial assistance rendered by the University of Cape Town and the University of Aberdeen in support of the research on which this article is based is gratefully acknowledged. Opinions herein expressed and conclusions arrived at are, however, those of the author and should not be attributed to the aforementioned institutions.
1 T.S. Eliot, 'Burnt Norton', *Collected Poems, 1909–1935.*

laws that impact drastically on their criminal justices systems and the way trials
are conducted. Furthermore both countries have 'mixed' legal systems, wherein
influences from 'Civilian' and 'Anglo-American' systems are incorporated, and
both faced similar challenges in the criminal justice sphere. In this paper the
different responses of the two systems to the notion of undue delay will be
examined and specific attention will be paid to the shortcomings of each system.

2 SCOTLAND

It would be fair to say that most of Scottish criminal law and procedure has
in the past been predominantly judge-made law with a peculiar Scottish flavour.[2]
The criminal process in Scotland afforded substantial protection to accused persons through the Scottish Criminal Procedure Act[3] long before any of the
human rights legislation came into operation.[4] Since delays involve the handling of matters before they reach court, it is important to note that in Scotland
the decision to prosecute in criminal matters, for practical purposes, lies in the
hands of the Crown.[5] The role of the police in Scotland is restricted as far as
the investigation is concerned. What is expected of the police is to report the
facts to the Procurator Fiscal and then to receive instruction from him for the
further investigation of the crime.[6] Absolute control is exercised over the proceedings by the Crown. It is the Lord Advocate, or the Procurator Fiscal acting
on his or her behalf, that has the discretion to decide whether an offence is sufficiently grave to justify the use of solemn procedure[7] or whether a summary
procedure[8] will be followed. Despite comprehensive protection afforded to
accused persons in criminal trials, constitutional changes and hence constitutional protection only came about in 1999.

   On 20 May 1999, section 44(1)(c) of the Scotland Act 1998 came into force
in Scotland and in terms of it the Lord Advocate became a member of the
Scottish executive. By virtue of section 57(2) of the Scotland Act 1998, he or
she has no power to do any act that is incompatible with any of the Convention
rights defined in section 1 of the Human Rights Act 1998, unless the act in

---

2 M.C. Meston et al., *The Scottish legal tradition* (Edinburgh, 1990), 25. **3** See Criminal Procedure
(Scotland) Act 1995 that governs criminal proceedings. **4** See *Buchanan v. McLean* 2000 SLT 928
and at 934 the views held by Lord Prosser with regard to the earlier concerns of the courts: 'Scots
law, prior to the Convention, was concerned with the principles of substantial justice, and with
a practical risk of real unfairness.' **5** Generic term for the state prosecution authorities in Scotland
including the Lord Advocate, the Crown Office and the Procurator Fiscal Service. **6** Op. cit. (n.
2) 27. **7** Solemn procedure refers to a trial, on indictment, before a judge and jury of 15 persons
who will decide upon the guilt or innocence of an accused person. **8** A summary procedure
refers to a trial heard before a judge, sheriff, magistrate or lay justice, but, most importantly, without a jury. The decision to indict is always one for Crown Counsel, not the Procurator Fiscal, but
the Fiscal may decide to delay initiating summary proceedings by placing the accused on a petition warrant, which is usually the first step in a solemn procedure.

question falls within section 57(3) of the Act.[9] The common law with regard to criminal procedure has been subjected to further constitutional change and is influenced by the Human Rights Act, 1998, which came into force only in October 2000. To understand the impact of these Acts, it is useful to know that the Human Rights Act of 1998 incorporated the European Convention for the Protection of Human Rights and Fundamental Freedoms (ECHR) into the law of Scotland, England, Wales and Northern-Ireland.[10] This Act requires all public authorities to comply with the provisions of the Convention and enables individuals to enforce Convention rights through domestic courts in the United Kingdom. For all practical purposes the Human Rights Act can be seen as a Bill of Rights for the United Kingdom, incorporating the ECHR into the domestic law of the countries concerned.

It is submitted that in practice the provisions of the European Convention should influence and shape the application of human rights in the Scottish criminal justice system. With reference to a trial right and the right to be heard without undue delay, the following articles of the ECHR should play a role: Article 5(3) that provides that an accused be 'brought to trial within a reasonable time or to release pending trial'; and Article 6(1) that requires that a criminal charge should be determined 'within a reasonable time'.[11] In light of these articles it will be incumbent on the Scottish courts to interpret an accused's rights in accordance with jurisprudence of the European Court of Human Rights and be guided by the principles set out in the ECHR.

The development of the right to be heard without undue delay will now be looked at and judged by reference to constitutional standards.

2.1 Undue delay prior to the inception of the Human Rights Act

Like the South African courts, the Scottish courts have also recognised the right to a 'speedy trial' as part of an accused's right to a fair trial even though the right was not statutorily regulated.

In the matter of *McNeillie v. Walkinshaw*[12] it was held with regard to a decision on undue delay that this remains a question of fact and degree and that the courts will be slow to interfere. With regard to onus it was held before the inception of the Human Rights Act that the Crown had to discharge the onus of showing that there has been no undue delay in bringing the matter to court.[13]

---

9 Prior to the Human Rights Act coming into force, the Scottish Parliament and the Scottish Executive were placed under a statutory obligation to comply with the terms of the European Convention by virtue of section 29 and 57 of the Scotland Act of 1998. **10** The Human Rights Act 1998, received Royal assent on 9 November 1998 and came into operation on 2 October 2000. **11** In international context it seems that criminal proceedings ought not to last beyond reasonable time. See Article 14(3) of the International Covenant of Civil and Political Rights, Article 8(1) of the American Convention on Human Rights and Article 7(1)(d) of the African Charter on Human and People's Rights. **12** 1990 SCCR 428. **13** See *McCartney v. Tudhope* 1985 SCCR 373.

2.2 Undue delay post the Human Rights Act

The development of Scots law with regard to Article 6 of the ECHR began with *Little v. HMA*[14] where the accused was charged with a number of sexual offences including the rape of children. Some of the offences were committed in the 1980s and in 1997 further allegations were made against the accused. The Crown chose to proceed in respect of the recent allegations and those that were reported in 1988. The defence then challenged the procedure on the basis of undue delay. Since this was a challenge before coming into force of section 57 of the Scotland Act the remedies included in Article 6 could not avail the accused. What was available was the procedure plea in bar of trial. The defence, however, was unsuccessful in its application for barring the trial. After the decision but before the trial section 57 of the Scotland Act came into operation and the accused relied on that section to challenge the intention of the Lord Advocate to proceed with the trial as *ultra vires*. When challenged, the Crown was not able to explain why the charges, laid in 1988, were not dealt with earlier. Lord Kingarth held that to proceed with the older charges would be *ultra vires*.

Shortly after the *Little* decision the matters of *McNab v. HMA*[15] and *HMA v. James Hynd* (unreported decision by Lord Bonomy on 9 May 2000) appeared before the courts and it was held that what was reasonable depended upon the particular circumstances of each case. The reasoning in *Little,* which was confirmed in *McNab,* showed a clear development in Scots law, with the High Court of Justiciary stating explicitly that existing Scots law and the Convention were not the same. The Court held in *McNab,* for example, that the question for the Court to decide was whether the accused had been brought to trial within a reasonable time of being charged, having regard to the *whole period* involved and the *whole procedure* involved. That question had to be determined not exclusively in the light of the time limits that apply in Scottish criminal procedure but by looking broadly at all circumstances of each case.[16] Lord Justice Clerk's view in *McNab* shows support for the proposition that the interests of all the parties should be considered in deciding upon undue delay:

> While the case appears to have been relatively straight forward it is necessary in our view to take into account not only the need to avoid delay in the particular case which is under consideration but also what is required in order to meet the needs of other cases and the interests of those who are involved in them.[17]

---

14 1999 SCCR 625. **15** 2000 SLT 99. **16** See *Reilly v. HMA* 2000 SLT 1330 at 1331J to 1332A where Lord Prosser held that 'charged' in the context of undue delay means 'that there has been an official notification given to the person by a competent authority of an allegation that he has committed a criminal offence'. See also *McLean v. HMA* 2000 SLT 299. **17** *McNab v. HMA supra* (n. 15) at 103D–E.

2.3 Reasonable time

In deciding whether there has been unreasonable delay in bringing cases to trial, the courts considered the meaning of 'reasonable time' as referred to in Article 6(1) of the European Convention.[18] While it is submitted that the notion of 'reasonable time' is a subjective one and that standards will inevitably differ from one system to another, it is also contended that the Scottish courts have not been consistent in their interpretation of the meaning of 'reasonable time'. Surely the fairness of the process should be considered? Specific attention should therefore be paid to whether the accused has suffered prejudice to the extent that he could no longer expect a fair trail. In deciding upon the reasonable time standard, due consideration should be given to the trite factors that need to play a role in determining what will be regarded as reasonable in a given proceeding.[19] It is submitted that these factors are: the complexity of the case; the way the authorities have handled the case; the way the applicant's own conduct contributed to the delay; and special circumstances that may justify the prolonged proceedings. Furthermore, that the aim of Article 6(1) is to protect all parties against excessive procedural delays. More explicitly,

> ... that in criminal matters, especially, it is designed to avoid that a person charged should remain too long in a state of uncertainty about his fate.[20]

In deciding whether the prosecution of a case had taken place within 'reasonable time' the Scottish courts found particularly guidance in *Eckle v. Federal Republic of Germany*[21] wherein the European Court of Human Rights considered the meaning of 'reasonable time' and ruled as follows:

> In criminal matters, the 'reasonable time' referred to in Article 6(1) begins to run as soon as a person is 'charged'; this may occur on a date prior to the case coming before the trial court, such as the date of arrest, the date when the person concerned was officially notified that he would be prosecuted or the date when preliminary investigations were opened. 'Charge', for the purposes of Article 6(1), may be defined as

18 Article 6(1) reads as follows: 'In the determination of his civil rights and obligations or of any criminal charge against him, everyone is entitled to a fair and public hearing within a reasonable time by an independent and impartial tribunal established by law. Judgment shall be pronounced publicly but the press and public may be excluded from all or part of the trial in the interest of morals, public order or national security in a democratic society, where the interests of juveniles or the protection of the private life of the parties so require, or to the extent strictly necessary in the opinion of the court in special circumstances where publicity would prejudice the interests of justice.' **19** See *Imbroscia v. Switserland* (1993) 17 EHRR 441 at para 36, where the Court made certain observations in relation to the 'reasonable time' requirement of Article 6(1). **20** See *Stögmüller v. Austria* (1969) 1 EHRR 191 at para. 5. **21** (1982) 5 EHRR 1.

'the official notification given to an individual by the competent authority of an allegation that he has committed a criminal offence', a definition that also corresponds to the test whether 'the situation of the [sus-
pect] has been substantially affected'.[22]

In the matter of *Boyle*[23] the Sheriff Court Glasgow and Strathkelvin considered
the meaning of 'reasonable time' and held, contra to *Eckle*,[24] that the important
date that denotes the 'start' of the proceedings is not the date when preliminary
investigations were commenced, but the date on which the accused is
'charged'.[25] The court also held that the test is not whether there has been an
inordinate delay, but whether the accused has received a hearing within a 'reasonable time'. In *casu* no explanation was tendered as to why it took the police
three months to report the case to the Procurator Fiscal, nor was there an explanation as to why no action had been taken by the Crown from August 1999
until November 1999 when the case was reported. The facts revealed that some
minor further information was required from the police. That information was
supplied on 26 November 1999, but there was no detailed explanation as to
why it took until 14 March 2000 to bring the case to court. The case has been
brought before the Court by summary prosecution and the facts were simple
indeed. The accused had allegedly encashed a stolen cheque. The Court held
that, *prima facie*, the ten-month period that had elapsed before bringing the
accused to court after he had been cautioned and charged involved unreasonable delay on the part of the authorities. In the opinion of the presiding sheriff,
no satisfactory explanation or reasons for the delay had been placed before the
court, and it held that a well-founded devolution issue was placed before it.
Sheriff Lockhart held that there had been a breach of Article 6(1) of the ECHR.
    Earlier, in the matter of *McNab* it had been held that the correct approach
for the courts to adopt in dealing with issues of delay was to consider whether
the period of time in question was unreasonable. Only if the period concerned
is *prima facie* unreasonable would the Crown be required to submit reasons for
such delay.[26] Recent cases, however, reveal a tendency amongst presiding officers to deal with the delays in a piecemeal fashion when evaluating the reasonableness of the elapsed time in determining the issue of delay.[27] The approach

22 Ibid. para. 73.   **23** See Scottish Courts website (www.scotcourts.gov.uk/opinions) Opinion
of the Sheriff Court in *Procurator Fiscal, Glasgow v. Boyle*, decided 14 June 2000.   **24** *Eckle v. Federal
Republic of Germany*, supra (n. 21).   **25** Cf. *Deweer v. Belgium* 1980 Series A no 35 at 22 where it
was held that being charged might occur on a date prior to the case coming before the court, such
as the date of arrest and the date when the person was officially notified that he would be prosecuted or the date when the preliminary investigations were opened.   **26** *McNab v. HMA, supra*
(n. 15).   **27** An interesting case dealing with 'reasonable time' is the decision of the Privy Council,
the 'Constitutional Court' of Scotland, in *Darmalingham v. The State* (2000) 2 Cr App R 445 (PC).
The House of Lords held that the right to a trial within a reasonable time in the constitution of
Mauritius (modelled on Article 6) was distinct form the right to a fair trial. Accordingly it was

of the Lord Coulsfield in *Kane v. HMA*[28] with regard to a 'reasonable' lapse of time is to be preferred where he stated:

> [The] judge erred in adopting the piecemeal approach suggested by the Solicitor General, and failing to give proper attention to the over-all period of delay, and the repeated and cumulative failure to progress the case. Each of the explanations for particular periods of delay put forward by the Crown might well have been sufficient if that period had been the only period which called for explanation. When, how-ever, the whole period is considered the explanations lose their force. In our view, that is an element which the judge did not take into account. In the whole circumstances, therefore, the overall period of delay has been unreasonable, and we shall sustain the minute of and dismiss the indictment.[29]

2.4 Reasonableness of the length of the proceedings

Considering the new constitutional order introduced by the Scotland Act, incorporating as it does section 6 of the Human Rights Act and the authority of Strasbourg jurisprudence, it is submitted that the reasonableness of the length of proceedings should be assessed in the light of the particular circumstances of each case. In each instance account should be taken of the complexity of the matter, the conduct of the accused and the conduct of the authorities, partic-ularly the Crown.[30]

The courts in Scotland have decided the issue in a somewhat arbitrary way. Their decisions lack consistency in the determination of what length of time would pass the standard of a 'reasonable time'. From the facts of *Gibson v. HMA*[31] it is apparent that the Court had been very sympathetic towards the Crown's conduct and had focused so much on the procedures preceding a trial that should be adhered to by the Crown in bringing a person to trial, within a reasonable time, that it had almost ignored the length of the period concerned. In *Gibson* the appellant appealed against the sheriff's refusal of his devolution minute con-tending that he had not been brought to trial within a reasonable period in terms of Article 6(1) of the ECHR. *In casu* 19 months had elapsed between the appel-lant being charged in January 1997 and the initiation of part of the proceedings in August 1998, with an indictment for trial only in May 2000.

The Court, per Lord Prosser, refused the appeal and held that the overall delay although unusual was not unreasonable and that the absence of a detailed chronology of events explaining what the Crown was doing with regard to the case, did not mean that the delay was *prima facie* unreasonable. He said that:

held, that a breach of the speedy trial right did not depend on proof of prejudice.   **28** See Scottish Courts website (www.scotcourts.gov.uk/opinions) Appeal No. 3296/2001, decided 4 May 2001. **29** *Kane v. HMA, supra* (n. 28) at para. 12.   **30** Cf. *Pélissier and Sassi v. France* (2000) 30 EHRR 715 at para. 67 and *Kemmache v. France* (1992) 14 EHRR 520 at 27.   **31** 2001 SCCR 51.

... if in any particular case it seems initially that the police or the Crown
have taken longer at some particular stage than is usual, it will often be
fairly evident what the reason or 'explanation' for this is likely to be,
having regard to the known circumstances of the case. Any suggestion
that in these familiar situations there has been even *prima facie* some
unreasonable delay appears to us to be without foundation. An assertion that there has been, even *prima facie*, some unreasonableness (and
of course any further assertion that unreasonableness at a particular stage
has produced an overall lapse of time which is not reasonable) will be
justified only if some factual basis for inferring such unreasonableness
can be identified and averred. In its ordinary English sense, even the
word 'delay' seems to us to imply some departure from some norm. It
appears to us that in quite a number of cases where Article 6(1) has
been invoked in this context, the expressions 'delay' and 'unreasonable delay' have been used with no apparent justification.[32]

He further observed that:

[I]t will be easy, but in our opinion quite wrong, to describe the
timescales achieved by, say, a busy Procurator Fiscal's department as
demonstrating some kind of 'failure', merely because greater resources
would have made it possible to deal with more cases faster.[33]

It is submitted that Lord Prosser's decision shows a judicial reluctance to criticise the handling of matters by the Crown's office and a tendency to view the
Scottish procedures as *per se* fair. The Court held that certain Scottish practices
and procedures may well be time-consuming but that such domestic practices
are needed so much in the system that they almost always will excuse a delay
by the Crown on the basis that appropriate time, irrespective of the length
thereof, is required at each stage and serves the interest of all the parties concerned.[34] How the court could come to such a finding in circumstances where

32 *Gibson v. HMA, supra* (n. 31) at para. 13.   33 Ibid., 14.   34 Ibid., 12: 'The normal and familiar is not, of course, necessarily reasonable; and scrutiny of our practices, in the light of provisions
such as Article 6(1), can of course be illuminating. But Scottish practice requires careful investigation and thought both before a matter is reported to the Procurator Fiscal, and thereafter, by
him and where appropriate by Crown counsel, before any charge is brought by way of complaint
or indictment. These careful procedures inevitably take some time. And in general it appears to
us that it is in the interests of accused persons, and a matter of public duty as well as public interest, that the appropriate time be taken at these stages. We are not aware of any case in which it
has been suggested by those representing an accused person that that approach itself is unreasonable. But it has been suggested in certain cases that the only reasonable course for either the police
or the Procurator Fiscal would have been to depart from normal practice, and to pass matters on
without the usual kind of investigation, on the basis perhaps of a mere sufficiency of evidence.
We find it hard to picture a situation in which that would be a reasonable course, far less the only

the Crown failed to give a detailed explanation[35] justifying the 19-month delay, which explanation would have been the very fact showing that the delay was excusable with particular regard being had to the facts of the specific case, is disconcerting in a human rights context. It appears from the judgment of Lord Prosser that it is unlikely that Scottish practitioners will be able to argue that the length of time in itself could give rise to trial prejudice and hence cause an unfair trial. In *Gibson* the court found that the reason for justifying the delay was to be found in the broader circumstances of the case. This decision is also in stark contrast to an earlier decision by the court in *Smith v. Peter Walker & Son (Edinburgh) Limited,*[36] given at a time before the courts were bound to sub-scribe to human rights norms and standards. Of particular importance is the opinion of Lord Justice General Emslie, approving the following passage:

> What constitutes undue delay must be a question of fact in each case. It must not be due to any act for which the prosecutor is responsible. The expression 'without undue delay' implies that there has been no slackness on his part and that any delay in execution is due to some circumstance for which he is not responsible, for instance, the conduct of the accused.[37]

In *Reilly v. HMA,*[38] also dealing with the reasonableness of the time taken to bring the accused person to trial, the Court held, per Lord Prosser, that the period from reporting the crime to the police in 1992 until the petition warrant was issued in 1999 was not unreasonable if note was taken of the complexity of the matter; and that there was thus no breach of Article 6(1) of the ECHR.

More recently Lord Bonomy dismissed an indictment as incompetent in *HMA v. H,*[39] a case where the delay was not extremely unreasonable but where the Crown failed to put forward good reasons for the delay. He held:

> The accused's trial has accordingly been delayed by about 10 months for no good reason. In my opinion, in the context of a straightforward case, which would ordinarily have been brought to trial within about 15 months of the accused being charged, that delay is unreasonable.[40]

reasonable course.'   **35** Ibid., para 17, where the following was stated by the court: 'This is in our opinion a case in which the question of whether there has been a breach of Article 6(1) in this respect necessitates scrutiny of the circumstances. But we reject the suggestion that in the absence of a detailed chronology of events, showing exactly what the Crown was doing, the period of delay was prima facie unreasonable. In some of the (quite rare) cases in which an explanation is needed from the Crown, that explanation may of course take the form of, or include, a detailed chronology. But in many cases the explanation may lie in the burden of work and necessary priorities. That is now a familiar explanation. It is a reason which will not usually need to be "explained".'   **36** 1978 JC 44.   **37** Renton and Brown's *Criminal procedure,* 4th ed, at 187 as quoted in the judgment of *Smith v. Peter Walker & Son (Edinburgh) Limited.*   **38** *Reilly v. HMA, supra* (n. 16).   **39** 2000 SLT 1321.   **40** *HMA v. H, supra* (n. 39) at 1323.

It is submitted that the approached followed by Lord Bonomy is to be preferred to the approached adopted by Lord Prosser in cases where the Crown fails to give cogent reasons for a delay in a particular matter.

2.5 Delays caused by the authorities

While it is submitted that institutional problems could justify a delay under certain circumstances, it is disturbing that a criminal justice system, like the Scottish system, tolerates almost every systemic delay at the cost of the right to a speedy trial. The Scottish courts have not been overly critical of systemic delays.[41] The facts of the appeal cases of *O'Brien and Michael Ryan*[42] reflect a clear systemic failure that led to an inordinate delay; yet the court, although it recognised the unreasonableness of such delay, held that under the circumstances that the overall delay did not breach the appellants' right to a fair trial. Lord Prosser considered the fact that such delays do not happen regularly as convincing enough to dismiss the appeals, despite the fact that the time elapsed was unreasonable. He held:

> ... Nonetheless, the time taken may be regarded as acceptable. As we have indicated, that does not seem to us to be the position in the present case. If delays such as these were identified as *occurring regularly and inevitably* as a consequence of the limited budget and manpower available to the forensic laboratory, or to the police, or indeed to the procurator fiscal, and nothing was done to alter that situation, then in our opinion there would be what could be described as systemic underfunding. And a failure on the part of Government to take steps to remedy such a systemic under-funding, and the unacceptable delays which it was seen to be producing, would in our opinion properly be described as unreasonable, in the context of any fair system of justice. Whether in any particular case this produced a breach of an accused's rights under Article 6(1) would be another and broader question, since any specific delay would have to be looked at in the context of the overall lapse of time. But the specific delay itself would be unreasonable, as flowing from an unreasonable failure to remedy the system.[43] [Own emphasis]

What is interesting in the comparison between the Scottish system and the South African system is that both systems, under very different circumstances (bearing in mind the fact that South Africa is a developing country compared to Scotland), recognise systemic failures in both systems but fail to act by grant-

---

41 *Alan O'Brien and Michael Ryan v. HMA* – see Scottish Courts website (www.scotcourts.gov.uk/opinions) Appeals Nos. C49/01 and 50/01, decided 7 June 2001. **42** *Alan O'Brien and Michael Ryan v. HMA, supra* (n. 41). **43** *Alan O'Brien and Michael Ryan v. HM, supra* (n. 41) at para. 11.

ing remedies that will put pressure on government to remedy the systemic under-funding of each justice system.

3 SOUTH AFRICA

The South African courts have always recognised that an expeditious conclusion of criminal proceedings was essential for a fair trial. Even prior to commencement of the interim Constitution,[44] the power of the courts to disallow or grant adjournments was governed by section 168[45] of the Criminal Procedure Act (CPA)[46] – a provision that is still in force. This section gives courts the power to adjourn proceedings if they deemed it necessary or expedient, and by implication, therefore, also the power to refuse to adjourn.[47] The discretion to postpone proceedings 'if the court deems it necessary' had to be exercised judicially. In exercising such discretion, two basic principles had to be borne in mind: 1) an accused person, deemed to be innocent, was entitled, once indicted, to be tried with expedition; and 2) the interests of society required that guilty persons should be duly convicted. The principle that an accused person is entitled to a speedy trial was therefore well established in the common law. The focus under the common law was on the reasonableness of the adjournment as determined in view of the proceedings. In *S v. Gerritis*[48] Vieyra J said:

> [T]he decision is one within the discretion of the judicial officer presiding at the trial and that it must be a judicial discretion. I venture to suggest that in exercising such discretion two basic principles must be borne in mind. The one is that it is in the interests of society and accordingly of the State that guilty men should be duly convicted and not escape by reason of any oversight or mistake which can be remedied. The other, no less valid, is that an accused person, deemed to be innocent, is entitled, once indicted, to be tried with expedition.[49]

In *S v. Magoda*[50] the court held that the appropriate remedy in matters of undue delay would be to refuse an adjournment and went as far as to deem the State's case closed in circumstances where the State refused to close its case.

---

44 Constitution of the Republic of South Africa, Act 200 of 1993.   **45** This section provides as follows: 'A court before which criminal proceedings are pending, may from time to time during such proceedings, if the court deems it necessary or expedient, adjourn the proceedings to any date on the terms which to the court may seem proper and which are not inconsistent with any provisions of this Act.'   **46** Act 51 of 1977.   **47** Cf. *S v. Scholtz and Others* 1996 (2) SACR 623 (C) at 626g–627a.   **48** 1966 (1) SA 753 (W).   **49** *S v. Gerritis, supra* (n. 48) at 754D.   **50** 1984 (4) SA 462 (C).

3.1 The right to a trial within a reasonable time post the Constitution

Both the interim Constitution and the final Constitution, in different terms, provide for the right that every accused person has the right to begin with his trial within a reasonable time after having been charged.[51] What becomes apparent from an analysis of the South African case law is that the courts were very cautions in determining the boundaries of the right, due to the extreme remedy claimed in the cases, namely, stay of prosecution and hence gave little recognition to the right to make it meaningful as a fair trial right. Some of the problems relating to delay have been addressed, however, by an amendment of the right in the final Constitution.[52] The new section 35(3)(d) now provides as follows:

> Every accused person has a right to a fair trial, which includes the right … (d) to have their trial begin and conclude without unreasonable delay

In the light of human rights documents, and in particular the European Convention, it seems that this right protects two interests, namely that an accused should be subjected for the shortest time possible to the uncertainty of a charge hanging over his or her head and that lengthy proceedings may impact on an accused's ability to effectively defend him or herself.[53]

3.2 'Charged'

The interim Constitution provided for the time period to start when an accused is 'charged with an offence', but the cases relating to the interpretation of this concept will be discussed even though they are less relevant after the amendment by the final Constitution.

In *Du Preez v. Attorney-General of the Eastern Cape*[54] the Court held that 20 months was not an unreasonable delay and did not justify the drastic remedy of a perpetual stay of the prosecution. The Court had difficulty in interpreting the meaning that should be given to the word 'charged' as it is used in section 25(3)(a) of the interim Constitution to determine the time when an applicant was 'charged'.[55] Consideration was given to the case of *Barker v. Wingo*[56] where

---

51 See s. 25(3)(a) and (j) of the interim Constitution. The provision which approximates most closely to s. 25(3)(a) is s. 11(b) of the Canadian Charter of Rights and Freedoms which provides: 'Any person charged with an offence has the right to be tried within a reasonable time'. **52** Constitution of the Republic of South Africa, Act 108 of 1996. **53** See N. Steytler, *Constitutional criminal procedure*, 270. **54** 1997 (3) BCLR 329 (E). **55** *Du Preez v. Attorney-General of the Eastern Cape*, supra (n. 54) at 335. 'Charge' has also been defined in section 1 of the CPA as 'charge' indicating an indictment and a summons. The word 'charged' is also in s 18(2) of the Declaration of Rights contained in the Zimbabwe Constitution. This section provides: 'If any person is charged with a criminal offence, then, unless the charge is withdrawn, the case shall be afforded a fair hearing within a reasonable time by an independent and impartial court established by law.' **56** (1972) 407 US 514. In the case of *United States v. Marion* 404 USA 301 the court stated that, irrespective of any prejudice that an accused person may experience by the conduct of his defence, certain interests of the accused are relevant such as those that 'seriously interfere with the defendant's lib-

the Supreme Court of the United States approved of a four-factor test in deciding upon speedy trial claims: 1) the length of the delay before the institution of the prosecution; 2) the reason for the delay; 3) the assertion by the accused of his or her rights; and 4) the prejudice to the accused.

In Canada the burden of proof to establish that an unreasonable delay has occurred rests upon the accused.[57] In *R v. Morin*, where the general purpose of a speedy trial right was been stated, McLachlin J agreed with the view relating to onus but held that a trial judge should first determine whether a *prima facie* or threshold case for unreasonable delay has been made out. If the threshold case is made out, the court must proceed to a closer consideration of the right of the accused to a trial within a reasonable time. In England the courts have developed, as part of their power to prevent an abuse of process, the principle that a prosecution may be stayed on the ground that there has been an undue delay which has prevented or is likely to prevent the accused from enjoying a fair trial.[58]

In Zimbabwe, in the case of *In re Mlambo*,[59] it was held that the time period starts to run when there is an official notification by a competent authority of an allegation that the accused person has committed a crime. It was held that this may not necessarily coincide with the person's arrest. It was also held in *Mlambo*'s case that if a charge against the accused is temporarily withdrawn such action does not stop the 'clock from ticking' against the state.

In the case of *Moeketsi v. Attorney-General, Bophuthatswana and Another*[60] the following was stated:

> In South African law the time period would commence when an accused person is served either with an indictment, or summons. That means from the time when an accused person had knowledge of the charge.[61]

erty, whether he is free on bail or not, and that may disrupt his employment, drain his financial resources, curtail his associations, subject him to public obloquy, and create anxiety in him, his family and his friends' (at 320). Also *Artico v. Italy* (1981) 3 EHRR 1 at para. 35 where the court has stated as a general proposition, in considering Article 6(3)(c), that the existence of a violation of the right is conceivable, even in the absence of prejudice. **57** *R v. Morin* (1992) 71 CCC (3d) 114; *R v. Askov* (1990) 74 DLR(4th) 355 (SCC) 381 at 459. **58** *Connelly v. Director of Public Prosecutions* 1964 AC 1254 (HL). In *R v. Horseferry Road Magistrate's Court, ex parte Bennett* [1993] 3 WLR 19 (HL) Lord Lowrie said, at 116: 'I consider that a court has a discretion to stay any criminal proceedings on the ground that to try those proceedings will amount to an abuse of its own process either (1) because it will be impossible (usually by reason of delay) to give the accused a fair trial or (2) because it offends the court's sense of justice and propriety to be asked to try the accused in the circumstances of a particular case. I agree that *prima facie* it is the duty of a court to try a person who is charged before it with an offence which the court has power to try and therefore that the jurisdiction to stay must be exercised carefully and sparingly and only for very compelling reasons. The discretion to stay is not a disciplinary jurisdiction and ought not to be exercised in order to express the court's disapproval of official conduct. Accordingly if the prosecuting authorities have been guilty of culpable delay but the prospect of a fair trial has not been prejudiced, the court ought not to stay the proceedings merely "pour encourager les autres".' **59** 1992 (2) SACR 245 (ZS). **60** 1996 (1) SACR 675 (B). **61** *Moeketsi v. Attorney-General,*

In examining the reasons for any delay, most courts had held that a distinction had to be made between four categories: 1) delays caused by the conduct of the State; 2) special circumstances relating to the case, such as complexity; 3) systemic delays; and 4) delays occasioned by the accused.

In *Berg v. Prokureur-Generaal, Gauteng*[62] the court held that a permanent stay of proceedings could be granted in appropriate cases, but should be reserved only for exceptional cases as it was an extreme remedy. In *Bate v. Regional Magistrate, Randburg and Another*[63] it was held that the date when the accused is 'charged' does not necessarily coincide with the commencement of the trial or the date when he is required to plead. The period commences with the start of the impairment of the accused's interests in his or her liberty and security of the person in the broad sense. The court quoted, with approval, from the case of *Foti v. Italy*:[64]

> Whilst 'charge', for the purposes of article 6(1), may in general be defined as 'the official notification given to an individual by the competent authority of an allegation that he has committed a criminal offence', it may in some instance take the form of other measures which carry the implication of such an allegation and which likewise substantially affect the situation of the suspect.[65]

In *Mlambo*'s case Gubbay CJ stresses the desirability of flexibility. His judgment is instructive:

> The time frame to be considered starts to run from the moment a person is charged. The key word is 'charged'. What does it mean in the context of section 18(2)? Does the provision envisage only the situation where the accused is called upon in court to plead to a formal charge? To my mind, such a restrictive construction has the effect of rendering the protection almost nugatory. It squares more with an arraignment. And, of course, it would be susceptible to untold abuse, permitting the State to delay inordinately before bringing a person before the trial court, happy in the knowledge that by so doing there has been no violation of a constitutional right.[66]

The judgment supports the proposition that this state of affairs begins with 'the official notification given to an individual by the (appropriate) competent authority of an allegation that he has committed a criminal offence', and that it may in some instances take the form of other measures which carry the impli-

---

Bophuthatswana and Another, supra (n. 60) at 963F. **62** 1995 (2) SACR 623 (T). **63** 1996 (7) BCLR 974 (W). **64** (1983) 5 EHRR 313. **65** *Foti v. Italy, supra* (n. 64) at 326. **66** *In re Mlambo, supra* (n. 59) at 249i–250g.

cation of such an allegation and which likewise substantially affect the situation of the suspect.

3.3 Reasonableness of the delay

In *Moeketsi v. Attorney-General, Bophuthatswana, and Another*[67] the court held that the right to trial within a reasonable time was 'indissolubly associated with the canon of a fair trial' and that an inordinately long and unexplained delay negated the concept. In assessing the reasonableness of a delay a court should consider *inter alia* the following factors: 1) the length of the delay; 2) reasons for the delay, including i) delay attributable to the State, ii) the complexity of the case, iii) institutional or systemic delay, iv) delay attributable to the accused; 3) waiver of time periods by the accused; and 4) prejudice to the accused.[68]

The analysis of the reasonableness test was based largely on Canadian authority.[69] Since *Moeketsi*, the courts have been distracted by the controversy surrounding permanent stays of prosecution and detailed inquiry into the test of reasonableness has been lacking. In *Sanderson v. Attorney-General, Eastern Cape*[70] the Constitutional Court held that the analysis of the United States Supreme Court in *Barker v. Wingo*[71] was decisive in determining reasonableness. The test outlined above was modified in line with the American approach at the third stage of the analysis to the assertion of the speedy trial right by the accused, and not simply waiver.[72]

In *Sanderson*, the Constitutional Court, in its only decision on this point, held that it was unnecessary to define 'charged'. The term was not repeated in the final Constitution, and derived much of its meaning from the context in which it was used. It was clear that the phrase encompassed an accused appearing in the dock to be formally remanded, which was the point in the case at issue.[73]

The starting point for the reasonableness enquiry is therefore still an unsettled issue. *Sanderson* indicated a preference by the Constitutional Court for a case-by-case approach without giving proper guidance to lower courts on issues of delay. In *Sanderson*, the Constitutional Court held that the amount of elapsed time was central to the reasonableness enquiry, and time had a pervasive significance that impacted upon all of the factors. The length of the delay was not to be considered as a threshold requirement, nor subsequently in isolation. The amount of time that had elapsed not only conditioned the relevant considerations, such as prejudice, but was itself conditioned by them.[74] It is submitted that it is appropriate to balance the length of the delay with all the other factors, par-

---

67 *Moeketsi v. Attorney-General, Bophuthatswana, and Another, supra* (n. 60). **68** Ibid. at 693 *et seq.* **69** More specifically *R v. Askov, supra* (n. 57). **70** 1998 (1) SACR 227 (CC) at para. 25. **71** 407 US 514 (1972) at 530–2. **72** Cf. *Du Preez v. Attorney-General, Eastern Cape* 1997 (2) SACR 375 (ECD) at 379d. **73** *Sanderson v. Attorney-General, Eastern Cape, supra* (n. 70) at para. 19. **74** Ibid. at paras 28–9.

ticularly prejudice, rather than to establish this factor as a barrier to relief when
the level of the threshold would be arbitrary. The courts are free to examine
delay at different stages of the case as well as the overall length of time. In *Wild*,
the Court considered various distinct phases to the proceedings and analysed
them individually, in the context of the overall delay in the proceedings.[75]

In *Sanderson* the Constitutional Court accepted that the State always requires
a certain amount of time to prepare a case for trial and this would vary according to the gravity, complexity and nature of the charges.[76] This category is akin
to the 'inherent time requirements' factor identified by the Supreme Court of
Canada. The Court in *Sanderson* refused to lay down semi-formal time constraints on the prosecution, and found that it was for the legislature to lay down
'normal delays' for specific kinds of cases. In calculating the inherent time
required by the case, there had to be some proportionality between the sentence available and the prejudice being suffered by the accused. Thus, a five-
month remand in custody pending trial, on an offence for which the maximum sentence was six months, would clearly point to unreasonableness.[77]
Exceptional circumstances that delayed the proceedings, such as civil unrest,
would also be balanced under this factor.[78]

In *Sanderson* the Constitutional Court held that, if the accused was the primary agent of delay, he or she should not be able to rely upon that period in
vindication of his or her speedy trial right. However, there was no need for
the accused to assert his or her right or actively compel the State to accelerate
its preparation of the case.[79] This position is not reflected in relation to interlocutory proceedings. In *Wild and Another v. Hoffert No and Others*,[80] the two
accused had challenged the proceedings in their case on a number of constitutional issues, prior to the trial being heard. The proceedings were for example
delayed by the dilatory response of the State. The Court, however, excused
the delay to a certain extent on the basis that the issues were new and important.[81] It is not clear that this was merited, however, since the State at no time
sought to explain its failure to respond. The Constitutional Court laid great
emphasis on the fact that the accused had chosen to take the proceedings and
had not tried to speed them up. The Court held that whilst the interlocutory
proceedings were underway the trial could not proceed.[82]

3.4 Delays attributable to State conduct

In *Wild* the Constitutional Court examined a four-month delay between the
case being struck off the role and the possibility of re-prosecuting the case. The

---

75 Ibid. at paras 22–5. Cf. *Moeketsi, supra* (n. 60) at 683h *et seq.*   **76** *Sanderson v. Attorney-General,
Eastern Cape, supra* (n. 70) at para. 34; *Mlambo, supra* (n. 59) at 249.   **77** Ibid. at paras. 30 and 34.
78 *Moeketsi, supra* (n. 60) at 699j.   **79** *Sanderson v. Attorney-General, Eastern Cape, supra* (n. 70) at
para. 33.   **80** 1998 (2) SACR 1 (CC).   **81** *Wild and Another v. Hoffert No and Others, supra* (n. 80)
at paras. 18–19.   **82** Ibid. at paras 23–4.

Attorney-General had offered no explanation for the delay. The court noted that, whilst the ultimate enquiry was whether the time which had elapsed was reasonable, it was relevant that one or other party was to blame in whole or in part for the delay.[83]

> In a case such as this where there is a period of ostensibly culpable inactivity on the part of the prosecution, an inference of unreasonableness can more readily be drawn if no explanation is proffered.[84]

The case law, however, indicates that the actions of the State do not weigh heavily in the balance with the court. In *Coetzee*, counsel for the defence argued that the Attorney-General should have re-appraised the case and commenced further investigations into the murder during 1993 when two of the accused had returned to South Africa and new evidence was emerging. The court held that whilst that might, with hindsight, have been an appropriate approach, there was no indication that an investigation would have turned up new evidence. This is in marked contrast to the Scottish High Court decision of *Little*,[85] where the court emphasised routine reviews by the Crown of the evidential position to avoid undue delay. The speedy trial guarantee would be far more efficacious if the State had to conduct regular reviews of the available evidence in historic serious cases to ensure that proceedings were held within a reasonable time of a sufficiency of evidence emerging.

Systemic or institutional delay is defined in South Africa as resource limitations that hamper the effectiveness of the police investigation or the prosecution of a case, and delay caused by court congestion.[86] The Constitutional Court in *Sanderson* recognised that the changes in modern South Africa had an historic legacy and imposed severe stress on the criminal justice system.[87] Whilst systemic problems could justify delay, it would be legitimate for an accused to adduce evidence to show that the average institutional delay for a particular jurisdiction had been exceeded. In the absence of such evidence, the court noted it might be hard to determine how much systemic delay to tolerate. Whilst no guidelines of acceptable delay have been issued and no cases decided on this basis, it is concerning that the court seems to limit itself to consideration of delay in the jurisdiction at issue. Whilst *Askov*[88] and *Morin* created dif-

---

83 *Wild and Another v. Hoffert No and Others, supra* (n. 80) at para 8.   **84** Ibid. at para 25. Cf. *Moeketsi, supra* (n. 61) at 695e and 700a; and *Mlambo, supra* (n. 59) at 254.   **85** *Little v. HMA, supra* (n. 14). **86** *Sanderson v. Attorney-General, Eastern Cape, supra* (n. 70) at para. 35. Cf. The narrower definition in *R v. Morin, supra* (n. 57).   **87** *Sanderson v. Attorney-General, Eastern Cape, supra* (n. 70) at para. 26.   **88** In the Canadian case of *R v. Askov, supra* (n. 57) at 449 Cory J formulated the factors which should be taken into account in considering whether the length of a delay of a trial has been unreasonable as follows at:

    (i) The length of the delay.
    (ii) The explanation for the delay which may take different forms, namely:

ficulties in Canada, the principle of seeking national standards by comparing different provincial jurisdictions is sound and ought to be followed.

3.5 Role of the new section 342A[89] of the CPA

The South African legislature has responded to the problem of delay by inserting a new section into the CPA, section 342A.[90] Section 342A (1) of the CPA provides as follows:

> A court before which criminal proceedings are pending shall investigate any delay in the completion of proceedings which appears to the court to be unreasonable and which could cause substantial prejudice to the prosecution, the accused or his or her legal adviser, the State or a witness.

In considering whether a delay is unreasonable, the court must have regard to all the relevant factors,[91] including the blame for the delay; actual or potential legal prejudice to the defence and the State; and the adverse effect on the public or victims should proceedings be stayed. If there is unreasonable delay, the court can order any remedy that will eliminate it.[92] This includes striking the case off the court roll. Such a step may be coupled with a prohibition of re-institution of the prosecution without the written authority of the Attorney-General. The matter may also be referred to the appropriate authority for investigation and disciplinary action. In addition, the court may order the party at fault to pay the wasted costs resulting from the delay to the other party.[93] As the State does not have a right to speedy proceedings, it is unclear on what basis an accused should have to pay such damages. In any event, the subsections dealing with the award of damages has not yet been brought into operation.[94]

In *S v. Motsasi*[95] the court ordered an investigation under section 342A of the CPA as the trial was being delayed by the fact that one of the accused was not brought to court on time from custody. The investigation revealed a sorry state of affairs in the justice system. Contributing to the delay were: the overpopulation in the prison; a lack of prison staff; the non-availability of the prosecutor due to other court commitments; and disorganisation in the transfer of warrants by court clerks. The court ordered urgent discussions on reme-

---

     (a) delays attributable to the prosecution;
     (b) systemic or institutional delays;
     (c) delays attributable to the accused;
   (iii) Waiver.
   (iv) Prejudice to the accused.

89 Introduced by the Criminal Procedure Amendment Act 86 of 1996 from 1 September 1997. **90** Section 342A of the CPA was inserted by s. 13 of Act 86 of 1996. **91** See s. 342A(2). **92** See s. 342A(3). **93** See s. 342A(3)(e). **94** Subsections 342A(3)(e) and 342A(5) are the ones not in force. **95** 1998 (2) SACR 35 (W).

dying the inadequacies and asked the Justice Department to explain why incompetent people had been appointed to office.[96]

It is submitted that this section is primarily aimed at curbing unreasonable delays in criminal trials. In *Wild*, the Constitutional Court described s 342A as;

> ... a major step in remedying the scourge of delays in criminal courts with practical tools that can be used in furthering the speedy trial objectives of section 25(3)(c).[97]

The provision is a step in the right direction. It is extensive in its ambit but it is no replacement of the constitutional right of a speedy trial, as it is limited to pending proceedings and excludes the conduct of the court and any appeal proceedings.

In a review matter, the High Court of Natal[98] held, per Hugo J, that in most cases with regard to reasons for a delay in criminal trials, the question of prejudice to an accused should take precedence in deciding upon the issue. The Court, unlike the Scottish court in *Gibson* where the delay by the Prosecution was excused despite the absence of a clear or justifiable explanation, held that the prosecution service should do more than merely 'explain' the reasons for delay. What would be required, it seems, is to place some evidence before the Court justifying the inordinate delay. In the words of Hugo J:

> I reiterate that had the prosecutor wished to put evidence before the Court to explain the delay and to argue that an inference of prejudice that arises from the delay in itself is not justified then she should at least have applied to do so. A refusal by the Magistrate to hear such evidence might have been a cause for appeal or review.[99]

---

96 See *S v. Maredi* 2000 (1) SACR 611 (T) depicting an equally sorry state of affairs. Mynhardt J described it at 613E–H as follows: 'This state of affairs is indeed shocking. Section 35(3)(d) of the Constitution of the Republic of South Africa Act 108 of 1996, provides that every accused person has a right to a fair trial, which includes the right to have their trial "begin and conclude without unreasonable delay". It seems to me, *prima facie*, that that right of the accused was ignored blatantly by not only the prosecutors who were involved in this matter, but also by the magistrates who presided over the court from time to time and who granted postponements of the case without enquiring whether or not the requests were reasonable and justified. The net result of the conduct of the prosecutors and the magistrates seems to be that a mockery was made of the accused's constitutional rights. That is to be deprecated. It seems to me, *prima facie*, that the conduct of the prosecutors involved in this matter was deplorable.' **97** *Wild and Another v. Hoffert No and Others*, supra (n. 80) at para 32. **98** See *The Director of Public Prosecutions, Kwazulu-Natal v. The Regional Magistrate, Durban and Dale Waters Allan*, Unreported Decision of the Natal High Court, Case Number AR/2001, dated April 2001. **99** *The Director of Public Prosecutions, Kwazulu-Natal v. The Regional Magistrate, Durban and Dale Waters Allan*, supra (n. 98) at 11.

4 CONCLUSION

In both systems there are elements of a serious commitment to a trial without unreasonable delay. However, this commitment is ambiguous. The ambiguity lies in the failure of the courts to give true meaning and hence true recognition to such commitment. As there are no discernible patterns in periods that are regarded as causing unreasonable delays, it is indeed unlikely that a catalogue of set periods will solve the issue. From some of the cases, however, it is apparent that the longer the delay suffered, the more likely it is that there will be prejudice suffered by an accused. It follows that the longer the delay in a case in bringing it to trial, the more difficult it should be for a court to condone the party causing such delay. In both systems, courts under different circumstances, were keen to excuse systemic delays or institutional delays caused by either a lack of resources available to the State, or the availability of sufficient personnel and courts. It is submitted that such delays should not constitute a justifiable excuse *per se*, rather the reasons for such systemic flaws should be analysed and reviewed by the court. This again involves a careful and sensitive balancing of all the facts, including the explanations afforded by the prosecution. It is ultimately the State's responsibility to bring an accused to trial and courts should, when deciding upon issues of undue delay, keep this uppermost in their mind. Time is too precious to be compromised in an arbitrary way.

3 THE EUROPEAN DIMENSION

Federalism and the European judiciary

NIAL FENNELLY

The word 'federalism' has to be employed with care in European debate. At the insistence of John Major, the British Prime Minister, the word 'federal' was deleted from the draft Treaty on European Union in 1991, even though, to the continentals, this was rightly seen as a purely semantic change. The objective of 'an ever closer union' remained. The Romans regulated their relations with the more distant parts of the empire by agreements or foedera. Federation is no more than an arrangement for distribution of powers between States by treaty.

The founding six Member States of the then European Economic Community founded their relationship on the Treaty of Rome of 1957. The ensuing decades have seen that Community enlarged geographically through Treaties of Accession: UK, Denmark and Ireland in 1973; Greece in 1981; Spain and Portugal in 1986; Austria, Sweden and Finland in 1995. The number of Member States is expected to grow to 25 to 30 in the next ten years or so. Over the same period, the powers of the Community have been expanded by successive treaties: the Single European Act in 1986; the Treaty on European Union in 1991; the Amsterdam Treaty in 1997.

Whether this is called a federation or not, there is a need to determine which powers are exclusive to the Community and which to the Member States. I intend to discuss the role played by the Court of Justice of the European Communities in allocating powers between the Community and the Member States. I propose, therefore, to explain and discuss briefly the following:

the nature and role of the Court of Justice;

some of the important principles established in its case law;

the particular importance of the internal market for issues of competence; the comparison with the experience of the United States of America; an evaluation of the current stance of the Court.

THE COURT OF JUSTICE

The European Court, the Court of Justice of the European Communities, to give it its full title, is one of the institutions established by the Treaties. The others are the Council of Ministers of the Member States; the Commission; the European Parliament and the Court of Auditors. It is comprised of 15 judges, one from each Member State, and eight Advocates General. Its seat is in

Luxembourg, the smallest Member State. The Treaty assigns to the Court the task of ensuring that in the 'interpretation and application of the treaties the law is observed.' In fulfilling this function the Court has naturally had to ascertain what the eponymous 'law' is. It has not restricted its inquiries to this effect to the words of the treaties and has, consequently, not been without its critics.

The Court chose from its earliest days a rule of interpretation generally applicable to international agreements. It is necessary according to this so-called teleological principle to consider the spirit, the general scheme and the wording of the provisions under consideration. It also speaks of 'the system and objectives of the Treaty',[1] or: 'not only its wording but also the context in which it occurs and the objects of the rules of which it is a part'.[2] In 1963, it decided the seminal case of *Van Gend en Loos*.[3] It held that:

> [T]he Community constitutes a new legal order of international law for the benefit of which the States have limited their sovereign rights, albeit within limited fields, and the subjects of which comprise not only Member States but also their nationals. Independently of the legislation of Member States Community law therefore not only imposes obligations on individuals but is also intended to confer upon them rights which become part of their legal heritage.

In this and subsequent cases, the Court developed propositions which have become the twin foundation stones of Community law. These are and were:

that the treaties may have direct effect in the legal systems of the Member States, thus conferring rights on individuals which the national courts must protect;

that Community law takes precedence over any conflicting provision of national law.

The Court based these principles very largely on one of the central legal mechanisms laid down in the Treaty. This is Article 234, which provides that any court at any level of the judicial hierarchy in any of the Member States may refer to the Court of Justice for preliminary ruling any question of interpretation of the treaties or of secondary Community legislation which is necessary for the determination of cases before them. Courts of final appeal are under a formal obligation to refer such questions whenever they arise. This mechanism has established a direct relationship between the Court of Justice and the courts of the Member States, effectively by-passing the governments of the Member States. Thus, a substantial and ever-expanding body of independent Community law has come into being. At the simplest level, it enables an individual to claim

---

1 Case 6/72 *Continental Can* [1973] ECR 215, para. 22 of the judgment. **2** Case 292/82 *Merck v. Hauptzollamt Hamburg-Jonas* [1983] ECR 1–3781, para. 12. **3** Case 26/62 [1963] ECR I.

rights against their own governments in their own courts and to call in aid the powerful support of the Court of Justice. Claimants alleging unlawful discrimination between men and women in employment and social security have resorted to this procedural mechanism successfully with almost monotonous regularity to the ill-concealed frustration and, it has to be said, cost of Member State governments. In summary, it is universally accepted that the preliminary ruling procedure is the foundation-stone of Community law.

The Court has enlarged on these first principles and has gone on to hold that:

the Community is one 'based on the rule of law' and that the Treaty is its 'basic constitutional charter;'[4]

the treaties must be interpreted so as to provide 'a complete system of legal remedies and procedures';[5]

Community law protects the fundamental human rights[6] of those coming within its scope.

Writing extra-judicially, the late Judge Fernand Schockweiler explained how 'the Court had acted as an engine for the building of the autonomous Community legal order'.[7] He thought that its most decisive contribution was its choice from the very beginning of the teleological method of interpretation. According to Judge Schockweiler: 'by favouring this method ... [t]he Court gave preference to the interpretation best fitted to promote the achievement of the objectives pursued by the Treaty'. Furthermore, it 'allowed a development beyond the literal meaning of the texts in a dynamic direction in the light of the purposes pursued by the [EC] Treaty in its entirety and in its context'.[8]

Not very surprisingly, there have been some who have seen the Court, not as a beneficent builder of a desirable European project, but rather as: 'a court with a mission; ... not an orthodox court'; as 'a potentially dangerous court – the danger being that inherent in uncontrolled judicial power'.[9] Professor T.C. Hartley has not minced his words either, stating, in 1986, that the Court 'has not hesitated to remodel the law even when this has entailed adopting a solu-

---

4 Case 294/83: *Partie Ecologiste 'Les Verts' v. European Parliament* [1986] ECR 1339. 5 Ibid. 6 Case 29/69 *Stauder v. Ulm* [1969] ECR 419; Case 11/70 *Internationale Handelsgesellschaft v. Einfuhr-und Vorratstelle Getreide* [1970] ECR 1125; Case 44/79 *Hauer v. Land Rheinland-Pfalz* [1979] ECR 3727. 7 See Judge Fernand Schockweiler, late judge at the Court of Justice, 'La Cour de justice des Communautes europeennes depasse-t-elle les limites de ses attributions?', 18 *Journal des Tribunaux, Droit Europeen* 73 Brussels 20 April 1995. 8 Fernand Schockweiler (Author's free translation of the text), loc. cit. 9 *The European Court of Justice: a case study in judicial activism* by Sir Patrick Neill QC, Warden of All Souls College, Oxford, presented as written evidence to the House of Lords Select Committee on the European Communities (HL Paper 88), Session 1994–95 18th Report 1996 Intergovernmental Conference, pp. 218–45.

tion different from that envisaged in the Treaties'[10] and, ten years later, of pursuing 'a settled and consistent policy of promoting European federalism, a policy which includes the extension of the powers of the Court itself'.[11] I will leave aside these entertaining contributions for later reflection.

THE INTERNAL MARKET

The internal market, originally called the common market, remains the central original project of the European Community, now the European Union. According to the Treaty (Article 14(2): 'The internal market shall comprise an area without internal frontiers in which the free movement of goods, persons, services and capital is ensured in accordance with the provisions of this Treaty.' It intersects in a particularly sensitive and acute way with the allocation of powers. It is first appropriate to recall the governing principle that the Community is one of attributed powers. Article 5 of the Treaty provides: 'The Community shall act within the limits of the powers conferred upon it by this Treaty and of the objectives assigned to it therein.' This principle draws into focus the especially important responsibility of the Court when it is asked to rule on the competence of the Community to legislate in relation to a particular subject-matter, where Community competence is disputed. That is quintessentially a constitutional function. It is analogous to that performed by the Supreme Court of the United States in its supervision of Congressional legislative action.

The internal market objective is to ensure that the commerce in goods and services in the Community market is unrestricted and undistorted. Obstacles to trade can arise not merely from border controls in the form of tariff or quota barriers, but from the internal product rules of the individual Member States. Divergent content, packaging, labelling or other product rules make it more difficult for products to circulate freely between the Member States and so they hinder the establishment of the internal market. It is for this reason that the Treaty authorises the Community to legislate so as to harmonise and approximate national laws or regulations by substituting uniform Community rules for diverse national ones and so permit products which comply to circulate freely throughout the Community.

When the Community is considering whether to enact harmonising legislation in pursuance of the internal market it is confronting a decision with an essentially federalist character. On the one hand, Community Competence exists only in order to pursue the 'object [of] the establishment and function-

---

10 Hartley, 'Federalism, courts and legal systems; the emerging constitution of the European Community', (1986) 34 *American Journal of Comparative Law* 229 at 247. 11 Hartley, 'The European Court, judicial objectivity and the Constitution of the European Union' (1996) LQR, p. 95.

ing of the internal market.'[12] Normally, the Community has no substantive competence in the subject-matter being regulated. On the other, the national rules which it is proposed to harmonise usually pursue such diverse national policy objectives as:

animal welfare: Council directive 91/629/EEC: laying down minimum standards for the protection of calves;

conservation of wild birds: Council Directive 70/409;

control of marketing of dangerous substances: Council Directive 67/548/EEC: on the approximation of laws relating to the classification, packaging and labelling of dangerous substances, considered in *Caldana*.[13]

The Community, in this situation, simultaneously pursues two objectives. Its competence and, hence, its power to act derive solely from the imperative of the internal market. However, once the pre-condition for internal-market action is satisfied and it commences to formulate the new Community rules, it necessarily substitutes itself for the Member States, both those which have and those which have not had rules affecting the subject-matter. In some respects, the Treaty mandates the adoption of a high level of protection. In that way, the subject-matter of the rules and not merely their prior trade-restricting features become, as a consequence of Community action, a matter of Community competence. Furthermore, there is no theoretical limit to Community internal-market competence. The Community's harmonising power is horizontal. It is capable, in principle, of applying to every subject of national legislation provided that it affects the functioning of the internal market.

This duality of objective is, however, an essentially legal analysis. The harmonising competence enables the Community to step into the shoes of, and to substitute itself for, the Member States in enacting rules affecting a wide and diverse range of substantive areas of policy. Member States may have different ideas about consumer protection, the environment, the sale of alcohol, the control of gambling and, to give the very concrete example of a recent important case, the advertising of tobacco products. It is natural, however, for the political actors at Community level to be less concerned with fine points of principle concerning Community or Member State competence than with their own policy views. The European Parliament has now become the joint legislator with the Council in all matters affecting the internal market. Lobby groups are much more likely to campaign vigorously for remedy of perceived social wrongs and in favour of health or environmental objectives. Such groups are not concerned with pursuit of an internal market objective, which is the legal basis for Community action, but see the Community and the European

12 Art. 95EC.   **13** Case 187/84 *Caldana* [1985] ECR 3013.

Parliament, in particular, as the most effective plane on which to promote their objectives at a European level.

At the same time, the possibility for such measures to be adopted by qualified majority vote at the Council means that Member States no longer have a veto over harmonising legislation as they did before the Single European Act. Consequently, dissenting Member States are more likely to be in a position, if they so wish, to apply to the Court for annulment of any such legislation. This has occurred, for example, where the United Kingdom challenged (unsuccessfully) the Working Time Directive, and when the Federal Republic of Germany challenged (successfully) the tobacco advertising ban.

The Court, thus, has the task both of overseeing and controlling the institutional balance between the Community institutions in the performance of their respective roles in the legislative process and also of policing the boundary between Community and Member State competence.

THE UNITED STATES: AN INSTRUCTIVE COMPARISON

It would be ridiculous to suggest that the European Union can be compared as a federal polity with the United States. There is, however, a real and substantial analogy between the so-called 'dormant' Commerce Clause in the United States Constitution and the Treaty provisions enabling the European Community to enact harmonising rules in furtherance of the internal market. Article I section 8, cl. 3 of the Constitution says, in material part: 'The Congress shall have power ... to regulate Commerce ... among the several States.' The United States over some two centuries of experience with its Constitution has seen its Supreme Court adopt widely divergent positions regarding the exercise of federal power by the Congress. However, it is not disputed that 'an expansive interpretation of the Commerce Clause'[14] has prevailed since the New Deal era under President Franklin D. Roosevelt. All this is in spite of the fact that the United States, like the European Union, follows a principle that the federal government enjoys only those enumerated powers which are attributed to it by the Constitution. Chief Justice Marshall, often seen as a great proponent of the power of the Union, said that the federal government could 'exercise only the powers granted to it.'[15]

The Congress has long since ceased to limit its use of the Commerce Clause to the direct regulation of trade, frequently adopting laws in respect of production and in particular labour regulation. The high water mark is usually considered to be the case of *Wickard v. Filburn*,[16] where the Supreme Court upheld a federal law which penalised a farmer for growing some wheat for home and family consumption on the basis that such activity, combined with others, could have a 'substantial effect on interstate commerce.'

14 See footnote 18, post.   **15** 17 U.S. 316,405 (1819).   **16** 317 U.S. 111 (1942).

The Supreme Court has, in more recent years preferred to emphasis the limits on the expansive use of the Commerce Clause. In 1995, it struck down a federal law prohibiting the use of firearms near schools.[17] In 2000, it struck down a federal statute which enacted a civil remedy for the victims of gender-related crimes of violence. The Court, through Chief Justice Rehnquist, emphasised in its judgment in *United States v. Morrison*,[18] its concern that 'Congress might use the Commerce Clause to obliterate the Constitution's distinction between national and local authority'. The Chief Justice emphasised the limits even to the 'modern expansionist interpretation of the Commerce Clause.' He recalled that, even at its high water-mark in the Roosevelt era, the Court had warned that the scope of the interstate commerce power 'must be considered in the light of our dual system of government and may not be extended so as to embrace effects upon interstate commerce so indirect and remote that to embrace them, in view of our complex society, would effectually obliterate the distinction between what is national and what is local and create a completely centralized government.'[19]

These recent signs of some retrenchment do not alter the long-established jurisprudence, which has caused such concern to proponents of the original understanding of the Constitution, and which effectively permits the Congress to legislate on the basis of a showing of some 'substantial effect' on interstate commerce. That means that the process of integration in the United States has proceeded much further than in the European Union.

THE VIEW FROM EUROPE: THE TOBACCO CASE

On 5 October 2000, the Court of Justice gave its judgment in two cases, which I will call together the Tobacco judgment.[20] The Court, at the instance of the Federal Republic of Germany in a direct action and certain tobacco manufacturers through an action referred from a London court, annulled the tobacco advertising Directive of 1998. That Directive would, if it had entered into force, have obliged Member States over time to prohibit, subject to narrowly drawn exceptions, all advertising of tobacco products in their territories. On July 6, 1998, the European Parliament and the Council had invoked their powers as Community legislator to enact Directive 98/43/EC on the approximation of the laws, regulations and administrative provisions of the Member States relating to the advertising and sponsorship of tobacco.

There was compelling evidence that the principal motivation of the proponents of the Directive had been the elimination of smoking to improve health

---

17 *U.S. v. Lopez* 514 U.S. 549 (1995). **18** 529 U.S. Judgment, 15 May 2000. **19** *NLRB v. Jones & Laughlin Steel Corp.*, 301 US. 1 (1937). **20** The cases are C–376/98 *Federal Republic of Germany v. European Parliament and Council of the European Union* and Case C–74/99 *The Queen v. Secretary of State for Health and others, ex parte Imperial Tobacco*, [2000] 3 Common Market L. Rpts. 1175.

and to reduce, in particular, the numbers of deaths from cancer. The stated purpose of the measure and its only possible legal basis was, however, the furtherance of the internal market and the removal of obstacles to trade in goods and services concerning the advertising of tobacco products. This was a position which was difficult to maintain since the entire burthen of the Directive was the almost total prohibition on the activity, the advertising of tobacco products, which was supposedly the object of its trade liberating provisions. It was reasonably clear as a matter of fact that it was health and not internal-market concerns that motivated the legislators. However, motivation was rightly considered to be irrelevant. The focus was on whether there was an objective internal market justification. The Community institutions, in the light of the more or less general prohibition enacted by the Directive, were forced to argue, and did so strenuously, that the Community power to harmonise permitted it generally to regulate trade in goods and services.

The Court described the relevant Treaty article, Article 95(4), as being 'intended to improve the conditions for the establishment and functioning of the internal market.' It then proceeded to reject the Council's claim to a general regulatory competence:

> To construe that Article as meaning that it vests in the Community legislature a general power to regulate the internal market would not only be contrary to the express wording of the provisions cited above but would also be incompatible with the principle embodied in [Article 5] that the powers of the Community are limited to those specifically conferred on it.[21]

The Court went on to assert a judicial position starkly at odds with the deferential approach to legislative choice which had been advocated by the Community institutions, enunciating the need for a measure claiming an internal market basis 'genuinely' to promote that object as defined in the preceding paragraph. It then indicated a willingness to investigate this issue substantively, stating:

> If a mere finding of disparities between national rules and of the abstract risk of obstacles to the exercise of fundamental freedoms or of distortions of competition liable to result therefrom were sufficient to justify the choice of Article 100a as a legal basis, judicial review of compliance with the proper legal basis might be rendered nugatory. The Court would then be prevented from discharging the function entrusted to it by … the Treaty of ensuring that the law is observed in the interpretation and application of the Treaty.[22]

21 Ibid., at 1265–1266. 22 Ibid., at 1266.

The Court expanded on its view of the judicial function emphasising the need for the Court to 'verify whether the measure whose validity is at issue in fact pursues the objectives stated by the Community legislature' and stating that 'the emergence of [alleged] obstacles [to trade] must be likely and the measure in question must be designed to prevent them.'[23]

SUBSIDIARITY

I should not end without a very brief reference to the principle of subsidiarity. This much lauded principle was inserted into the Treaty by the Treaty on European Union, but has disappointed the hopes of its political progenitors. One might have thought that this much proclaimed innovation of the Treaty on European Union could perform a useful function in guiding decisions as to whether action should be taken at Community or Member State level precisely in the context of internal market action and precisely by reason of the complex and sensitive inter-reaction between the two planes of competence which I have discussed. However, the operative range of the principle is drastically limited by the Treaty rule that it applies in 'areas which do not fall within [the] exclusive competence' of the Community. The general view is that Article 95 harmonising action in pursuit of the internal market is inherently an 'exclusive competence' of the Community. It is hard to resist the conclusion that subsidiarity is a dead letter.

CONCLUSION

The judgment of the Court of Justice in the tobacco cases must be regarded as a positive development in Community law. There have been earlier cases where the Court has annulled Community acts, but this was the first time that it declared a Community measure to have been adopted without any legal basis. The Court has rightly held that, when called upon, it should itself positively verify whether the impugned measure genuinely pursues a claimed internal objective. Admittedly, there is a danger of the Court becoming involved in passing judgment on the assessment by the Community legislature of complex factual and economic data, which it traditionally and carefully refrains from doing. However, it must at a minimum be allowed to pass judgment on whether a genuine basis for legislation exists. To do otherwise would risk allowing the Community to usurp the powers of the Member States and to expand its own powers beyond those provided by the Treaty. At the very least, the Court has answered those critics who believed that the Court would in every case uphold Community action in preference to the prerogatives of the Member States.

23 Ibid.

It is, to the present writer, to read these important passages in the judgment of the Court of Justice as an acceptance of the view expressed by the
Advocate General in his Opinion that it is the 'task of the Court, as the repos-
itory of the trust and confidence of the Community institutions, the Member
States and the citizens of the Union, to perform [the] difficult function of
upholding the constitutional division of powers between the Community and
the Member States on the basis of objective criteria.'[24] It demonstrates, in other
words, that the Court can act as the federal Constitutional Court of the
European Union and not merely as a promoter of European integration.

---

24 Ibid., at 1184.

Incorporation of the European Convention on Human Rights into Irish domestic law

WILLIAM BINCHY

Ireland is at present in the middle of an important debate, centring on the role of the judiciary in the development of a society's legal culture. The debate has been prompted by a Bill,[1] now before the Irish Parliament, giving some effect to the European Convention on Human Rights in Irish domestic law.

Ireland was one of the first states to ratify the Convention[2] and to accept the right of individual petition. The first judgment handed down by the European Convention of Human Rights related to Ireland.[3] Yet Ireland is one of the last states to engage in the process of domestic incorporation.

Several reasons explain this delay. The first, and most obvious, is that the Irish Constitution already contains effective protection for the rights specified and protected under the European Convention. Explicit recognition is afforded by the Constitution to the right to life, freedom of assembly, association, speech and religion, the ownership of property, the family, equality and personal liberty, for example, and a strong jurisprudence on access to the courts, due process and privacy has been developed by the courts. These rights are not coextensive with those protected in the Convention[4] but they cover much the same ground and are in some respects broader in their scope than the rights prescribed by the Convention.

The breadth of protection of constitutional rights is radical. The State is treated in the same way as a private citizen in that it has no immunity from suit[5] and the Constitution applies horizontally: thus one citizen can sue another citizen for infringement of a constitutional right to the same extent as he or she

---

1 The European Convention on Human Rights Bill 2001. 2 See Connelly, 'Ireland and the European Convention', Chapter 6 of Brice Dickson (ed.), *Human rights and the European Convention* (1997). 3 The *Lawless* case, ECHR Series A Vol. 3 (1961). 4 Perhaps the most obvious area of dissonance concerns the scope of protection of family rights. Articles 41 and 42 of the Constitution protect the family and prescribe the rights and duties of parents. The 'family' here has been interpreted as meaning the family based on marriage. This has led to problems under the Convention: *Johnson v. Ireland*, 9 EHRR 203 (1986) and *Keegan v. Ireland*, 18 EHRR 342 (1994). These problems have proved at least partially susceptible to legislative resolution: Status of Children Act 1987; Adoption Act 1987. 5 *Byrne v. Ireland*, [1972] IR 241.

can sue the State.[6] It has to be admitted that the courts themselves have baulked at the formidable juridical implications of such an entitlement[7] but it still remains at the centre of Irish constitutional jurisprudence.[8]

A second reason why politicians might hesitate about incorporating the Convention domestically springs from changing mores in Europe on issues with a human rights dimension, especially those relating to life, death and sexual conduct. In contrast to the Supreme Court of the United States of America, the European Court of Human Rights has generally been circumspect in these sensitive areas. Nevertheless, this is a political factor which has to be taken into account.

First let us note briefly the existing position. The courts have made it clear that he Convention, not being part of Irish domestic law, should not be considered to be a determinant of the validity of any aspect of Irish law, so far as the domestic order is concerned. In *In re Ó Laighleis*,[9] Maguire CJ stated:

> The Oireachtas has not determined that the Convention of Human Rights and Fundamental Freedoms is to be part of the domestic law of the State, and accordingly this Court cannot give effect to the Convention if it be contrary to domestic law or purports to grant rights or impose obligations additional to those of domestic law.
>
> No argument can prevail against the express command of section 6 of the Article 29 of Constitution before judges whose declared duty it is to uphold the Constitution and the laws.
>
> The Court accordingly cannot accept the idea that the primacy of domestic legislation is displaced by the State becoming a party to the Convention for Protection of Human Rights and Fundamental Freedoms. Nor can the Court accede to the view that in the domestic forum the Executive is in any way estopped from relying on the domestic law.

In the Supreme Court case of *Norris v. Attorney General*,[10] O'Higgins CJ agreed with the statement. In *Norris*, the plaintiff unsuccessfully challenged the consistency of nineteenth-century criminal prohibitions on private homosexual conduct with the Constitution. His counsel invoked a recent decision[11] of the European Court of Human rights which had found these prohibitions viola-

---

6 *Meskell v. Coras Iompair Eireann* [1973] IR 121.   **7** Cf *McDonnell v. Ireland* [1998] 1 IR 134, *W v. Ireland (No 2)* [1997] 2 IR 142; *Hanrahan v. Merck Sharp & Dohme (Ireland)* [1988] ILRM 629. **8** See Binchy, 'Constitutional Remedies and the Law of Torts', in J. O'Reilly (ed.), *Human rights and constitutional law: essays in honour of Brian Walsh* (Dublin, 1992), p. 201 and Butler 'Private litigation and constitutional rights under sections 8 and 9 of the Constitution – assistance from Ireland', *S. Afr. LJ* 77 (1999).   **9** [1960] IR 93.   **10** [1984] IR 36.   **11** *Dudgeon v. United Kingdom*, 4 EHRR 149 (1982).

tive of the right to a private life guaranteed by Article 8 of the Convention. Counsel argued that this decision should be regarded by the Supreme Court as more than a persuasive precedent and should be followed, on the basis that, since Ireland had ratified the Convention, a presumption arose that the Constitution was compatible with the Convention and that, in considering a question as to inconsistency under Article 50 of the Constitution, regard should be had to whether the laws under scrutiny were consistent with the Convention. The Chief Justice was of the view that to accept this submission:

> would be contrary to the provisions of the Constitution itself and would accord to the government the power, by an executive act, to change both the Constitution and the law. The Convention is an international agreement to which Ireland is a subscribing party. As such, however, it does not affect in any way questions which arise thereunder. This is made quite clear by Article 29, s. 6 of the Constitution which declares: 'No international agreement shall be part of the domestic law of the State save as may be determined by the Oireachtas.[12]

Nevertheless the Convention has had some influence on the development of judicial analysis of the Constitution. Thus, for example, in *Murphy v. IRTC*,[13] Geoghegan J observed:

> Although the European Convention on Human Rights is not part of Irish municipal law, regard can be had to its provisions when considering the nature of a fundamental right and perhaps more particularly the reasonable limitations which can be placed on the exercise of that right.

In the Supreme Court decision of *de Rossa v. Independent Newspapers Plc*,[14] Hamilton CJ quoted this passage with approval.

More recently, in *Kelly v. O'Neill*,[15] Denham J considered there to be:

> no doubt that, when considering the balance which is required to be struck between the protection of the due administration of justice and freedom of expression, the jurisprudence of the European Convention of Human Rights may provide helpful guidelines.

OPTIONS FOR INCORPORATION OF THE CONVENTION INTO DOMESTIC IRISH LAW

Speaking in broad terms, there are three ways in which the European Convention might be incorporated into domestic law. The first, and most rad-

---

12 [1984] IR 36, at 66.   **13** [1997] 2 ILRM 467, at 476.   **14** [1999] 4 IR 432, at 450.   **15** [1999] 4 IR 432.

ical, would be by way of constitutional amendment. The second would be by
direct legislative incorporation, subject to the Constitution. The third, more
modest, approach is to introduce an interpretative principle whereby legislation and common law rules would be interpreted, as far as possible, in the light
of Convention norms. As we shall see, the Bill, controversially, has adopted
the last of these options. It must be acknowledged that none of the three is free
from controversy. Let us consider each of them in turn.

Incorporation by way of constitutional amendment
Let us first consider the option of incorporation by way of constitutional amendment. The advantage to this approach would, on first reflection, appear to be
obvious. The Convention would become part of Irish law with the security
that the application of none of its provisions could be found incompatible with
the Constitution. Applicants such as Mrs Airey, Senator Norris and Mr Keegan
would find satisfaction in the Four Courts without the delay and expense of
having to go to Strasbourg.

Further reflection reveals the complexity of this apparently straightforward
option. The Convention is an international treaty under which States give certain undertakings to protect particular specified rights. It is not, in its express
terms, a traditional schema of constitutional rights.[16] Of course, its application will yield protection overlapping greatly with such a traditional schema
but its introduction into the Irish constitutional framework would raise a host
of important questions, some of a theoretical jurisprudential nature, others of
a practical character, still others in the realm of politics.

Under the Irish Constitution, there is already a range of rights which are
protected expressly or which have been found to exist by the courts. Some
of these rights have been well developed in jurisprudence; others less so. They
extend over much of the corpus of rights protected by the Convention. Neither
body of rights is static so the task is to compare two systems of thought that are
in motion, sometimes in the same direction, sometimes at different speeds.

Thus, one could make somewhat crude observations such as that the right
to privacy has been more fully developed under the Convention,[17] that the

---

16 Cf. Puddephat, 'Incorporating the European Convention on Human Rights', Ch. 18 of Angela
Hegarty & Siobhán Leonard (eds.), *Human rights: an agenda for the 21st century* (London, 1999), at
334: '[T]he Convention is an international treaty and was drafted as such. It was meant to be the
backstop to a domestic Bill of Rights, the lowest common denominator below which no country should fall. To imagine it is satisfactory as a domestic instrument is to misunderstand its purpose. Secondly, it was drafted some time ago at the end of the Second World War. While imag-
inative and progressive in its day, it is not the last word in human rights thinking ... Since it was
drafted, a number of more comprehensive human rights treaties have been produced ...' See also
Lyell, 'Whither Strasbourg? Why Britain should think long and hard before incorporating the
European Convention on Human Rights', 2 EHRLR 132, at 138 (1997).   **17** Thus, in *Norris v.
Ireland* 13 EHRR 186 (1988), the European Court of Human Rights held that the criminal prohibitions on homosexual conduct by adults in private violated Article 8 of the Convention whereas

right to freedom of speech under the Convention has a more clearly broad remit than under the Constitution,[18] that fair trial rights under the Constitution are both of narrower[19] and broader[20] scope than under the Convention, that the principle of non-retroactivity under the Constitution is narrower than under the Convention,[21] and so on.

the Supreme Court in *Norris v. Attorney General* [1984] I.R. 36 had rejected a privacy-based challenge to the consistency of these legislative provisions with the Constitution: see Donncha O'Connell, 'Ireland', Ch. 18 of Robert Blackburn & Jörg Polakiewicz (eds), *Fundamental rights in Europe: the European Convention on Human Rights and its member states, 1950–2000* (2001) at 456–457; Richard Clayton & Hugh Tomlinson, *The law of human rights* (2000), Chapter 12, especially paras. 12.84–12.94; McMahon & Binchy, *Irish law of torts* (3rd ed., 2000), Chapter 17, especially paras. 37.60ff. **18** The Irish courts have been struggling to rationalise the effect of Article 40.6.1.1. of the Constitution as being in harmony with Article 10 of the Convention. In *de Rossa v. Independent Newspapers plc* [1999] 4 IR 432, Hamilton CJ observed that '[t]here does not appear to be any conflict between Article 10 and the common law or the Constitution'. Whether this is actually the case will in due course be determined by the European Court of Human Rights in the *de Rossa* litigation. See further Binchy, 'Some Unanswered Questions in Irish Defamation Law', in J. Sarkin & W. Binchy (eds), *Human rights, the citizen and the state: South African and Irish perspectives* (2001), 243; Leonard, 'Irish Libel Law and the European Convention on Human Rights', 5 *Bar Rev.* 410 (2000). As to the consistency of the Irish law on contempt of court with Article 10, Henchy J made observations similar to those of Hamilton CJ, in *de Rossa*, in *The State (D.P.P.) v. Walsh and Conneely* [1981] IR 412, at 440. See also *Desmond v. Glackin* [1992] ILRM 490, at 512–13, where O'Hanlon J sought inspiration from the jurisprudence of the European Court of Human Rights. This approach found favour with Denham J in *Wong v. Minister for Justice* [1994] 1 IR 223; cf., however, Flynn, 'The significance of the European Convention on Human Rights in the Irish legal order', 3 *Ir. J. of Eur. L.* 4, at 14 (1994). See further Dillon-Malone, 'Mrs Nevin's pictures – a European gloss', 5 *Bar Rev.* 510 (2000); Alpha Connelly, 'Ireland and the European Convention', Ch. 6 of Brice Dickson (ed.), *Human Rights and the European Convention* (1997), at 202–3. **19** For example, in respect of access to civil legal aid: cf. *M.C. v. Legal Aid Board* [1991] 2 I.R. 43 *Airey v. Ireland*, 2 EHRR 305 (1979). See further Flynn, op. cit., at 19–20. There are many areas where Irish criminal law and procedure and the law of evidence run the risk of being found incompatible with Article 6. Examples include the abrogation or modification of the presumption of innocence or the right to silence and lack of 'equality of arms' in relation to disclosure of evidence and forfeiture provisions. The reason why it is hard to identify cases of compatibility with the Constitution combined with incompatibility with the Convention is that the Irish law is itself uncertain and highly mobile. The courts, having declared a principle that seems destined to send Irish law into collision with the European Court of Human Rights, resort to the handbrake and send our law spinning off, temporarily at least, in a different direction. Cf. *Heaney v. Ireland* [1996] 1 IR 580, *Rock v. Ireland* [1997] 3 IR 484, *In re National Irish Banks Ltd*, [1999] 1 ILRM 321, Casey, op. cit., 535–8. See generally Una Ní Raifeartaigh, 'The European Convention on Human Rights and the Irish Criminal Justice System' 7 *Bar Review* 111 (2001). **20** There is, of course, a right to trial by jury for non-minor offences (subject to certain controversial exceptional instances) under Article 38.5 of the Constitution: see J.Kelly, *The Irish Constitution* (3rd ed., by G. Hogan & G. Whyte, 1994), 657–668, J. Casey, *Constitutional law in Ireland* (3rd ed., 2000), 324–327. No such right is guaranteed by Article 6 of the Convention, though, in States which have juries, the manner of their operation must comply with Article 6 values: Clayton & Tomlinson, op. cit., para. 11.2.90. Delay is treated somewhat more leniently under Article 6 of the Convention than under Article 38.1 of the Constitution: cf. Casey, op. cit., 522–4. **21** Cf. Casey, op. cit., 102, the Constitution Review Group *Report* (Pn 2632), p. 43.

The benefit to be derived from this process of comparison is not to award higher marks to one or other instrument on the basis of the great remit of a particular right: that would be a naive and futile exercise since any system for the protection of rights cannot treat any right in isolation: it must have a coherent philosophy for the reconciliation of all of these rights in a harmonious larger unity. The extension of one right – speech, for example – may inevitably trench upon and ultimately diminish another right – such as the right to one's good name, overtly recognised and protected under the Irish Constitution (but not overtly under the Convention).

One should also be conscious of the dynamism of any living system for the protection of human rights, which I have already mentioned. The calibration of potentially competing rights is an ongoing process and we can be sure that yesterday's precise determination will not necessarily stand today and almost certainly not tomorrow. The reasons for changes in calibration are complex and will be affected by social, economic and broader cultural influences. In seeking, therefore, to compare the respective remits of Constitution-based and Convention rights, one has to attempt to take account of these influences and to predict how they will operate in the future. No one could claim that this is an easy or a certain process.

Another approach may be mentioned briefly. This would be to examine the Constitution comprehensively in the light of Convention norms and add to the Constitution those norms that are at present in the Convention but not the Constitution. Whether this would be feasible may be debated in view of the changing normative content of both instruments and the implications for the corpus of rights and their relationship with each other of the addition of particular rights.

It must also be borne in mind that our Constitution has been interpreted as involving, not merely the protection of rights of citizens (and in some instances others) from violation by the State and its agents, but also the protection of constitutional rights from infringement by other individuals, whether personal or corporate. This horizontal effect of rights-protection has yet to be fully developed by our courts, and there are many signs that the courts do not savour the task. From the standpoint of incorporating the Convention by way of constitutional amendment, a large question has to be addressed. Should the Convention rights, when incorporated in this manner, be restricted to rights enforceable only against the State? If so, should the existing horizontal effect of equivalent constitutional rights be removed? Or are we to have a new constitutional order in which Convention rights will be incorporated at a constitutional level, limited so as only to be enforceable against the State, where 'traditional' constitutional rights encompassing largely the same area – life, speech, assembly, and so on – will be retained, with their continuing horizontal effect? Or should the Convention rights be incorporated at a constitutional level in replacement of the existing 'traditional' constitutional rights and given horizontal effect?

All of these questions are of course capable of resolution but there is no one obvious answer: people of goodwill who are strongly in favour of the idea of domestic incorporation of the Convention at a constitutional level may find themselves in disagreement as to the best way of doing so. In truth this is not a difference of opinion merely about some technical procedural question but rather one of a substantive character, in which important issues of constitutional law and jurisprudence have to be addressed.

I should mention another factor which must exercise the minds of politicians. This is the need for any strategy of incorporation of the Convention by way of constitutional amendment to have the support of the People. Unless a majority of those who vote in such a referendum favours the initiative, it will not succeed. The Convention involves value-positions on a range of issues on which there may be no consensus and which are considered to be of great importance by many voters. Almost inevitably, debate would arise about some of these issues and analysis and prediction would be met by counter-analysis and counter-prediction. Neither side of these arguments would be able to refute the other's position completely since there would indeed be some element of uncertainty about how such a momentous change in the constitutional order would work out in practice. It is quite understandable that politicians might hesitate before embarking down this road.

Direct incorporation by way of legislation

Let us now consider the second option: of directly incorporating the Convention into Irish law by way of legislation.

As with the first option, the idea is a simple one but is capable of execution in more than one way. The Oireachtas could, for example, contemplate a simple piece of legislation providing that the rights prescribed and protected under the Convention are to be protected under the domestic law of the State. This would mean that the legislation would be treated as any other Act of the Oireachtas. It would be given the benefit of the presumption of constitutional validity afforded all such Acts and would be interpreted in a way favouring its validity where two interpretations, one constitutional, the other not, were open to the court. Crucially, it would not be afforded a *guarantee* of constitutional validity. If any of its provisions were found to conflict with the Constitution in any way, it would have to be declared invalid on that account.

Some may consider this model for direct incorporation by legislation to be quite unsatisfactory. There are, of course, many situations where the Convention may require a particular outcome which will not be *required* by the Constitution but equally not be *contrary* to the Constitution. A situation may arise, however, where the Convention requires a particular outcome which is contrary to a provision in the Constitution. In such circumstances, the legislation incorporating the Convention would be struck down as unconstitutional by the courts. Far from effectively incorporating the Convention into domestic law, this approach would stigmatise the Convention and enhance the potential for conflict at a political level between Ireland and the Council of Europe.

Putting it in blunt terms, there is no merit in incorporating the Convention directly at a legislative level and leaving its constitutional status unresolved. If incorporation by way of constitutional amendment, which is the only way of resolving that issue in advance, is not to be contemplated, then it is essential that the option of direct incorporation by way of legislation should specify clearly that the Convention's provisions are subject, rather than superior, to the provisions of the Constitution.

Such a mode of direct incorporation does not in any way denigrate the Convention: on the contrary, it gives the courts the opportunity to clarify the relationship between the Convention and the Constitution. Far from defeating the application of the Convention, such a strategy maximises the potential to highlight any differences that exist between the Convention and the Constitution. Of course, the party whose Convention rights give way to the Constitution will have the burden of making the trip to Strasbourg but he or she will be doing so with the documentary evidence, provided by the Irish courts themselves, of an incompatibility between the Constitution and the Convention. What better legal argument could a litigant have? So potent is it that the political process for addressing the incompatibility would in some instances be likely to start even before (or without) the trek to Strasbourg. In upholding the constitutionality of an impugned aspect of Irish law, the courts would in effect be anticipating the work of the Strasbourg Court.

It would be possible for the legislation to provide that any enactment passed *or to be passed* is to be construed and have effect subject to the provision of the Convention.[22] This would not offend against any entitlement on the part of the Oireachtas subsequently to introduce legislation inconsistent with the legislation incorporating the Convention by inserting an express provision stating clearly that the new legislation is to have effect notwithstanding any provision in the earlier Act.[23]

Let us now consider whether this model of direct legislative incorporation of the Convention, subject to the Constitution, presents any hidden constitutional difficulty. In particular, is there a credible concern that, by introducing the requirement to scrutinise the corpus of Irish legislation in the light of the broad provisions of the Convention, the Act of incorporation would be guilty of violating some constitutional principle by inserting an *ersatz* Constitution, or at least an *ersatz* Bill of Rights, into the existing Constitution?

I will try to express this concern in its strongest form. It appears to be as follows. The courts have the function of determining the validity of the corpus

---

22 Cf. Emmerson, 'Opinion: this year's model – the options for incorporation', 3 EHRLR 313, at 318–19 (1997), using sections 2(1) and 2(4) of Britain's European Communities Act 1972 as a model.   **23** Cf. id., at 319.

of Irish statutory and common law in the light of the Constitution; to impose on the courts an extra function, derived from statute, of assessing the validity of that corpus in the light of a similar, but not identical, normative cluster of rights represented by the Convention is not permissible. In any legal system, there can be only one coherent philosophy of human rights protection and of calibration of the relationships between the respective organs of State, between the State and its citizens and between citizens (or, indeed, between non-citizens).

I believe that this concern is fundamentally misconceived. Article 29.6 of the Constitution specifically envisages the incorporation into domestic law of international treaties. Many treaties set out broad principles of general application which are presumed to be harmonious with, or similar to, principles at the core of the Constitution. Even before any consideration is given to the actual content of the European Convention, it may be observed that the courts would not be called on to choose, at their option, between competing norms: if the Convention norm is incompatible with the Constitution it would have to give way.[24] Nor would the courts be required to construct some new normative structure, separate from the Convention and the Constitution. Rather would they have to engage in the simpler process of examining a particular legislative provision or common law rule in the light of the requirements of the Convention before going on, in appropriate cases, to address the question whether a provision or rule of law that is incompatible with the Convention is nonetheless required by the Constitution. The two normative systems are separate from each other and judicial consideration of them is equally separate. This is not a new legal phenomenon. In private international law courts are often called on to examine a factual situation from the standpoint of more than one legal system. Indeed, they may even have to choose between the application of one or other of them on the basis of complex criteria.[25] None of these complications will arise under a model of direct legislative incorporation of the Convention, subject to the Constitution.[26]

---

24 There will, of course, be far more cases where this clash will not occur either because the Convention or the Constitution (or both the Convention and the Constitution) would support, but not require, legislation of a particular character. For example, the Constitution supports, but does not require, discrimination in the law of succession in favour of the marital family: *O'B. v. S.* [1984] IR 316. If the Status of Children Act 1987 had not been passed and (let us assume) the Convention's provisions were incorporated directly into law in the manner of statutory interpretation now proposed, the effect of Article 8, thus incorporated, might be considered to have impliedly repealed (or possibly modified) the original provisions of the Succession Act 1965 and the fact that the Oireachtas, according to *O'B. v. S*, is entitled to discriminate in favour of the marital family would not be relevant. Similarly, *Norris v. Attorney General* [1984] IR 316 would be decided differently since its rationale was based on the State's entitlement, but not obligation, to maintain legislative provisions of the kind held to be incompatible with the Convention in *Norris v. Ireland*, 13 EHRR 186 (1988). **25** Cf. *Grehan v. Medical Incorporated Inc.,* [1986] IR 528. **26** It is possible in theory to envisage a case where the Oireachtas enacts a statute containing a set of

When one considers the actual normative content of the Convention and compares it to that of the Constitution, the manner in which this model of incorporation would be likely to work out in practice is not too difficult to discern. The Human Rights Commission has observed:

> So far as coherence of philosophies is concerned, in point of fact the fundamental rights section of Constitution and the ECHR do adhere well and could be taken as two complementary expressions of one foundational philosophy. The doctrine of the 'margin of appreciation', which is regularly applied by the Strasbourg Court, is generally elastic enough to allow for local variations.[27]

Some opponents of direct incorporation by way of legislation have argued that it would offend against the principle of the separation of powers by permitting the courts to interfere with the legislation enacted by the Oireachtas which is compatible with the Constitution. To this argument, the Human Rights Commission has responded robustly:

> [I]f it is constitutional for the courts to have recourse to the Convention in judging administrative actions why is it unconstitutional for them to have regard to the Convention in judging legislative action? If one is not a violation of the discretion of the courts under the Constitution, neither is the other.[28]

A more technical and formal refutation of the argument can also be made. Far from surrendering its legislative function to the courts, the Oireachtas would be *exercising* that function and prescribing the criteria by which previous and future[29] legislation is to be assessed in terms of its compatibility with the Convention. The courts would not be trespassing on the legislative domain but rather acting under the statutory authority of the Oireachtas.[30] The

principles, against which all statutory provisions and common law rules must be judged (subject only to the Constitution), and the principles are so unclear or mutually contradictory as to render the statute itself unconstitutional. No such charge has been, or could credibly be, brought against the European Convention.   **27** *Submission*, pp. 6–7.   **28** *Submission*, p. 7. The precise way in which the margin of appreciation doctrine should operate in the context of legislative incorporation needs to be considered. It may be argued that the domestic courts should, as it were, accept a *renvoi* from Strasbourg and apply what they perceive to be the appropriate margin in the light of the norms and culture of their particular society.   **29** I have already addressed this aspect of the legislation. The Oireachtas, if it chose a mode of incorporation that purported to apply to future legislation, would not be restricting its constitutionally-based entitlement to enact legislation subsequently that would not be affected by the Act of incorporation.   **30** It is possible to conceive of legislation which *would* be unconstitutional as involving a surrender to the judiciary of the legislative function. If the Oireachtas passed an Act providing that the courts should be entitled to hold unlawful (or otherwise legally ineffective) any legislative provision on the statute book which

Oireachtas is perfectly free to repeal legislation in the exercise of its legislative function. The Oireachtas is also free to pass a law suspending the operation of, or otherwise rendering ineffective, any earlier or subsequent piece of legislation, either subject to some condition precedent or not. If the Oireachtas enacts a law incorporating the provisions of the European Convention on Human Rights and providing that laws (past or future) incompatible with these provisions are not to have legal effect[31], that is within its prerogative.

I leave the last word on this matter to the Human Rights Commission:

> It is, in the Commission's view, quite unconvincing to argue that the infusion into domestic law of the Convention would contaminate our law so as to render the legislation unconstitutional. On the contrary, the Commission considers that our jurisprudence would be greatly enriched. The Convention, and the body of law that has been developed under the European Convention of Human Rights, represent a treasury of human rights protection. The Commission does not argue that this corpus of human rights protection has to be regarded as better in every respect than what is provided by the Irish Constitution. Clearly no such contention could be sustained. The Commission is, however, firmly of the view that its incorporation by legislation, subject to the Constitution, would strengthen the protection of human rights measurably.[32]

Indirect incorporation of the convention

Let us now consider the third option, which is indirect incorporation of the Convention by legislation that contains an interpretative provision designed to encourage harmonising domestic law with Convention norms, supplemented

they did not like, that Act would clearly be unconstitutional. If the Act gave the courts a somewhat narrower power, to render inoperative any statutory provision that they considered to be unjust, that could also be unconstitutional in inhibiting the efficacy of the legislative function. **31** It should be noted that a court's finding that a particular statutory provision is incompatible with the Convention and accordingly of no legal effect is not the same, juridically speaking, as a finding that a legislative provision is not valid having regard to the Constitution. In the latter case the invalidity follows from the terms of the Constitution itself and the court, in making such a finding, is discharging an obligation and exercising a right deriving from the Constitution. Moreover, the nature of the invalidity and the effect of a finding of invalidity on the rights of non-parties to the litigation in question are matters whose resolution derives from the Constitution. In stark contrast, the Oireachtas, when enacting legislation, is perfectly free to define the extent of its capacity to repeal or otherwise render ineffective earlier legislation or to delimit the legal effectiveness of future legislation (subject, of course, in the latter instance, to its power to change its mind in the future). A court making a finding of legal ineffectiveness ('invalidity', 'incompatibility', etc.) of a statutory provision by reason of its failure to comply with the principles of the European Convention on Human Rights is not, therefore, engaging in some illegitimate exercise of judicial power mimicking its mandate to strike down unconstitutional legislation but is instead merely doing the task of interpretation prescribed by the Oireachtas in the exercise of its legislative function and having effects also specified by the Oireachtas. **32** *Submission*, p. 7.

by a sanction against State organs for failure to perform their functions in a manner compatible with the State's obligations under the Convention, as well as declarations of incompatibility, backed by provision for *ex gratia* payments. This, of course, is the option that has found favour in the Bill as initiated. Does it represent the best way forward?

I do not believe that it does but let us be gracious enough to acknowledge that it improves the present position by giving some domestic acknowledgment, half-hearted though it may be, to the Convention. The interpretative provision, if it becomes law, is likely to have the considerable, albeit stealthy, effect of encouraging the courts to interpret Irish law, including the provisions of the Constitution, in a manner compatible with the Convention. It requires less effort to take this course than to present a detailed judgment, which would almost inevitably be appealed, finding a particular provision incompatible with the Convention. Section 3, the narrow scope of which I will criticise in a moment, introduces a genuine remedy in domestic law for certain violations of the Convention and section 5, which I will also be criticising, is likely in practice to result in compensation being made to some victims of breaches of the Convention. The political reality may turn out to be that the *ex gratia* form will not deprive many claimants of their due.

The threshold question, however, is whether this modest strategy of indirect incorporation is the best one. I am frankly unable to conjure up any convincing argument that it is. This approach may have suited the distinctive constitutional culture of Britain, with its strong tradition of parliamentary supremacy, but it seems quite foreign to our legal environment, with a written Constitution and wide-ranging powers of judicial review. I can only see weaknesses, anomalies and drawbacks with this mode of incorporation. Let me mention some of the more obvious ones.

The Bill, as drafted, fails to provide an effective remedy for violations of the Convention in domestic law. Section 3 is hedged about with significant qualifications, being '[s]ubject to any statutory provision ... or rule of law.' Section 5 gives no right to a remedy following a declaration of incompatibility and the possibility of an *ex gratia* payment may be of no assistance in many cases, where the violation of the Convention will not be cured by the transfer of money to the claimant. The Human Rights Commission put its critique in strong, but clear, terms:

> It is unacceptable to place the courts in a position where they can identify a breach of human rights and not be in a position to give an effective remedy. The whole procedure set out in Section 5 of the Bill is of questionable constitutional validity. Moreover, the Commission finds it difficult to understand how one can purport to incorporate Article 13 of the European Convention on Human Rights ... which requires the provision of an effective remedy at national level, into

domestic law while withholding a judicial remedy for a breach of the Convention. Strasbourg case-law establishes the principle that a discretionary remedy is no remedy.[33]

THE HUMAN RIGHTS COMMISSION'S CRITIQUE OF THE BILL

The Human Rights Commission's strong preference is for legislative incorporation of the Convention rather than the model adopted in the Bill. Indeed, the Commission expresses the view that 'it would be quite wrong to reject [the option of constitutional incorporation] out of hand and ... on the contrary, it merits serious consideration'.[34] It regards the Convention as a rich source of human rights protection which in many ways can supplement the protection afforded by the Constitution. It considers that there is much to be gained from Ireland's active participation in the developing community of legal rights in Europe and contributing to improving the jurisprudence on the Convention's provisions.

Having clarified its general view, the Commission goes on to make a number of criticisms of specific provisions in the Bill. I will mention several of them here.

Narrow definition of 'organs of the State'
The Commission recommends that the definition of 'organs of the State' should be expanded to encompass the courts and semi-public authorities, such as regulatory bodies, privately-owned hospitals and schools. The crucial test should relate to whether the organ is engaging, in part or in whole, in public functions.

So far as the courts are concerned, the Commission is conscious of the need to preserve judicial independence but equally acknowledges that the performance of judicial functions falls within the scope of Convention obligations. Judicial delay or failure to give adequate reasons for decisions are examples of breaches of these obligations. If the Oireachtas thought it necessary, it could protect judges from being sued whilst retaining the availability of remedies against the State, such as damages or release from prison.[35]

In relation to the debate on the horizontal protection of human rights, the Commission considers that bringing the courts within the scope of section 3 will not determine the issue:

> It raises a distinctive policy choice which the legislation incorporating the Convention will have to resolve, one way or the other. The Commission's own preference is that the legislation should prescribe that it does not have direct horizontal effect.[36]

33 *Submission*, pp. 4–5. 34 *Submission*, p. 3. 35 *Submission*, pp. 7–8. 36 Id., p. 9. The Commission

Extending the remedies

The Commission proposes[37] a radical expansion of the remedies under the Bill. The court should have power under section 3 to make orders other than simply for damages. These should include injunctions (including mandatory injunctions) and orders for the release of people from custody, for example. Later, I will be discussing in more detail the drafting of section 3 and considering how it may be interpreted on the question of remedies.

With regard to section 5, the Commission considers that the system for *ex gratia* payments by the Government should be replaced by compensation as of right. It does not see any constitutional difficulty in giving the courts the power to make such awards, limited only to exclude instances where the incompatibility with the Convention springs from a constitutional imperative.[38]

Restriction on remedies in the Circuit and District Courts

Sections 3 and 5 of the Bill exclude the District Court as a forum where a remedy can be sought for breaches of the Convention. Moreover section 5 also excludes the Circuit Court.

The Human Rights Commission does not support these restrictions. It believes that it should be possible to raise Convention points in all courts and to plead breach of the Convention as a general shield in the lower courts[39]. To facilitate this, the Commission recommends that the Bill should provide for a case stated procedure when this raises a new issue not previously decided and on which the lower court may wish to seek guidance.[40]

Time limits

Section 3(5) of the Bill prescribes a one-year time limit for initiating claims for a contravention of section 3(1), subject to a judicial power – unusual in Irish limitations law – to extend the period if the Court considers it 'appropriate to do so in the interests of justice'. The Human Rights Commission considers[41] that this is too short and that the limitation period should be extended to six years, which is the general limitation period for tort claims.[42] It regards a section 3 claim as analogous to a claim in tort for breach of statutory duty[43]. It notes that, in *McDonnell v. Ireland*,[44] the Supreme Court characterised the action

---

considers (id.) that the Oireachtas can revisit the question, perhaps in five years' time, after the provisions of the Convention have become familiar to Irish lawyers and the courts.   **37** *Submission*, p. 9.   **38** Id.   **39** *Submission*, p. 13.   **40** Id.   **41** *Submission*, p. 11.   **42** Cf. McMahon & Binchy, *Irish law of torts* (3rd ed., 2000), para. 46.03.   **43** Cf. McMahon & Binchy, op. cit., Chapter 21.   **44** [1998] IR 34. For more than a decade, the courts have been evincing some discomfort with the principle, articulated without qualification in *Meskell v. Coras Iompair Eireann* [1973] IR 121, that infringement of a constitutional right should occasion an award of damages in appropriate cases, not just against the State but also non-State actors. *McDonnell v. Ireland* leaves important limitations issues unresolved. Three are of present relevance. Should the analogy with tort carry to the point of differentiating claims for damages for infringement of constitutional rights involving

for damages for infringement of a constitutional right, for the purposes of the Statute of Limitations 1957, as a tort. There are, of course, parallels with a claim based on violation of the European Convention.

The Commission goes on to deal with a more subtle aspect of the subject. This is where there has been a failure to respect the *positive* obligations under the Convention,[45] such as where the Oireachtas fails to introduce legislation providing an appropriate remedy for breach of a Convention right by private individuals. The Commission recommends that a right to take a claim for such failure to respect positive obligations should also be expressly guaranteed 'with its own appropriate limitation period'.[46]

Finally, one may reflect on the power given to the court to extend the limitation period where it considers it appropriate to do so. How is the court to exercise this broad power? The word 'appropriate' is very general. Questions will arise as to whether it is open to courts to make what might be called a generic value judgment that it will always be appropriate to extend the period where the claimant could not reasonably have been aware of his or her entitlement to make a claim against the defendant within the one-year period. Irish limitations law is at present in a somewhat unfinished and anomalous state. Where claims for personal injury are concerned, the 'discoverability' test has been applied by legislation enacted in 1991[47] but other claims may be defeated by the Statute of Limitations before the victim of the tort could reasonably have become aware of the entitlement to sue,[48] The Supreme Court has taken a quiescent stance, deferential to policy choices made (or neglected to be made) by the Oireachtas.[49] We can only speculate on whether the courts would be disposed to take a more interested and active role under the discretion conferred on them by section 3(5) of the Bill.

Extending the notice requirement under section 6

Section 6 requires notice to be given to the Attorney General of proceedings before a court decides to make a declaration of incompatibility. The Attorney

---

personal injuries from other claims? Should any difference be made between intentional and negligent infringement of constitutional rights for the purposes of limitation of actions? And is it possible to characterise an infringement of a constitutional right as a 'breach of duty' for the purposes of the Statute of Limitations 1957, as amended by the Statute of Limitations (Amendment) Act 1991? As to the latter question, cf. Byrne & Binchy, *Annual Review of Irish Law 2001*, 439–40. **45** Cf. David Feldman, *Civil liberties and human rights in England and Wales* (2nd ed., 2002), 53–5. **46** *Submission*, p. 11. **47** Statute of Limitations (Amendment) Act 1991. **48** Cf. McMahon & Binchy, op. cit., paras. 46.04ff. Carroll J, quite understandably, regarded this outcome as inconsistent with the requirements of the Constitution, in *Morgan v. Park Developments* [1983] ILRM 156, but the Supreme Court, in *Hegarty v. O'Loughran* [1990] 1 IR 148, did not agree. The Law Reform Commission in its recent *Report on the Statute of Limitations* has recommended that the discoverability principle should apply to certain claims not involving personal injury. **49** Cf. *Hegarty v. O'Loughran, supra, Tuohy v. Courtney* [1994] 3 IR 1.

General is thereupon entitled to appear in the proceedings and to become a party to them as regards the issue of the declaration of incompatibility.

The Attorney General performs several functions. One is to defend the validity of legislation from attack. Another is to protect the constitutional rights of citizens (and, it seems, others). In cases where a person is attacking the constitutional validity of legislation or, in the context which we are considering, the compatibility of legislation with the European Convention, the Attorney General is placed in what the Human Rights Commission has described as a 'somewhat ambiguous role'.[50] Accordingly the Commission has recommended[51] that it should be made a notice party under section 6. This would enable the Commission to perform its functions under its statutory mandate, especially section 8, paragraph (4) of the Human Rights Commission Act 2000.[52]

Enlarging the duty to report

Section 5(3) of the Bill requires the Taoiseach to lay before each House of the Oireacthas a copy of an order containing a declaration of incompatibility. This is a fairly minimal obligation. The Human Rights Commission has argued[53] that the provision should go further and require the Taoiseach to say what the Government proposes to do about the situation. This would encourage political attention and debate.

Human rights proofing for legislative proposals

In Britain, Government Ministers introducing legislative proposals must either state that, in their view, the Bill is compatible with the Convention rights[54] or that they are unable to do so but that nevertheless the Government wishes the House to proceed with the Bill.[55] This statement must be in writing. The practice is for it to appear on the front cover of the printed version of the Bill.[56]

---

50 *Submission*, p. 12. 51 Id. 52 The Commission goes on to comment (id.) that: '[i]t is desirable that a litigant should be enabled, if he or she wishes, to claim relief under the existing law, the Constitution, and the Convention as alternative reliefs in the one action and that he or she should not have to exhaust the procedures under the law and the Constitution before raising the question of a breach of the Convention. At the same time it does appear that if a litigant wishes to challenge the validity of an Act of the Oireachtas he or she should only be allowed to do so in the High Court or the Supreme Court and on notice to the Attorney General. If the litigant wishes to challenge a statute in the light of the European Convention he or she should also be obliged to notify the Human Rights Commission.' 53 *Submission*, p. 12. 54 Human Rights Act 1998, section 19(1)(a). 55 Human Rights Act 1998, section 19(1)(b). 56 Cf. David Feldman, *Civil liberties and human rights in England and Wales* (2nd ed., 2002), 93: 'This focuses the Minister's and the drafter's minds, and Parliament's attention, on Convention rights. Where (in the light of appropriate advice) it is impossible to make a statement of compatibility, section 19(1) makes it clear that the government is collectively responsible for the serious step of inviting the House to proceed with a Bill which probably violates a Convention right. The statement may also guide courts or tribunals which have to decide how strenuously to seek an interpretation of the provision which is compatible with Convention rights. A more rights–centered interpretation will be justified where

The Human Rights Commission considers[57] that the Bill should contain a similar requirement. If the Government persists with the narrow model of the legislation, with declarations of incompatibility rather than a more robust mode of incorporation, it would seem logical and desirable to have such a requirement as part of the legislation.

The need for an ongoing monitoring obligation

The trend in human rights protection internationally is to place an obligation on those in authority – national or even private organs – to monitor their organisation, its system of operation and the practical day-to-day application of management principles in order to ensure compliance with human rights standards. The Bill does not include a provision of this type. There is much to be said for section 3 being amended to require organs of State to monitor periodically and report on their compliance with the provisions of the Convention in the performance of their functions.[58]

Legal aid

The Bill contains no provision enabling claimants to have access to legal aid. The Human Rights Commission has recommended that the Minister for Justice, Equality and Law Reform should issue a policy directive under section 7 of the Civil Legal Aid Act 1995 to the effect that applications for legal aid will be considered in suitable cases under the Bill.[59]

Duplication of proceedings

Section 3(2) of the Bill provides in part that a person who has suffered injury, loss or damage as a result of a contravention of section 3(1) may, 'if no other remedy is available', institute proceedings to recover damages. This raises the question as to how the non-availability of any other remedy is to be established. The most obvious way is by having taken unsuccessful proceedings already. The subjective belief on the part of the claimant that no other remedy is available would not suffice.

The redundancy, futility and expense of forcing claimants to take successive proceedings led the Human Rights Commission to recommend that the

---

the Minister has made a statement of compatibility than where Parliament has proceeded having recognised the likelihood of incompatibility, although the court need not accept the correctness of the Minister's view.' **57** *Submission*, p. 12. **58** The Human Rights Commission so recommended in its *Submission*, p. 12. It considered (*id*.) that this monitoring requirement should include an anti-discrimination clause. **59** *Submission*, p. 11. The Commission goes on to state (id): 'Consequential amendments of sections 24(a) and 28(c) may be necessary in the light of the practice of the Legal Aid Board in interpreting these provisions and the dearth of constitutional actions which have been legally aided. If a constitutional-type action is necessary under the Human Rights Commission Acts 2000 and 2001 and the present Bill, it is essential to establish who has the primary responsibility for funding the action'.

Bill be amended to provide that claims under the Bill may be initiated in conjunction with other proceedings.[60]

SOME ISSUES OF INTERPRETATION

Let me now mention some issues of interpretation that arise in relation to sections 2 and 3 of the Bill.

Section 2

Section 2 requires the court, when interpreting and applying any statutory provision or rule of law, already in force or coming into force after the passage of the legislation, to do so, 'in so far as is possible, subject to the rules of law relating to such interpretation and application', in a manner compatible with the State's obligations under the Convention provisions. This section is somewhat similar to section 3 of Britain's Human Rights Act 1998 but the differences are striking. Section 2 applies, not only to statutory provisions but also rules of law. This means that the corpus of common law is to be 'interpreted' as far as possible, in a manner compatible with the State's obligations under the Convention. One does not usually speak of courts interpreting rules that they themselves have created; this would suggest that the interpretation process is capable of embracing the modification of a common law rule, whether the court so describes the process.

Again in contrast to section 3 of the 1998 Act, section 2 is subject to a qualification that the court's function is 'subject to the rules of law relating to such interpretation and application'. The scope of this qualification is completely obscure. There is no packet of pre-ordained, self-contained rules of law relating to interpretation of statutes. (*A fortiori*, there are no rules of law relating to the interpretation of common law rules.) It is of course true that, over the years, the courts have developed principles or rules for the interpretation of constitutional and statutory provisions. These are not inflexible and unchanging and certainly they are not so complete and final as to prevent a court, faced with the task of interpreting a statutory provision, 'in so far as is possible', in a manner compatible with the State's obligations under the Convention provisions, from asking itself how it should interpret the phrase 'in so far as is possible'. If the qualification 'subject to the rules of law relating to such interpretation...' had not been included in section 2, no doubt the court would have embarked on the task of interpretation desirous of respecting the pre-existing rules of interpretation but not so servile to them as to deny itself the entitlement of modifying those rules or fashioning a distinctive rule or rules of interpretation in response to the novel elements of the new legislation. The ques-

60 *Submission*, p. 11.

tion, therefore, is whether the inclusion of the qualification prevents the court from this element of creativity which is inherent in the judicial function. I think that the answer is no, because the rules of statutory interpretation are themselves sufficiently dynamic to permit such a course; but the inclusion of the qualification does create uncertainty, especially where the judicial function under section 2 is expressed as being 'subject to', rather than 'in accordance with', the rules of statutory interpretation.

Section 3

It is generally considered that section 3 restricts the remedy under it to one of damages, and only in cases where no other remedy in damages is available to the victim of the contravention of section 3(1). Looking closely at the text of section 3 another interpretation may be hazarded. The section first imposes a duty on every organ of the State to perform its functions in a manner compatible with the State's obligations under the Convention provisions. This duty is expressed in clear peremptory terms. If the section stopped there, a question of statutory interpretation would arise as to the nature and scope of the sanctions (if any) for breaking that duty. It could be argued that victims of a breach would be entitled to an action for damages under traditional principles[61], as well (perhaps) as the right to an injunction[62] against conduct – whether by way of act or omission – by the State organ that is incompatible with the State's obligations under the Convention's provisions. When one examines subsection (2), one discovers that it does not, in express terms, provide that the *only* remedy for violation of subsection (1) is an action for damages. On the contrary, it can be regarded as a supplementary remedy, focused on the context of damages claims, in that it provides a default damages remedy if no other remedy in damages 'is available'.[63] It does not profess to restrict, or even address, the range of potential remedies for breach of subsection (1) other than ones sounding in damages.

When one examines subsection (4), which provides that nothing in the section is to be construed as creating a criminal offence, one is perhaps entitled to draw the conclusion that this adds reasonably strong weight to the broader interpretation of the section that I have indicated. If it was considered neces-

61 Cf. McMahon & Binchy, op. cit., Chapter 21.   **62** Cf. *Lovett v. Grogan* [1995] 1 ILRM 12, *Wall v. Feeley* High Ct, 26 October 1983, *Stelzer v. Wexford Slob Commissioners*, [1988] ILRM 279, *Mourneview Estate Ltd. v. Dundalk U.D.C.*, 101 ILTR 189 (High Ct., 1967).   **63** Against this interpretation, it may be argued that the references in subsection (5) to '[p]roceedings under this section' and in subsection (3) to '[t]he damages recoverable under this section' envisage that the section limits the remedy for breach of subsection (1) to the proceedings for damages prescribed in subsection (2). It can, however, be replied that the references in subsections (3) and (5) are merely seeking to identify the remedy prescribed in subsection (2) for the purposes of settling issues of jurisdiction and limitation of actions and that they add no weight to the argument that the subsection (2) remedy is the only one flowing from a breach of subsection (1).

sary to clarify that the remit of the section did not run to creating a criminal offence, one may infer that the legislator proceeded on the basis that subsection (1) established a duty carrying with it remedies and sanctions not necessarily determined definitively by subsection (2).

The new European Regulation on public access to documents

ALEX SCHUSTER

Under the laws of many democratic States, the right of public access to documents is perceived both as an intrinsic element of a thriving democracy and as a means of citizens' control of the executive. The climate of openness engendered by this right enables citizens to participate more closely in the decision-making process and guarantees that the administration enjoys greater legitimacy (insofar as it is more effective and more accountable to the citizen).

The Treaty on European Union was designed to create 'an ever closer Union amongst the peoples of Europe, in which decisions are taken as openly ... and as closely as possible to the citizen'. Article 1 of the Treaty raised the concept of openness to the constitutional level and introduced the citizen's right of access to European Union documents. Both the European Commission and the Council initially gave effect to this right through a Code of Conduct concerning public access to Council and Commission documents. In order to implement this Code of Conduct, both institutions adopted separate decisions on public access to documents.

But both the European Commission and the Council recognised that this piecemeal regulation of public access to documents was only intended as a stop-gap measure and that a more comprehensive regime would have to be introduced to comply with constitutional imperatives. On 30 May 2001 EC Regulation No. 1049/2001 was adopted in order 'to give the fullest possible effect to the right of public access to documents and to lay down the general principles and limits on such access'. This Regulation also consolidated the initiatives that the Community institutions had already taken in order to improve the transparency of the decision-making process.

Although Regulation 1049/2001 entered into force on 3 June 2001, the Community institutions were afforded a six-month moratorium during which to adapt their rules of procedure to comply with the new legislative regime.

One of the core principles which underpins the new Regulation is that wider access should be granted to documents in cases where the Community institutions are acting in a legislative capacity (including under delegated powers). Although the need to preserve the effectiveness of the institutions' decision-making processes is expressly recognised in the Regulation, this is counterbalanced by the principle that documents linked to the legislative process should be made directly accessible to the greatest possible extent.

The community institutions covered by regulation 1049/2001

The new Regulation applies to the European Parliament, the Council and the Commission. It is appropriate, at this juncture, to explain briefly the different tasks undertaken by these Community institutions.

The Commission is effectively the civil service of the Community. There are twenty Commissioners (two each for France, Italy, Spain, the United Kingdom and Germany and one each for the other ten Member States). The members of the Commission are required to be persons 'whose independence is beyond doubt', and the Treaty stipulates that they shall 'in the general interest of the Community, be completely independent in the performance of their duties'.

The role of the Commission may be divided into six different categories: (i) to design policies which flow from the provisions of the Treaty; (ii) to initiate or promote Community legislation; (iii) to act as as watchdog in ensuring that the Member States comply with Community legislation; (iv) to bring Member States before the European Court of Justice in the event of non-compliance with the Treaty or Community legislation; (v) to act as a mediator when inter-governmental disputes between Member States arise; (vi) to legislate in its own right within the limited powers vested in it by the Treaty in relation to Competition Policy, or when authorised by the Council of Ministers in relation to the Common Agricultural Policy.

The Council is made up of representatives of the governments of the fifteen Member States of the European Community. Council membership tends to depend on the subject matter under discussion. So, for example, the General Affairs Council, which brings together the fifteen Foreign Ministers of the Member States, deals, *inter alia,* with the external relations of the European Community as a whole. The Agriculture Ministers of the Member States may be called upon to discuss matters relating to the Common Agricultural Policy, and so on. The Council is the principal law-making body in the European Community.

The European Parliament is a body of representatives from the Member States which is directly elected by universal suffrage. Although the Parliament is not the primary law-making body in the European Community, it is the beneficiary of significant powers in the legislative sphere. Viewed from a strictly legal perspective, the European Parliament is the equal legislative partner of the Council in many of the areas of competence covered by the EC Treaty. The final product of the law-making process is often a joint act of both the Parliament and the Council, to which the President of each institution must append his signature. In reality, however, both the Council and the Commission have a much greater influence in shaping the substance of Community legislation.

The purpose of regulation 1049/2001

The objectives behind Regulation 1049/2001 are threefold. First, it strikes a balance between the various public and private interest grounds (which may justifiably be relied upon to curb or limit public access to European Parliament, Council and Commission documents) and the need to 'ensure the widest possible access to documents'. Secondly, and as a corollary to the first objective, it establishes rules designed to facilitate the 'easiest possible' exercise of the right of public access to documents. Thirdly, it is designed to promote good administrative practice on access to documents.

The new Regulation applies to all documents relating to policies, activities and decisions falling within the respective spheres of responsibility of the European Parliament, Council and Commission. The word 'document' encompasses anything containing substantive content whatever its medium, whether 'written on paper or stored in electronic form or as a sound, visual or audio-visual recording'.

Beneficiaries and scope of regulation 1049/2001

The right of access to the documents of the Community institutions is almost universal insofar as it vested in any 'citizen of the Union', and 'any natural or legal person residing or having its registered office in a Member State' of the Union (subject, of course, to the principles, conditions and limits set out in the Regulation). Although the aforementioned beneficiaries of the Regulation are defined in terms of European citizenship or residence, the institutions have a discretion to grant access to documents to any natural or legal person *not* residing or *not* having its registered office in a Member State.

Regulation 1049/2001 is far-reaching insofar as it applies to 'all documents held by an institution' including 'documents drawn up or received by it and in its possession' relating to 'all areas of the European Union'. As a general rule, documents must be made accessible to the public either following a written application or directly in electronic form or through a register. Given the importance attached to the twin concepts of openness and transparency in the context of the EU law-making process, it is scarcely surprising that all documents 'drawn up or received in the course of a legislative procedure' must be made 'directly accessible' (in accordance with a procedure which will be outlined at a later stage of this paper).

Special procedures operate in relation to public access to 'Top Secret', 'Secret' and 'Confidential' documents of a 'sensitive' nature. The rules governing access to such documents will be explained at a later juncture.

Exceptions to the right of public access to documents

Although the public is supposed to enjoy the 'widest possible access' to documents, there are two main categories of exceptions to the general rule. The first category comprises documents whose disclosure would undermine the protection of public interests such as public security, defence and military matters, international relations, financial, monetary or economic stability as well as the protection of the privacy and integrity of individuals in general (including documents relating to personal data). In these cases, the Community institutions are under an obligation to deny access, once the relevant circumstances have been substantiated.

The second category attributes a certain degree of discretion to the institution from which access to documents is requested. This category encompasses documents which would undermine: (i) the protection of the commercial interests of a natural or a legal person (including intellectual property), (ii) court proceedings and legal advice, (iii) the purpose of inspections, investigations and audits. The institutions are obliged to refuse access to such documents 'unless there is an overriding public interest in disclosure'. This proviso precludes institutions, such as the Council, from taking a blanket decision to refuse access to its documents under the discretionary exemption. Instead, the Council has to balance in each case its own interests in protecting confidentiality against the public's interest in access to Council documents. The same balancing exercise has to be performed in relation to documents drawn up by an institution for its own internal use (or received by an institution) in the context of its own decision-making process. If the institution concerned has yet to take a decision, it is obliged (subject, of course, to the overriding public interest in disclosure) to deny access to such documents in order to prevent its own decision-making process from being undermined.

The above exceptions only apply for the period during which protection is justified on the basis of the contents of the relevant documents. In any event, there is a thirty year cut-off period, after which the documents no longer enjoy any protection (save for documents relating to privacy or commercial interests and sensitive documents, all of which may, if necessary, benefit from protection from disclosure *after* the expiry of this period).

Documents in the possession of the Community institutions are often generated by third parties. In this context, 'third party' means any natural or legal person, or any entity outside the institution concerned, including the Member States, other Community or non-Community institutions and bodies and third countries. With regard to such documents, the institution concerned is obliged to consult with the third party with a view to ascertaining whether the documents comes within either of the exceptions outlined above, unless it is clear that access to the documents in question should be either granted or denied.

Documents emanating from or in the possession of Member States
It is important to point out that a Member State may request the European Parliament, Council or Commission (whichever is relevant) to refrain from disclosing a document originating from the Member State concerned to third parties without its prior agreement.

If a Member State receives a request for a European Community document in its possession, the Member State in question is obliged to consult with the institution from whence it originated in order to take a decision that would not 'jeopardise the attainment of the objectives of this Regulation'. If, however, it is clear from the content of the document that access to it should be either refused or denied, the Member State has the capacity to grant or refuse access. It is also open to the Member State concerned to refer the request for such documentation directly to the institution concerned.

The making and processing of applications

All applications for access to a document must be made in a written form (including electronic writing) in a sufficiently precise manner to enable the institution concerned to identify the document in question. If the application is imprecise, the institution concerned can request clarification from the applicant and/or provide information and assistance on how and where applications for access to documents can be made (including information and assistance relating to the existence and use of Community registers of documents). If the applicant refers, in his or her application, to a lengthy document or numerous documents, the institution concerned is entitled to confer with the applicant informally, 'with a view to finding a fair solution'.

The applicant is not obliged to provide reasons for his or her application. The institutions concerned will not inquire into the motives for which access is required. On the contrary, the twin principles of openness and transparency – which operate to monitor the use and abuse of powers by the institutions – dictate that no specific interest in the information has to be shown.

The institution concerned must handle all applications for access to documents promptly. Within fifteen working days of the registration of the application, the institution in question must: *either* (i) grant access to the document requested and provide access to it within that period or (ii) state, in writing, the reasons for a total or partial refusal to grant access and inform the applicant of his or her right to make a confirmatory application within fifteen working days of such total or partial refusal. In essence, a confirmatory application is a request from an applicant asking the institution concerned to re-consider a negative decision or to rectify a failure on its part to reply to an initial request for documents within the time limit of fifteen working days.

Similar time constraints operate in relation to the processing of confirmatory applications. The institution concerned must either provide access to the document requested within fifteen working days of the receipt of a confirmatory application or, in a written reply, state the reasons for a either a total or partial refusal to grant access. In the event of a total or partial refusal, the institution concerned must inform the applicant of the remedies open to him or her, 'namely instituting court proceeedings against the institution and/or making a complaint to the Ombudsman'. A failure on the part of the institution to reply will be construed as a negative reply and entitle the applicant to institute court proceedings against the institution concerned and/or make a complaint to the Ombudsman.

In exceptional cases involving lengthy documents or large numbers of documents the time limit of fifteen working days – which is normally applicable to both initial and confirmatory applications – may be extended by a further period of fifteen working days. This right to an extension of time is, however, subject to the proviso that the applicant be notified in advance and that detailed reasons to explain the necessity for an extension of time are given to him or her.

Treatment of sensitive documents

Sensitive documents are documents classified as 'Top Secret', 'Secret' or 'Confidential' in accordance with the rules of the Community institution concerned. Such documents generally originate from the Community institutions or the agencies established by them, from Member States, third countries or international organisations and relate mainly to 'public security, defence and military matters'. Applications for access to sensitive documents may only be handled by persons who have a right to acquaint themselves with such documents. Sensitive documents may only be released to an applicant with the consent of the originator. An institution which decides to refuse access to a sensitive document must give the reasons for its decision in a manner which is not detrimental to the interests which it is seeking to protect.

The scope and extent of public access to documents

The applicant is, according to his or her preference, entitled to either on the spot access to documents or a written copy of such documents (including, where available, an electronic copy or, if the applicant is blind or visually handicapped, in Braille, large print or on tape). Although the cost of producing and sending copies may be charged to the applicant, consultation on the spot, copies of less than twenty A4 pages and direct access in electronic form or through the register will all be made available to the applicant free of charge. If, however, a document has already been released by the institution concerned and is easily accessible to the applicant, it can fulfil its obligation of granting access to documents by informing the applicant how to obtain the requested document. All of the above provisions are without prejudice to any existing rules on copyright which may limit a third party's right to reproduce or exploit released documents.

Registers

To enhance the citizen's right of access to documents, the European Parliament, Council and Commission were all obliged to produce a register of documents relating to their respective institutions. The deadline date for the creation of fully operational registers (with electronic access) was 3 June 2002. With regard to each and every document which is registered, the register contains a reference number, the subject matter and/or a short description of the content of the document and the date on which it was received or drawn up and recorded in the register. Although each institution has its own separate register, where documents overlap as between two or more institutions the inter-institutional reference to such documents is recorded in all relevant registers.

There is also a provision in the Regulation which provides that the Community institutions shall, as far as possible, make documents directly accessible to the public in electronic form or through a register in accordance with the rules of the institution concerned. In particular, the Regulation emphasises the importance of making legislative documents (*viz.* 'documents received in the course of procedures for the adoption of acts which are legally binding in or for the Member States') directly accessible to the public. If direct access to a document is not available through the register, then the register itself must, so far as possible, indicate where the document is located.

Administrative practice in the institutions

The European Parliament, Council and Commission are all obliged to 'develop good administrative practices' in order to 'facilitate the right of access' enshrined in the Regulation. To this end, they have to establish an inter-institutional committee 'to examine best practice, address possible conflicts and discuss future developments on public access to documents'.

Each institution is also obliged to produce an annual report setting out the number of cases in which the institution concerned refused to grant access to documents, the reasons for such refusals and the number of sensitive documents not recorded in the register. The Commission is also obliged to undertake a review of the workings of the Regulation by 31 January 2004 at the latest and, if appropriate, make proposals for its revision and put forward an action programme of reforms to be undertaken by the institutions.

Conclusion

Many, if not all, of the recipients of the Nobel Prize for Literature have produced works which embody universal themes which hold good throughout the world. The reader in Cape Town or Nairobi is just as likely to identify with their work as the reader in Borris-in-Ossory or Abbeyfeale. Although the new Regulation on public access to documents could never, under any circumstances, be described as literature, its importance stems from the fact that the principles of openness and transparency embodied therein *might*, with appropriate modifications, be successfully adapted to serve the needs of many democracies and multi-national institutions currently without freedom of information legislation. Against this, however, the success of such initiatives depends, in substantial measure, on public participation and on the culture of the country or institution in which the initiative is being introduced. To date, the Commission has discovered that its openness initiatives have generated relatively little impact on the European public. Perhaps the more formalised struc-

ture (including the establishment of document registers) established by the new
Regulation and the advent of the electronic age will encourage greater public
participation in challenging the more questionable aspects of the Community
law-making and decision-making processes.

Judicial review by the Federal Constitutional Court in Germany

ELIZABETH MAYER

INTRODUCTION AND HISTORY

Often when one refers to the Federal Constitutional Court of Germany it is called the 'German Supreme Court' or the 'Federal Supreme Court', but both are incorrect even though it is the highest court in the country. It is not an ordinary court above all the other appeal courts within the judicial system. The Federal Constitutional Court (FFC) is only competent to decide on constitutional issues, to interpret if the constitutional rights of a person or a constitutional body have been infringed by an act or an action of the State or any public body acting on behalf of the State. In this paper the main tasks of the FCC will be described and the development of the FCC dispensation will be discussed.

German Basic Law (BL), when first announced on 23 May 1949, was conceived as an interim solution applicable only until German reunification should happen and so, it was not explicitly called the German Constitution at that time. However, under this Basic Law, the FCC has the power of final decision affecting all other constitutional bodies, even the democratic legislator, the Bundestag (BT), the Federal Parliament. This makes the FCC a very important and powerful constitutional organ that can control all other constitutional organs thoroughly. To understand the logic behind the FCC, it is worth looking at the development and history of the Basic Law.

After the capitulation of Germany on May 8 1945, the country was divided into four different zones each of which was governed by one of the Allied Forces. Because of tensions between the Western powers and the Soviet Union, the United States, France and Great Britain decided to strengthen the West German State, which was created to function as a stronghold against the communist East. In 1948 the western allies vested the power to convene a constitutional assembly to draft a constitution in the Minister Presidents of the remodelled States (Lander). The three western zones were meant to be joined together on a federal basis. The Minister Presidents of the West German Lander decided to convene an expert committee to draft recommendations that would then be submitted to the Parliamentary Council to be installed. At the Herrenchiemsee Constititional Convention a draft of the Basic Law was developed within two weeks.

There were two important influences on the draft of the BL. First, the Allied Powers strongly influenced the content of the Basic Law. They demanded restrictions on the powers of the federation, and were in favour of more legal competences for the Lander. They also influenced the financial order of the federation. Secondly, the Herrenchiemsee Constitutional Convention was convinced that there had been major flaws in the Constitution of Weimar and that it was partly due to these that Hitler had been able to gain power. Therefore, the Convention aimed to create a constitution that would limit the powers of the head of State, decentralise the country and establish a constitutional court the main task of which was to be to be the 'Huter der Verfassung', 'Guardian of the Constitution'.

There was also a lot of mistrust of the German people at that time as it was felt that they first had to be educated as democrats before they could be expected to act democratically. For that reason and also because the Basic Law was meant to be for an interim period only, there was no referendum by the German people to adopt that Basic Law as a constitution. The preamble of the Basic Law and Article 146 confirmed that interim status by stating that the German people are called upon to 'achieve in free self determination the unity and freedom of Germany' and that at the day on which the entire German people adopted a constitution, the Basic Law would cease to be in force. This, however, never happened as the reunification never occurred in the way foreseen by the members of the Constitutional Convention.

The members of the Constitutional Convention, in approving the Basic Law, had in mind the reunification of the German people within the territory of the German Reich of 1937, thus including not only the territory of the German Democratic Republic, but also the eastern territories that were occupied by either Soviet Russia or Poland. Instead, however, on 24 May 1949 the Basic Law came into force only within the boundaries of the States occupied by the western Allies, after all of these States, except the Free State of Bavaria, had agreed to approve the Basic Law.[1] Further, when the reunification of 'West' and 'East' Germany took place on 3 October 1990, it was not based on Article 146. The German Democratic Republic was unified with the Federal Republic of Germany by the Act of Accession pursuant to Article 23 of the Basic Law and Article 1 of the Unification Treaty. The two German States and the Allies signed the 'Two plus Four Treaty' of 12 September 1990; by this Treaty Germany signed away the claims on its eastern territories under occupation and became a sovereign State.

THE CONSTITUTIONAL ORDER AND TASKS AND POSITION OF THE FCC

The most important constitutional organs are the Federal Parliament (Bundestag),[2] the Federal Council (Bundesrat),[3] the Federal President,[4] the Federal

---

1 According to art. 144 BL the approval of only two thirds of the Lander was necessary for the BL to come into force. 2 Arts. 38–48 BL. 3 Arts. 50–53 BL. 4 Arts. 54–61 BL.

Government,[5] and the Federal Constitutional Court (FCC).[6] The five most important principles of the German State are defined in Article 20 section 2 BL: democracy; republicanism; governance of the rule of law, (separation of power, supremacy of the law); federalism; and social market economy. While the Basic Law in general can be changed by a two-thirds majority in both the Federal Parliament and the Federal Council, Article 20 cannot be changed at all, but is guaranteed and known as a so-called 'Ewigkeitsklausel', 'eternity clause'.

The FCC's position can be regarded as exceptional as it is the most independent and autonomous of the federal constitutional organs with the capacity to control all the other constitutional bodies and to check their actions according to their constitutionality. It is the highest body of jurisdiction and administration of justice within Germany and its rulings are binding for all federal constitutional organs, for the Lander and for all courts and public authorities. Thus, even the democratically elected Parliament as the authorised legislative body is controlled by the FCC's interpretation of the constitutionality of an act or any issue. No statutes can be enacted that contrave the Basic Law as all are subject to constitutional review. The Bundesverfassungsgerichtgesetz, Code of the Federal Constitutional Court, governs the organisation and competences of the FCC. It is not attached to any ministry, but has its own administration and a budget that in 1997 amounted to 26 million DM. Even though the FCC has its special status as a constitutional organ, it is not a political organ, but a court. It must not act *ex officio*, but solely when called upon by an authorised body. It is not the last stage of appeal in a sequence within the court system, but it is rather a sole instance different from the ordinary court system.

The ordinary court system is split into five different sections of jurisdiction: the administrative courts, headed by the Federal Administrative Court in Leipzig; the so called 'ordinary jurisdiction' dealing with civil and penal law, headed by the Federal Court of Justice in Karlsruhe; the financial jurisdiction with the Federal Finance Court in Munich; the labour jurisdiction and the Federal Labour Court in Erfurt; the social jurisdiction with the Federal Social Court in Kassel. In contrast to these courts the task of the FCC is to monitor that all State organs and acts observe the constitution. It is the first and final instance for constitutional issues only.

The FCC consists of two senates each of them composed of eight professional judges. The FCC judges are elected by the Bundestag and the Bundesrat that each determine one half of the judges. According to §§ 5 to 7 of the Code of the Federal Constitutional Court a two-thirds majority is required for the election of a FCC judge. So far in the history of Germany neither one individual party nor a government coalition of two or more parties has ever had a two thirds majority in either the Bundestag or the Bundesrat.[7] Therefore,

---

5 Arts. 62 –69 BL. **6** Arts. 93, 94, 99, 100 BL. **7** The judges who are elected by the Bundesrat are elected directly, the ones that are selected by the Bundestag are indirectly elected by a twelve-man board consisting of Bundestag members.

even though the election of the FCC judges is a political one, it is far from the situation in the United States, where either ultra conservative or very progressive candidates are appointed.

In Germany the two big parties, the conservative Christian Democratic Union, CDU (together with its Bavarian sister party, the Christian Social Union) and the Social Democratic Party of Germany, SPD, always have to seek a compromise when electing an FCC judge as only the consensus of the two big players will guarantee a two-third majority. This leads to the result that no 'extreme' candidate has a real chance to get elected as he or she would be refused by either the SPD or the CDU. In practise, alternately the SPD and the CDU would come forward with a candidate, but the candidate must be able to find approval from both. When the SPD had proposed Frau Herta Daubler-Gmelin (Minister of Justice in the current SPD / Green Government) to be elected as FCC judge, the CDU felt that she was not an acceptable candidate, so the Social Democrats suggested Professor Jutta Limbach instead who is now the President of the FCC. This regulation has led to a political balance within the FCC so far and has proven to be a useful instrument to prevent hardliners from filling these responsible positions.

The judges are elected for twelve years, but cannot be re-elected after their term. According to Article 4 section 3 of the Code of the FCC, a judge will retire at the end of the month in which he or she reaches the age of 68.

TYPES OF PROCEEDINGS OF THE FCC

In regard to the powers of the FCC the principle of enumeration (*Enumerationsprinzip*) applies. This determines that the FCC does not automatically have jurisdiction for all possible disputes on constitutional issues, but may only act by operation of law. The competences of the FCC are enumerated in Article 93 BL and Article 13 of the Code of the FCC. These provisions enumerate in numbers 1 to 15 the proceedings to be adjudicated by the FCC. The FCC cannot act on its own initiative, but only in pursuance of an external application. The eligibility to make such an application varies from procedure to procedure as there are particular preconditions for the admissibility of certain procedures. The applicant initiating proceedings must be an entitled person or organ for filing the application with the legal ability to institute proceedings. An application generally can only then be admissible if the applicant asserts that his or her constitutional rights have been infringed by a measure or omission of the respondent. The BL Article that is thought to be infringed must be specified in the application. Only if the application is admissible will the Court decide if it is well-founded.

The most important proceedings before the FCC shall now be explained.

A. Disputes between constitutional organs

According to Article 93 section 1–1 BL a dispute on any question between constitutional organs concerning their respective constitutional rights and obligations can be brought to the FCC. As the principle of the separation of powers applies, no constitutional organ shall exceed or abuse its own power to the disadvantage of another constitutional body.

One example of a dispute between organs was the decision of the FCC of 29 September 1990,[8] that, during the unique and special circumstances of the first federal election after reunification, the five per cent hurdle for a party to enter the Bundestag was unconstitutional. As the reunification had only taken place shortly before the federal election, not all parties would equally have the chance to campaign pan-German wide. So, in the first federal election after reunification, the five per cent hurdle was amended in the following way: a party needed to gain five per cent of the votes either in the territory of former East or West Germany to get into the Bundestag.

Another example of great political controversy was the decision of the FCC of 12 July 1994 on the participation of German soldiers in either NATO or WEU missions aimed at implementing UN Security Council resolutions or in peace-keeping forces created by the UN, in both the former Yugoslavia and in Somalia. The Federal Government had decided to send German soldiers to these areas without seeking the consent of the Bundestag. As German troops had been in the Balkans during WW II committing horrendous crimes there, this caused concern within large parts of the German population, which was articulated by demonstrations and a new debate about Germany's political role within Europe and the world.

The Social Democrats and the Liberal Democrats initiated the proceedings, raising two issues. First, can German soldiers take part in armed missions at all according to the BL? Secondly, are the constitutional rights of the Bundestag infringed by the Federal Government sending off troops without the consent of the Bundestag? The FCC decided that German troops may participate in armed NATO and UN missions, under the BL, but that the consent of the Bundestag must be sought before sending these out. Thus, the Federal Government had exceeded its power when it had sent out the troops without consent.

This issue became topical again when a debate started about the potential participation of German troops in a mission to Macedonia. The Bundestag and the Federal Government were again disagreeing on policy. However, on 18 August 2001, the CDU opposition leader, Schauble, came forward with the idea to change the constitution in regard to the participation of the German army in NATO or UN missions. He suggested changing the BL in a way that

---

8 Decisions of the FCC vol. 82 n322.

would allow the Federal Government the sole decision on such an action without seeking consent of the Bundestag. If there was a majority within the SPD and CDU/CSU for this suggestion in the Bundestag and the Bundesrat of two thirds, this change could be made to the BL. That would allow for more flexible and quicker decisions on these, often urgent matters. However, it would lead to a new era of post-war German politics by empowering the Government in disadvantage to the Parliament, when in the beginning purposely the powers had been strongly limited.

B. Disputes between the Federation and the Lander
In these disputes the parties can only be the Federation on the one side and a Land or some Lander on the other, or a Land/some Lander versus one other Land or Lander. Matters of controversy are constitutional rights and obligations between the Federation and the Lander or any legal dispute between them in general if no other recourse to the courts is at hand. By this means, the FCC can ensure that the principle of federalism will be complied with.

In a decision of 26 March 1957 the FCC ruled that the Lander are not bound by an international treaty of the federation in regard to matters concerning education. The object of the legal dispute was the difference of opinion between the Federation and the Land of Lower Saxony as to whether it had contravened the Concordat between the Holy See and the German Reich of 20 July 1933 by enacting the Act on Public Schooling of 14 September 1954 thereby infringing the right of the Federation to respect by the Lander for international treaties binding upon it.

After the Land of Lower Saxony had enacted the Public Schooling Act, the Apostolic Nuncio complained to the Federal Government against a number of provisions of the Act, because of their incompatibility with the Reich Concordat. On behalf of the Federation, the Federal Government called for a decision of the FCC on the difference of opinion that had arisen with the Land of Lower Saxony. The proceedings were joined by the Land of Hesse and the Free Hanseatic City of Bremen, both supporting Lower Saxony's petition.

The FCC ruled that the Lander cannot be bound by the schooling provisions of the Reich Concordat (or any international treaty) as the Lander are solely entitled to decide on education. The Reich Concordat signed by the Nazi Government and the Holy See therefore contradicted the basic principles of the BL that shape the relationship of Federation and Lander in a different way. The FCC confirmed that according to Articles 7, 30 and 70 ff BL the Lander are the sole bearers of cultural sovereignty.

At the time of writing, a similar topic is under review of the FCC. The Land of Brandenburg has decided not to offer religion classes separated by faith, but a general 'ethics' class instead as over 80 per cent of the students are not members of any church.

C. General norm control proceedings

The Constitutional Law provides for two types of proceedings to review the constitutionality of laws: the abstract or general norm control and the concrete or specific norm control. Up to January 2004 there have been 3377 norm control proceedings; of these only 125 were general. The organs which are entitled to file an abstract norm control proceeding are restricted to the Federal Government, the Government of a region or one-third of the members of the Bundestag only. As a certain peculiarity there is no respondent in this sort of proceeding, but if the application is legally justified because the norm in question violated the BL, the FCC will declare that norm as void or incompatible with the BL. In that case, the statute would not be void immediately, but the legislator instead would be asked to either abrogate the statute or to amend it in a way to make it compatible with the BL. If a statute can be interpreted in different ways and partly the interpretation would 'lead to an unconstitutional result, but partly to a constitutional result, the provision is constitutional and must be interpreted (only) in a constitutional manner.' If only one provision of a statute is found to be unconstitutional, there are no means by which the whole statute could be found void.

The most prominent and controversial examples of general norm control proceedings are the FCC decisions on abortion.

In 1974 the Social Democratic and Liberal Government enacted the Abortion Law Reform Act under which, even though abortion in general remained criminalized, it was provided that an abortion performed by a physician with the pregnant woman's consent would be legal during the first twelve weeks of pregnancy. Before the statute came into force, 193 members of the Bundestag and some State governments initiated abstract norm control proceedings that led to the so-called First Abortion Decision of the FCC. The FCC declared the Abortion Law Reform Act as unconstitutional as it held that Article 2 section 2 of the BL 'also protects the developing life within the womb as an independent value', and that the State had to protect the foetus against 'third parties' including the pregnant woman in an efficient way. It states that the legislator 'can be under an obligation to use the criminal law as a means of protecting the developing life'.

Here, the FCC not only declared a statute unconstitutional, but went further, recommending the use of the criminal law to the legislator. This dictates to the legislator not only 'what' had to be done: to protect the right to life of the unborn child against third parties, which logically fits into the system, but also the 'how' by which this protection could be reached: this would fall under the competence of the Bundestag as the democratically legitimated legislator only, but here the 'Guardian of the Constitutional Order' takes this right into his own hands by prescribing the criminal law to the legislator as the way of protection.

But the FCC in that decision marches further into the direction of legislation by listing reasons for the legality of an abortion. It states that if there are 'circumstances of considerable weight which make the fulfilment of this duty [continuation with the pregnancy] so extraordinarily difficult', it cannot reasonably be expected. These circumstances include 'aversion of a danger for the woman's life' or health, genetic abnormalities of the foetus, pregnancy as a consequence of rape or social hardship due to the pregnancy.

It is unclear what gives the FCC the competence to dictate the conditions under which the protection of the child can be abandoned so specifically. It is completely incomprehensible how the FCC could have been entitled to the value judgement that the genetic abnormality of an unborn child is a justification for an abortion, as the FCC stated that the unborn child is included in the 'everybody' in the meaning of Article 2, section 2 BL and there is no difference in the protection of the right to life for a person who is already born with a genetic abnormality to one without it.

However, as the FCC is the one and last resort in any constitutional issue, there is no way of controlling the FCC itself and little can be done if the FCC itself perhaps exceeds or even abuses its power, even if the principle of separation of power might be at risk. After the First Abortion Decision, the Bundestag enacted an amended Abortion Law Reform Act that included all the points mentioned by the FCC as indications for a legal abortion.

After the reunification a new abortion law needed to be negotiated, as in the Reunification Treaty no compromise was found between the position of the German Democratic Republic (abortion legal within the first 12 weeks of the pregnancy) and that of the Federal Republic of Germany. Under a conservative Government of the CDU/CSU and the Liberal Democrats, a compromise was reached that made abortions lawful within the first trimester of the pregnancy if the pregnant woman had sought and received counselling prior to the abortion. The Bavarian Government and 249 members of the Bundestag filed a norm control proceeding against that reform, and again with the Second Abortion Decision, the FCC confirmed that the State must protect the unborn life, but changed its position to the use of the criminal law:

> It accords with the respect owed to a woman and expectant mother that the State does not … evade their maternal tasks by a general threat with punishment, but by individual counselling and an appeal to their responsibility for the unborn life, by economic and social support and by particular information referring thereto. The legislator can rightly be of the opinion that [the attainment of this goal] would be hindered rather than promoted if a third party had to examine and assess the reasons for which a woman finds it unreasonable to carry her child to term.

The FCC obliged the legislator to change its Abortion Reform Act again, by describing almost verbally what could and would be accepted by the Court, for example, that merely informative counselling was not sufficient, but that the counsellor 'must have motivation to encourage the woman to continue her pregnancy and to provide perspectives for her life with a child'.

When reading the First and Second Abortion Decision, one wonders what Germany needs its legislative body for as, at least for politically controversial issues, it is almost certain that a decision will be sought by the FCC in the end. As the FCC in its decisions does almost dictate what is acceptable and what is not, it might as well draft the Statute in the first place. In any case the boundaries between the judiciary and the legislature are at risk, or at least under question, when an institution as powerful as the FCC almost becomes the legislator. On the other hand, it can be seen that responsibility is pushed away by other constitutional organs to the FCC that has to decide on any controversial topic.

D. *Specific norm proceedings*

A case of this type occurs when any court in Germany (except the FCC) considers a statute or provision to be unconstitutional if that law is relevant to its specific decision in a case. In such a situation, the court cannot itself declare that law invalid, but must transmit the file of that case to the FCC and state both why the decision of the case depends on the validity of the statute submitted for review and why it considers that law to be unconstitutional. The FCC is the only court that can declare a democratically enacted law (any post-constitutional law as opposed to either pre-constitutional ones or governmental ordinances that can be reviewed by any court) null and void.

These proceedings account for the second largest share of the FCC's activities. By the end of 2003, more than 3,200 cases were pending before the court, 1,065 decisions had been handed down and about 400 statutory provisions had been found void. One of the most famous specific norm proceedings is the FCC ruling on the constitutionality of the integration of Germany into the European Community, the so-called 'Solange I' Decision. Here, the administrative court of Frankfurt/Main dealt with an application of a German import/export company. The administrative court had first obtained a preliminary ruling from the European Court of Justice under Article 177 of the Treaty establishing the EEC as to whether some rules referring to the case were lawful under the law of the EEC. Then the administrative court stayed its proceedings and requested a ruling of the FCC under Article 100 BL as to whether the obligation to export existing under ECC law was compatible with the BL.

The administrative court took the view that ECC law could be examined for its compatibility with the BL as it is not entitled to take precedence over national law in its entirety. The Second Senate of the FCC decided that as long as the integration process has not progressed so far that Community law incorporates a catalogue of rights comparable with the one of the BL, a reference by a German court to the FCC in judicial review proceedings, following the obtaining of a ruling of the ECC, is admissible and necessary if the German court regards the rule of Community law which is relevant to the decision as inapplicable in the interpretation given by the European

Court, because and insofar as it conflicts with one of the fundamental rights of the BL.

Thus, we find again that the FCC in its unique power can even decide whether or not the German constitution has some priority over European laws, even though there are binding treaties providing the European law's superiority. Further attempts of EU opponents to have, for example, the Treaty of Maastricht and Amsterdam declared unconstitutional by the FCC have been unsuccessful, but it is still possible that the ruling of the FCC could stop the further integration of Germany into the European Union by a Court decision.

E. Article 100 section 2 and section 3 BL procedure

There are only a small number of cases that have ever come up under either Article 100 section 2 or section 3 BL. At the end of 2002, there were 24 Article 100 section 2 BL cases pending before the FCC and seven had been decided; eight Article 100 section 3 BL cases were pending before the FCC and five decisions had been handed down.

Pursuant to Article 100 section 2 BL, the FCC will decide on the request of a court if an act or a rule of public international law can be an integral part of German Federal law, and if so, whether that law can directly create obligations and rights for an individual. The incorporation of general rules of public international law into the law of the German Federation would lead to those rules taking precedence over German national law. But by giving the FCC the right to control even those laws by checking their constitutionality, we can see again that the authority of the FCC is large and even international treaties can be found in breach of Federal Constitutional law and, therefore, invalid insofar as they would, for instance, oblige an individual to act accordingly.

Pursuant to Article 100 section 3 BL, the constitutional court of a German State that in interpreting the Basic Law by itself proposes to deviate from a decision of the FCC must obtain a decision from the FCC to find out if that interpretation is to be found constitutional by the FCC. The same decision by the FCC has to be sought by a State constitutional court that proposes to deviate from a decision of the constitutional court of another State.

F. Constitutional Complaint, 'Verfassungsbeschwerde'

The Constitutional Complaint is governed by Article 93 section 1 No 4a BL and it is a complaint against an Act of the State infringing the basic rights of another person. Constitutional complaints are of utmost importance in the constitutional order of Germany as they ensure the constitutional rights of the individual versus the State. Up to January 2004, there were almost 147,000 cases pending before the FCC of which more than 141,000 were constitutional complaints. Only 2.5% of the complaints had been successful. Even so, the impact of the FCC decisions on constitutional complaints is far reaching as a decision does not only concern the two parties involved in the procedure, but the general population, as the decisions are binding on all public authorities in the interpretation of constitutional rights. Even a case that has been unsuccessful can lead to some sort of change as often the FCC would give a certain opinion in the statement of the reasons for the decision that can have an impact on the legislature, the executive and the judiciary.

There are also a number of successful cases that are not included in the three per cent, because they were settled by the public bodies involved to the advantage of the complainant e.g., when the State body has sought legal opinions while the case is pending at the FCC that convinced them to rethink their interpretation of the law in favour of the complainant.

Admissibility of a constitutional complaint
There are strict, exclusive preconditions of a constitutional complaint that have to be met in order that it is admissible at all and will be heard by the FCC:

(1) A complainant must show that there is at least a theoretical possibility that his or her Basic Rights have been infringed. A Basic Right can be any one right included in the catalogue of Articles 1 to 19 BL. A complaint concerning any other violation of rights would not be accepted by the FCC as the violation of Basic Rights is the FCC's one and only subject.

(2) The violation must be 'direct, personal and present'. A constitutional complaint can only challenge an act that directly violates a basic right. That means that a complainant must challenge an act the State has taken against him or her, by the execution or implementation of a statute, rather than challenging the statute itself as the abstract statute itself normally cannot harm the citizen directly. This means, for example, that in the case of Paragraph 1355 section 2 of the Civil Code that obliged a wife to take her husband's name when they got married, no woman could file a complaint just because she felt that this rule violated her basic right of Article 3 BL concerning equality of men and women. Only when she got married and was forced to accept her husband's name at the civil marriage, could she fight this implementation of that rule. This was done successfully only in 1991, when the FCC ruled that Paragraph 1355 section 2 Civil Code was in breach of Article 3 BL and therefore void, after a constitutional complaint in the 1950s on the same issue had been unsuccessful.[9]

The only exception to that rule is when the statute describes a criminal offence. Then a complainant would not have to wait until the rule was implemented against him or her as that could cause too much hardship on a person. Thus, a statute criminalising an action could be taken to the FCC by a complainant before a 'direct' act by the State had caused him or her damage. The

9 BVerfGE 84, 9 1991, Surname of Married Couples Decision.

complainant must also show that the violation of right concerns him or her personally, but no infringements of third parties can be challenged. As an exception again, parents can complain if their children's rights are infringed when these children are minors and can only be represented in court by their parents.

The violation of rights must be present. It is not enough that the violation is likely to happen in the future. For example, in the *Surname of Married Couples Case*, it would not have been possible for the woman who was only planning to marry to file the constitutional complaint, even though it was certain that she would be forced to accept her husband's surname when she got married. Her constitutional complaint was admissible only when the violation was present, when she got married and her name and personal papers were changed against her wish.

(3) The violation must be an act of a State body The notion of a State or public body is very broad and includes any executive or legislative organ as well as the judiciary. Thus, any act by a civil servant acting on behalf of the State can be challenged.

(4) Before a complainant can seek an FCC decision, all ordinary court remedies must have been unsuccessfully sought. Only after there are no more appeals possible is the way to the FCC open.

Constitutional court decisions on complaints
Human dignity Article 1 BL states that 'Human dignity shall be inviolable. To respect and protect it shall be the duty of all State authority.' This rule opens the canon of Human and Civil Rights articles that come first in the German Basic Law before the rules concerning the State beginning with Article 20 BL. Article 1 BL together with Article 20 BL are the only regulations that cannot be changed under Article 79 section 3 BL that guarantees them for 'eternity'.

Even though Article 1 BL sounds rather abstract, it puts specific and legally enforceable obligations on the State towards the protection of its citizens, and the FCC held that the individual dignity of people is to be the main principle of the German constitution.[10] All other articles depend on Article 1 BL and have to be interpreted with it in mind. The FCC interpreted Article 1 very early in a constitutional complaint and stated that 'no person shall be handled in a way that merely degrades him to be the object of certain steps taken by the State and its organs;'[11] Human dignity is seen by the FCC as a:

> fundamental principle within the system of basic rights … It is not only the individual dignity of every person, but also the dignity of the human

10 BverfGE 32, 98–110. 11 BVerfGE 9, 95.

> being as a species. Everybody possesses human dignity, regardless of his characteristics ... Those who cannot act in a meaningful way because of their ... condition also possess human dignity. It is not even forfeited by means of undignified behaviour; and it cannot be taken away from any human being.

This means that human dignity can not be given or taken away, but is based on the very existence of a human person. In many decisions on complaints the FCC has developed a framework of standards that have to be guaranteed to ensure the dignity of human beings:

Guarantee of minimal standard of life Germany has the principle of being a social welfare state as one of its five main State principles and Article 1 BL, as the main human rights article, has to guarantee at least a minimal standard of life for everybody. That means that anybody who cannot provide for his or her own life has a constitutional right to receive social welfare payments that enable him or her to live a dignified life. Thus, the costs for housing, clothes, food, and also for some basic participation in social or religious life, have to be met by the State.[12] This is true especially for prisoners. In a case where a prison cell had been flooded occasionally with faeces from a blocked waste pipe, the FCC held that these conditions were incompatible with respect for human dignity.[13]

Equality There are also many decisions on Article 3 BL which states:

(1) All persons shall be equal before the law.
(2) Men and women shall have equal rights. The State shall promote the actual implementation of equal rights for women and men and take steps to eliminate disadvantages that now exist.
(3) No person shall be favoured or disfavoured because of sex, parentage, race, language, homeland and origin, faith, or religious or political opinions. No person shall be disfavoured because of disability.

In the *Housework Day Case*[14] the FCC decided that it was unconstitutional to grant female employees one free day for household work, when men were not given the same option. That household work had traditionally been the work of women could not matter, as there were no biological differences that could possibly justify the different treatment. The FCC also declared a rule unconstitutional that had determined that women were not allowed to work during the night as that rule would prevent equal job opportunities for women and men, because women were legally excluded from access to any of those jobs.[15]

12 BverfGE 84, 133, 1991. 13 BverfG NJW 1993,3190. 14 BVerfGE 52, 369, 1979. 15 BVerfGE 85, 191, 1992.

Religion The FCC has been criticised greatly by the Free State of Bavaria for its decision on religious neutrality of the State in the *Crucifix Decision*.[16] Article 4 section 1 BL states that: 'Freedom of faith and conscience, and freedom to profess a religion or philosophical creed, shall be inviolable.' That guarantees positive and negative freedom of religion. However, the Bavarian authorities had ordered a crucifix put up in every classroom. A family with children who were attending a Bavarian State school protested against the crucifixes in the school rooms and asked for their removal. The school authorities refused to remove the crucifixes arguing that they were obliged to put them up. The administrative courts in Bavaria confirmed their decision, but the FCC decided that: 'Freedom of religion corresponds with the freedom to keep away from religious actions of a belief that one does not share. This freedom extends to religious symbols. Article 4 section 1 BL leaves it to the individual to decide which religious symbols he recognises and worships and which he rejects.'

Thus, it did not matter that the majority of school children and their parents were Catholic and in favour of a crucifix in the classroom. The State has to show neutrality as this is the idea of the German secular State. The argument by the Bavarian government that the cross was merely a cultural symbol was rejected as well. The FCC held that it was not a symbol of western culture, but a religious one. At the time of writing, a case is pending at the FCC concerning an Islamic woman who wishes to teach in a State school wearing a scarf. She was refused a job as a teacher in the civil service citing State neutrality towards religion as the reason.

Freedom of expression Article 5 section 1 BL states that: 'Every person shall have the right to freely express and disseminate his opinions in speech, writing, and pictures and to inform himself without hindrance from generally accessible sources.' In the *Soldiers Are Murderers* decision,[17] the FCC held that the complainants, three people who had previously been convicted for slander (insult) of German Bundeswehr soldiers, had a right to express their opinion on soldiers, even in the radical way of either using a sticker that said 'Soldiers Are Murderers', or writing a leaflet that stated 'Soldiers are trained to be murderers. You shall not kill turns into you have to kill. World wide. In the Bundeswehr, too,' or sending a letter to the editor that said 'All soldiers are potential murderers.' It cannot depend on the content of the opinion, but the freedom of opinion is safeguarded no matter whether the content is 'desirable' or 'undesirable'.

Finally, there are also interim decisions that can be sought by the FCC.

G. Provisional orders
If there is an urgent reason for the issue of a provisional order, the FCC may issue such an order according to § 32 FCC Code. The FCC can do so with

16 BVerfGE, 93,1, 1995. 17 BVerfGE, 93, 266, 1995.

respect to any type of procedure, but there is a high standard to be met to issue a provisional order. Only if the consequences of not issuing an interim order would make it almost impossible to be corrected later, could such an order shall be granted.

The Bavarian Government asked for an interim order to prevent the enactment of a federal law on 1 August 2001, that allows homosexuals to get married (by civil registration). The Bavarian Government felt that an interim order was necessary as a decision after the first marriages would have taken place might be too late. However, the FCC held that the claim of the Bavarian Government would not warrant the granting of an interim order.

There are a few other procedures of lesser importance, such as a constitutional complaint of a local authority; the forfeiture of basic rights (no decision ever by the FCC); the prohibition of a party (five occasions so far with one pending against a nationalist right wing party, the NPD); scrutiny of elections; and the impeachment of the Federal President or Federal judges (no case ever). There are far more cases concerning the articles mentioned and concerning the other basic rights that have not been mentioned here, but the ones demonstrated show that the general and the political impact of the FCC decisions, especially because of constitutional complaints, is very strong.

The FCC has the last say in any constitutional matter and has often corrected the executive, the judiciary and even the legislature, sometimes by unpopular decisions. Often it has protected minority rights versus the majority. This is a particular model of democracy, different for example to the one traditionally favoured in Great Britain, where the democratically elected legislative body is the supreme body and the judiciary cannot control the parliament. (The Human Rights Act 1998 has tempered, but not completely abolished, this philosophy). The German system has been created that way to ensure the utmost division of power. Thus, the German Chancellor is weaker than the British Prime Minister, and the German President is Head of State, but cannot at all be compared with the French or the American President. It must be remembered that when the German State had been created, there was a huge distrust in the German people and in their representatives as well.

However, the FCC with all its competence and power has so far proven that it is doing its job efficiently and effectively and has not abused its power. It seems to get used by the other constitutional bodies more and more to decide on any major critical issue, which can lead to responsibility that should be taken up by the parliament pushed over to this specific court. But as the FCC has so far shown that it has the capability to do its job well and it has upheld and safeguarded the constitutional principles, the model might not be a bad one in the end.

The FCC has been the Guardian of the Constitution, but the success of democracy in Germany still might have less to do with the constitutional model of the BL versus the 'flawed' one from Weimar than with the successful implementation of the Marshall Plan in the 1950s. It is this that has convinced the

German people of the value of western democracy more than any constitution could possibly have done. However, the FCC has the benefit of having been neutral, safeguarding minority rights and having gained the reputation of a liberal interpretation of the German constitution. Without it, family law, labour law, for example, would not have developed so progressively as seemingly individuals were quicker in asking for their constitutional rights than the legislature granting them.

4 SOCIAL AND POLITICAL DIMENSIONS

The work of the Irish Law Reform Commission: an overview

DECLAN BUDD

FUNCTION AND COMPOSITION

The Law Reform Commission was established as a statutory body corporate, by the Law Reform Commission Act of 1975. The essential function of the Commission, as described by section 4 of that Act, is:

(a) to undertake examination and conduct research with a view to reforming the law;
(b) to formulate proposals for reform.

Reform, for the purposes of the Act, is defined broadly to include the 'development' of the law as well as the revision and codification of statute law.[1] The Commission is comprised of a President, who, so far has always been a serving or retired Supreme Court or High Court Judge, a whole-time Commissioner and four part-time Commissioners, all being practising or academic lawyers of distinction and experience.

SOURCES OF WORK

There are two sources of work for the Commission. First, topics emanate from a general 'Programme of Work'. Provision is made under section 4(2)(a) for the establishment of such a Programme. This is prepared in consultation with the Attorney General for submission by the Taoiseach to Government.

The second source of work is from 'ad hoc references' sent by the Attorney General. Authority is conferred on the Attorney General to forward such references under section 4(2)(c) of the Act. Referred matters need not fall within the Work Programme.

THE METHOD OF WORK

Once a decision is taken to research a particular subject then consideration is given by the Commission as to how best to proceed. The normal practice is

1 Law Reform Commission Act 1975, section 2.

to issue a consultation paper.[2] This may be given limited circulation or may be broadly circulated depending on the topic and the likely level of interest. The Commission looks for submissions in response to the Paper from interested members of the public and experts, including practitioners, government departments and academics. Often a seminar is convened to stimulate discussion of contentious issues and to elicit suggestions. After considering the various submissions, the Commission formulates its final recommendations and prepares a Report, and in recent times has drafted and appended appropriate statutory provisions.

In some instances the Commission may decide it is more appropriate to dispense with the Consultation Paper and proceed directly to drafting and considering a final Report. The preparation of either a Working Paper or a Report often entails extensive comparative research,[3] and the framing of a draft Bill.[4]

The Commission is authorised to convene 'working parties or advisory committees' if deemed necessary.[5] Such advisory committees are usually made up of leading experts and practitioners in a particular field and are convened by a member of the Commission. A standing working group was set up in 1987 in the field of Land Law and Conveyancing. In 1999 a special working group was formed to prepare for the Hague Convention on International Jurisdiction and the Effects of Foreign Judgments in Civil and Commercial Matters. In 2001, both a Landlord and Tenant working group and a Judicial Review group were established. Groups to tackle the Law of Charities and the Codification of the Law in respect of Limitations periods have also been set up.

The Commission is obliged under the Act to produce an annual report. This report is furnished to the Attorney General in the first instance and is then forwarded to the Taoiseach who lays it before both Houses of the Oireachtas. Among other things, the annual report contains information about legislation passed following the recommendations of the Commission.[6]

THE RESEARCH PROCESS

Responsibility for conducting research and producing texts rests with the research side of the house. It is directed by the Director of Research and carried out by several researchers. The Commission also contracts out the preparation of draft Consultation Papers and Reports to academics and practitioners with specialised knowledge in particular fields. The actual research conducted is generally historical, contemporary and comparative in scope. It looks at the developments in other common law jurisdictions and also increasingly at the law in civil law jurisdictions like France, Italy and Germany.

---

2 Strictly speaking, a Working Paper as set out in section 4(3)(f) of the Act.   3 S. 4(3)(b).   4 S. 4(3)(c).   5 S. 4(3)(b)(e).   6 S. 6.

The responsibility for debating, modifying and adopting Consultation Papers and Reports rests with the Commission as a collegiate body.

THE WORK TO DATE

The Commission was operating under its first Working Programme between 1977 and 2000. Over 60 Consultation Papers and Reports have been adopted on topics as diverse as plain language and statutory interpretation; defamation; personal injuries; family courts; sentencing; privacy; and the law governing inter-country adoption.

Much of this work has led to reforming legislation. For example, the important Report on *Statutory Drafting and Interpretation: Plain Language and the Law*[7] recommended some reform measures of fundamental importance. First, the Commission accepted that the literal rule should remain the primary rule of statutory interpretation. However, it recommended that a court should be enabled to depart from the literal interpretation and prefer an interpretation based on the plain intention of the legislature in cases where a legislative provision is ambiguous or obscure, or when a literal interpretation would be absurd or would fail to reflect the plain intention of the legislature.

The Commission recommended that in construing a provision of any Act, a court should be able to make allowances for any changes in the law, social conditions, technology, the meaning of words and other relevant matters, which have occurred since the date of the passing of the Act, so far as its text, purpose and context permit.

There is an existing statutory provision in Irish law,[8] which states that marginal notes and cross-headings which appear with the text of an Act when it is published should not 'be taken to be part of the Act ... or be considered or judicially noticed in relation to the construction or interpretation of the Act'. The Commission recommended the repeal of this provision and considered that in construing the provisions of an Act, a court ought to be able to make use of all matters that are set out in the document containing the text of the Act as officially printed.

A final recommendation made by the Commission in its Report related to the use of 'extrinsic aids' to statutory interpretation. These include: relevant reports of committees of the Irish legislature; treaties and international agreements to which reference is made in an Act; official explanatory memoranda; speeches made by a Minister on the second reading of a Bill in Parliament; and publications of such bodies as the Law Reform Commission. The Commission considered the use of such material in statutory interpretation and provided an exhaustive list of the types of material to which a court should, in its view,

---

7 LRC 61–2000. 8 S. 11 (g), Interpretation Act, 1937.

be entitled to refer. However, it recommended that in considering the weight
to be accorded to such material, a court should have regard to the desirability
of persons being able to rely on the ordinary meaning of the words of an Act,
and the need to avoid prolonging any legal or other proceedings without com-
pensating advantage.

SOME OF THE AREAS UNDER REVIEW

In December 2000 the Second Working Programme was established. The
Programme's contents reflect the rapid changes in Irish society. It includes topics
such as government accountability; judicial review; the law in respect of privacy on the internet and encryption; the law and the elderly; and restorative
justice.

Some topics under research are set out in synopsis below.

Homicide: the mental element in murder; provocation; legitimate defence
The Consultation Paper was published in 2001 and subsequently the
Commission held a seminar to gauge reaction from the legal community and
the public to the Commission's provisional recommendations on the reform
of the law of homicide. The Commission's principal proposal is that the net of
liability for murder should be widened to include the reckless killer who exhibits
extreme indifference to the taking of human life. As the law stands, the definition of murder is confined to intentional killings and may not cover situations
where the defendant bombs or burns a building knowing the actions pose a
grave peril to human life. The Commission's proposal, if accepted, would enable
defendants of this type to be convicted of murder. In the Commission's opinion, the justification for extending the definition of murder to such killers is
that, by showing extreme indifference to the value of human life, they are no
less culpable than the intentional killer.

The Consultation Paper on Provocation traces its early development
through to modern times and looks comparatively at other jurisdictions to
examine whether Irish law should be changed or improved in light of the various models employed in those other jurisdictions.

The Consultation Paper in relation to legitimate defence in cases involving homicide is currently being prepared. The paper examines the traditional
rules for the defence, including the threat requirements (namely, that life is
endangered, and the threat is imminent and unlawful), and the response requirements (namely, that the defender's response is necessity and proportionate).
The paper also considers which standard is most appropriate to the defence,
namely an objective, a subjective, or a mixed or dual standard.

Corporate homicide

A Consultation Paper is currently being prepared which deals with the liability of corporations for the death of human persons. It is widely perceived that the law does not deal appropriately with corporations and the persons who control them in circumstances where corporate wrongs result in death. The Paper will review the current law and consider whether a new corporate offence should be introduced or whether the existing law should be extended to take account, in either case, of corporate practice in the formation of policy and intent.

Prosecution appeals

A consultation paper is currently being prepared in relation to whether the prosecution should have broader rights to appeal against trial rulings. Currently, the prosecution has a limited *without prejudice* right to appeal in cases where a trial judge directs the jury to acquit the accused. Hence, notwithstanding a finding by the appellate court that the trial judge was in error, the acquittal cannot be disturbed. Furthermore, rulings other than directed verdicts are not subject to prosecution appeal, yet may create precedents for future cases. The paper considers whether reform is needed and, if so, whether prosecution appeals should be on a *with prejudice* basis or whether the current *without prejudice* right of appeal should be expanded to encompass a wider range of trial rulings.

Restorative justice and alternatives to custodial sentencing

The Consultation Paper is in its early stages. Restorative Justice is effectively a problem- solving approach to crime involving the parties themselves and the community generally. Restorative Justice views crime as a breakdown in relationships which causes harm to the victim and the community. Restorative Justice seeks to repair this harm by attending to the needs of the victim and by trying to reintegrate the offender into the community and, thus, preventing re-offending. The Commission is assessing the developments in Restorative Justice in this jurisdiction and in other jurisdictions such as New Zealand and Australia where it is already an integral part of the criminal justice system. The Paper also examines alternatives to custodial sentencing.

Indexation of fines, penalties for minor offences

The Consultation Paper on the Indexation of Fines is in its final stages. A Consultation Paper is being prepared on Penalties for Minor Offences. This Paper considers whether the amount of a fine should be proportionate to the accused's means. It looks at how this system works in other jurisdictions and also examines the implications of a similar system here.

Public inquiries

The Commission is preparing a Consultation Paper on the subject of public inquiries. In recent years such inquiries have been established in Ireland to inquire into various matters of public concern. Most are conducted under the auspices of a British (pre-independence) statute that dates back to 1921 and which has been subject to piecemeal amendment. The Commission is undertaking a review of this legislation, which is perceived by some to produce inquiries that are excessively costly, and is considering alternative models.

The deductibility of collateral benefits from awards of damages
Section 2 of the Civil Liability (Amendment) Act, 1964, provides as follows:

> In assessing damages in an action to recover damages in respect of a wrongful act (including a crime) resulting in personal injury not causing death, account shall not be taken of:
> (a) any sum payable in respect of the injury under any contract of insurance,
> (b) any pension, gratuity or other like benefit payable under statute or otherwise in consequence of the injury.'

In essence, section 2 lays down the rule that certain payments which individuals may receive in connection with personal injury, for example, insurance payments, shall not be deducted from any subsequent award of damages that they may receive as plaintiff in a civil suit from the defendant-tortfeasor. These external payments have come to be termed 'collateral benefits'. To the extent that these collateral benefits compensate for the loss met by awards of damages in tort they result in double compensation for the same loss.

Under a reference from the Attorney-General, the Commission was asked to address the question of repealing or amending this provision 'with a view to ensuring that a plaintiff does not receive double compensation in respect of the same loss', and to submit to the Attorney General such proposals for reform as the Commission thinks appropriate.

Law and the elderly
The work currently underway at the Commission in relation to law and the elderly reflects an increasing social awareness of the plight of vulnerable groups in our society. It is now recognised that there is a need to provide adequate legal safeguards for citizens who are themselves unable to vindicate their legal rights, whether because of advanced age, ill-health, mental incapacity, lack of education, or lack of familiarity with our legal structures.

The increasing proportion of elderly people in our society makes this review of the law in this area a timely one. While individual elderly citizens may be affected by almost every branch of law, the Consultation Paper being prepared by the Commission will address some of the areas of law which impact most frequently on our elderly population. Some of the important subjects to be examined are: the problems experienced by the elderly in relation to legal matters; legal protections of vulnerable elderly people with respect to property transactions; the law governing wills and testamentary capacity; care of the elderly person, including the law governing residential care facilities; decision-making on behalf of the incapacitated elderly person; 'advance care directives'; and the problems of elder abuse and crimes against the elderly.

Taking evidence abroad in Irish proceedings and vice versa

A Consultation Paper is in its final stages which looks at the present procedures for taking evidence from a witness abroad for use in proceedings in an Irish Court and vice versa. It examines ways of making this procedure more efficient. It also looks at the obstacles posed by the viva voce rule to using deposition evidence in Irish proceedings. Solutions such as the use of a video link, transporting the Irish Court to the State where the evidence is being taken, and the development of an extra-territorial subpoena are discussed in the paper.

PROCEDURAL DEVELOPMENTS

A Consultative Committee, under the aegis of the Attorney General, was established by a government decision in 1998. The Committee consists of representatives of interested government departments, the Bar Council, the Law Society and the Law Reform Commission. Its remit is to assist the Attorney General in his functions under the Act with regard both to research programmes and particular references by the Attorney General to the Commission; it is also to monitor the implementation of recommendations of the Commission by the relevant government department and the legislature.

As a result of the establishment of this Consultative Committee, regular meetings have been arranged between the Law Reform Commission and the Department of Justice. This has helped increase awareness at Government level of the research being done at the Commission and the progress of work on the enactment of recommendations for reform.

The Commission has also made an effort to draw media attention to its Reports and Consultation Papers by organising press releases and interviews to explain its recommendations. This helps to keep the importance of law reform before those interested and the broader public.

The role of the future African Human Rights Court

CHRISTOF HEYNS

Africa will soon have its own regional human rights court, comparable in structure to the European and Inter-American Human Rights Courts. The Protocol to the African Charter on Human and Peoples' Rights on the Establishment of an African Court on Human and Peoples' Rights (the 'African Human Rights Court Protocol' or 'Protocol') that will create the African Court on Human and Peoples' Rights was opened for signature in 1998. It has, by early 2004, been signed and ratified by fifteen States. Fifteen ratifications are required for the Protocol to enter into force.[1] The Organization of African Unity (OAU) initiated the process that will lead to the creation of the African Human Rights Court. The OAU is in the process of being replaced by the African Union (AU), and it is assumed that the AU will take the place of the OAU as the parent body in respect of the Court.[2]

The creation of the African Court on Human and Peoples' Rights (the 'African Human Rights Court') is aimed at strengthening the supervising mechanism of the African Charter on Human and Peoples' Rights (the 'African Charter'). The ability of the African Commission on Human and Peoples' Rights (the 'African Commission') to deliver authoritative, yet non-binding decisions will be supplemented by the power of the Court to deliver judgments that will bind those States that have ratified the Protocol and thus accepted the jurisdiction of the African Court.

The European system has provided for the creation of a Court in addition to the Commission of Human Rights since the European Convention on Human Rights was accepted in 1950; the Court was established in 1959. In 1998 the single Court was established as the sole monitoring mechanism in that system and the Commission was phased out.[3]

The Inter-American system still uses the two-tiered system of a Commission, established in 1960, and a Court, installed in 1980.[4]

---

1 Art. 34(3). 2 See Evarist Baimu, 'The African Union: hope for better protection of human rights in Africa?' (2001) 1 *African Human Rights Law Journal* 299. 3 See Erika de Wet, 'The present control machinery under the European Convention on Human Rights: its future reform and the possible implications for the African Court on Human Rights' (1996) 29 *Comparative and International Law Journal of Southern Africa* 338. 4 See Frans Viljoen, 'The relevance of the Inter-American human rights system for Africa' (1999) 11 *African Journal of International and Comparative Law* 659.

The attempt to create an African Human Rights Court has faced many obstacles. Some commentators see in the process to establish the Court the emergence of the 'teeth' that the system needs in order to have a significant impact on the protection of human rights in Africa. Others are sceptical, and see the prospect of an efficient court as yet another pipedream at best, and as a threat to the Commission at worst.

There has been a widespread belief that the concept of human rights is 'non-African' and largely a legacy of colonial domination. Even to the extent that the notion of human rights is accepted, the idea that it should be enforced by a court of law has for a long time been rejected, both because litigation is seen as un-African[5] and because notions of sovereignty still play a strong role on the continent – often as a shield for leaders with scant regard for human rights.[6]

Even if one accepts the legitimacy of the idea of human rights and agrees that it may legitimately be enforced by a supra-national court in Africa, the idea of establishing such a court in Africa at this moment in time may still be contested. The African Charter system has not been a shining success so far, and the question is asked whether creating yet another monitoring institution within that framework is wise. The Court may dilute the power and relevance – not to mention resources – of the already struggling Commission.

It could also be asked whether the conditions required for such a court to function exist in Africa. The other regional systems depend for the success of their courts on the existence of a relatively strong regional 'parent' body, while the OAU/AU is weak. An elaborate network of trade and other relations exists in the other regions, but it does not exist in Africa. The building blocks of State parties in whose domestic legal systems human rights have gained a minimum level of official acceptance and enforcement exist in large parts of the area covered by the Inter-American and certainly the European systems, but it is a rare occurrence on the African continent.

The worst possible scenario would be the creation of a human rights court for Africa whose judgments are not complied with, or whose judgments are toned down in advance by the judges because of fear of non-compliance. The decisions of the African Commission have regularly been ignored, but since they are not technically binding in the first place, that does not mean the end of the Commission.[7] A court whose decisions are ignored even once with impunity will find it very difficult to maintain its legitimacy.

---

5 See A.A. An-Na'im and F.M. Deng (eds), *Human rights in Africa* (Washington, 1990), especially parts 3 and 4.   6 See U. Oji Umozurike, *The African Charter on Human and Peoples' Rights* (The Hague, 1997) 9 and Evelyn A. Ankumah, *The African Commission on Human and Peoples' Rights* (The Hague, 1996) 4, 193.   7 The African Commission has found it hard to cite even one example where its decisions have made an actual difference in respect of the observation of human rights. See 'Non-compliance of State Parties to adopted recommendations of the African Commission: a legal approach' Twenty-fourth Ordinary Session, Banjul, 22–31 October 1998 DOC/OS/50b (XXIV). On the possible implications of such a court for State sovereignty, see

There is consequently great uncertainty about the future role of the Court. In this contribution the following issues will be considered briefly: The process leading up to the creation of the Court; the main features of the envisaged Court; the relationship between the Commission and the Court; the enforcement of the decisions of the Court; and the likely impact of the Court on the realisation of human rights in Africa.

THE PROCESS LEADING UP TO THE CREATION OF THE COURT

The Charter of the Organisation of African Unity of 1963 made only passing reference to the concept of human rights. In the Preamble it was stated that 'freedom, equality, justice and dignity are essential objectives for the legitimate aspirations of the African peoples', and it was observed that 'the Charter of the United Nations and the Universal Declaration of Human Rights, to the principles of which we reaffirm our adherence, provide a solid foundation for peaceful and positive cooperation among States'.

Although there had been voices calling for the creation of an African Court on Human and Peoples' Rights even before the creation of the OAU,[8] this idea received little support when the African Charter was drafted and adopted in 1981, and only a Commission was provided for.[9]

The early 1990s saw major changes in the world,[10] and a wave of democratisation in Africa,[11] with a concomitant greater acceptance of the idea of human rights and a willingness to accept stronger enforcement mechanisms.

In January and December 1993, meetings convened by the International Commission of Jurists (ICJ), the OAU General Secretariat and the African Commission were held in Senegal and Addis Ababa to explore the possibility of the establishment of an African Human Rights Court.[12] In June 1994, the OAU Assembly of Heads of State and Government, meeting in Tunis, Tunisia, approved a Resolution[13] requesting the Secretary General to convene a government experts' meeting to 'ponder over ways and means of strengthening

Andre Stemmet, 'A future African Court for Human and Peoples' Rights and domestic human rights norms' (1998) 23 *South African Yearbook of International Law* 233.   **8** For example, at the 'Law of Lagos' Conference in 1961, organised by the International Commission of Jurists.   **9** See Evelyn A. Ankumah *The African Commission on Human and Peoples' Rights* (1996) 194.   **10** See the Declaration on the Political and Socio-Economic Situation in Africa and the Fundamental Changes Taking Place in the World, adopted by the OAU Assembly of Heads of State and Government in 1990 [Reference to be provided], in which the implications of the fall of the Berlin Wall for Africa were considered.   **11** Benin, for example, held free elections in 1991 in which an incumbent regime on continental Africa was removed through the ballot box for the first time since the 1960s. See Christof Heyns, *Human rights law in Africa 1998* (2001) 238.   **12** See Ben Kioko, 'The road to the African Court on Human and Peoples' Rights', *Proceedings of the Tenth Annual Conference of the African Society of International and Comparative Law*, 3–5 August 1998 70 at 75.   **13** AHG.230 (XXX).

the African Commission on Human and Peoples' Rights in considering particularly the establishment of an African Court on Human and Peoples' Rights'.

The First Government Legal Experts' Meeting was held in Cape Town, South Africa, from 6 to 12 September 1995. They produced the 'Cape Town Draft Protocol' on the African Court.[14] Responses from States were received, and the Second Government Legal Experts' Meeting was held in Nouakchott, Mauritania, from 11 to 14 April 1997, where the 'Nouakchott Draft Protocol' was produced.[15] The Third Legal Experts' Meeting (enlarged to include diplomats) was held in Addis Ababa from 8 to 11 December 1997, which resulted in the Addis Ababa Draft Protocol.[16] A slightly amended version of that Draft was subsequently endorsed by the Council of Ministers[17] and, on 8 to 10 June 1998, accepted by the Assembly of Heads of State and Government in Addis Ababa.

As was alluded to earlier the OAU has subsequently, in 2001, been replaced by the African Union. The Constitutive Act of the African Union,[18] in a number of provisions, recognises the role and importance of human rights in the work of the new continental body.[19] Although no explicit reference is made to the African Human Rights Court in the Constitutive Act, the African Charter is explicitly recognised, together with 'other relevant human rights instruments'.[20]

THE MAIN FEATURES OF THE AFRICAN HUMAN RIGHTS COURT

We now turn to the main features of the African Human Rights Court.[21] The Court will consist of 11 judges, all of whom must be jurists,[22] serving (once renewable) six year terms.[23] The judges on the Court will elect a President for a two-year period.[24] The judges will be part-time, except for the President who will be full-time and who will reside at the seat of the Court.[25] The seat of the Court is to be determined by the Assembly of Heads of State and Government of the OAU/AU.[26]

The judges must be nationals of member States of the OAU,[27] and no two judges may be nationals of the same State.[28] Only State parties to the Protocol may nominate judges,[29] but the entire Assembly eventually elects the judges.[30]

---

14 OAU/LEG/EXP/AFCHPR/PROT (I) Rev 1.   **15** OAU/LEG/EXP/AFCHRP/PROT (2)
16 OAU/LEG/EXP/AFCHPR/PROT (III) Rev 1.   **17** OAU/LEG/MIN/AFCHPR/PROT (1)
Rev 2.   **18** CAB/LEG/23.15, adopted on 11 July 2001 and entered into force on 26 May 2001.
19 In the Preamble; as an objective in art 3(h); in art 4(h); and indirectly in arts 23 & 30.   **20** Art.
3(h).   **21** See Gino J. Naldi & Konstantinos Magliveras, 'The proposed African Court of Human and Peoples' Rights: Evaluation and comparison' (1996) 8 *African Journal of International and Comparative Law/RADIC* 944; John Mubangizi & Andreas O'Shea, 'An African Court on Human and Peoples' Rights' (1999) 24 *South African Yearbook of International Law* 256; and Gino J. Naldi, *The Organization of African Unity* (The Hague, 1999) 148.   **22** Art. 11.   **23** Art. 15.   **24** Art. 21(1).   **25** Art. 21(2).
26 Art. 25.   **27** Art. 11(1).   **28** Art .11(2).   **29** Art. 12(1). They may nominate up to three candidates, at least two of them being their own nationals (art. 12(2)).   **30** Art. 14.

Both in the nomination and electoral process, emphasis is placed by the Protocol on the need for adequate gender representation.[31] Emphasis is also placed on the independence of the judges.[32] The Protocol provides that a judge who is a national of any State that is a party to a case may not hear such a case.[33]

According to the Protocol, the Court has jurisdiction over 'all cases and disputes submitted to it concerning the interpretation and application of the Charter, this Protocol and any other relevant human rights instrument ratified by the States concerned'.[34] Some commentators believe that the phrase 'any other relevant human rights instrument ratified by the States concerned' implies that the jurisdiction of the Court is extended to all human rights treaties ratified by the States concerned, irrespective of their origin and whether they were intended to be justiciable by their drafters or by the States that have ratified them.[35] I have argued elsewhere that such an interpretation would lead to absurd results, and that the inclusion of the word 'relevant' in the phrase should be understood to limit the jurisdiction of the Court to treaties (in addition to the African Charter and the Court Protocol) that explicitly grant jurisdiction to the Court.[36]

The Court will have both advisory and contentious jurisdiction. Advisory opinions may be requested by 'a member State of the OAU, the OAU, any of its organs, or any African organisation recognised by the OAU'.[37] The situation in respect of contentious cases is more complex. Access to the Court, and in particular the ability of the individual to subject his or her government to the binding decisions of a supra-national court, affects the sensitive issue of State sovereignty head-on. It has consequently been the subject of much debate as the Protocol was being drafted.[38] An uncertain compromise was eventually reached, which may be set out as follows:

A distinction should be made between *indirect* access to the Court (that is, the ability to approach the Court after the case has been dealt with by the Commission) and *direct* access to the Court (approaching the Court without approaching the Commission first). Who will have such powers, and under what circumstances?

---

31 Arts. 12(2) & 14(3). **32** Arts. 17 & 18. **33** Art. 22. **34** Art. 3(1). **35** See Gino J. Naldi & Konstantinos Magliveras, 'Reinforcing the African system of human rights: The Protocol on the establishment of a regional court of human and peoples' rights' (1998) 16 *Netherlands Quarterly of Human Rights* 431–4. **36** See Christof Heyns, 'The African regional human rights system: In need of reform?' (2001) 1 *African Human Rights Law Journal* 155. The Draft Protocol to the African Charter on Human and Peoples' Rights on the Rights of Women in Africa, as adopted by the Meeting of Government Experts in Addis Ababa on 16 November 2001 CAB/LEG/66.6/Rev1, art 23 does provide for an interpretative role for the African Court. **37** Art. 4. **38** For commentary on an early draft of the Court Protocol, see Abdelsalom A. Mohamed, 'Individual and NGO participation in human rights litigation before the African Court of Human and Peoples' Rights: Lessons from the European and Inter-American Courts of Human Rights' (1999) 43 *Journal of African Law* 201. See also Makau Mutua, 'The African Human Rights Court: a two-legged stool?' (1999) 21 *Human Rights Quarterly* 342–55.

Indirect access will be automatically possible in respect of all States that have accepted the jurisdiction of the Court by ratifying the African Human Rights Court Protocol, but only a carefully selected number of institutions will have the power to pursue this course. Cases may be taken from the Commission to the Court by the Commission itself; the States that have lodged the complaint with the Commission or against whom the complaint was lodged; the State whose citizen is a victim of a human rights violation, and African intergovernmental organisations.[39] In other words, the standard position will be that individuals will not have the power, by themselves, to proceed from the Commission to the Court. They will only have indirect access, mediated by State or State-related institutions.

However, where the State in question has, in addition to having ratified the Protocol, also made a special, optional declaration in terms of article 34(6) of the Protocol,[40] individuals and NGOs with observer status before the Commission will have the option not to go to the Commission in the first place but instead to approach the Court directly.

To draw a brief comparison with the other regional systems: Mere ratification of the Protocol will result in the same kind of situation that has traditionally prevailed in the Inter-American system as well as the European system, where individuals, by themselves, do not have the power to proceed beyond the Commission to the Court. Only the State and other similar actors have this power. Where a State has ratified the African Human Rights Court Protocol and has made the additional declaration, States and other similar actors are still the only ones who can approach the Court indirectly, but individuals and NGOs are authorised, as is the case in Europe.

THE RELATIONSHIP BETWEEN THE COMMISSION AND THE COURT

According to the Preamble of the Protocol, the Court is established to 'complement and reinforce the functions' of the Commission. The Protocol provides that '[t]he Court shall ... complement the protective mandate ...' of the Commission,[41] and refers to the 'complementarity' between the Commission and the Court.[42] In cases of direct access to the Court by individuals, the Court may consider cases or refer them to the Commission.[43] It is not clear on what basis the Court will exercise this discretion.

The above suggests that the Court has no explicit promotional mandate in respect of the African Charter – that remains the domain of the Commission. The Court supplements, but does not replace, the protective mandate of the Commission.

At the same time, the emergence of the Court may undermine the position and work of the Commission. For example, the Commission has the quasi-

---

39 Art. 5(1).   **40** Art. 5(3).   **41** Art. 2.   **42** Art. 8.   **43** Art. 6(3).

judicial function to interpret the Charter.[44] It is not clear how this will tie in with the mandate of the Court to render advisory opinions.

It is not likely that many States will at the outset make the declaration recognising the right of individuals to have direct access to the Court, but to the extent that this is done, the Commission could be sidelined when individuals who have the choice between approaching the Commission or the Court first approach the Court directly. It is worth noting here as well that in cases of direct access by individuals the Court is not bound by the same admissibility criteria as the Commission, such as the exhaustion of domestic remedies. The Court is merely required to '[t]ake into account' those criteria.[45] The Court is clearly in a potentially very powerful position in those cases where direct access is possible and the Court could, if it wanted to, marginalise the Commission and even the domestic courts by exercising jurisdiction.

The creation of the Court could also undermine the position of the Commission in other ways. The budget available to the OAU/AU to support the Charter system is limited. The Commission is already grossly underfunded, and it could now be required to forfeit some of those resources to the Court.

ENFORCEMENT OF THE DECISIONS OF THE COURT

The African Charter, like other similar regional instruments, does not require State parties to incorporate the Charter into domestic law – as long as the end result is the realisation of the rights in question.[46]

The Protocol provides that:[47]

> If the Court finds that there has been a violation of a human or peoples' right, it shall make appropriate orders to remedy the violation, including the payment of fair compensation or reparation.

The responsibility of State parties to the Protocol in respect of judgments of the Court is set out in the following terms:[48]

> The States Parties to the present Protocol undertake to comply with the judgement in any case to which they are parties within the time stipulated by the Court and to guarantee its execution.

The Council of Ministers are to be notified of the judgment and 'shall monitor its execution on behalf of the Assembly'.[49] Moreover:[50]

---

44 Art. 45(3) of the African Charter.   **45** Art. 6(2) of the African Human Rights Court Protocol.
46 See Art. 1 of the African Charter.   **47** Art. 27(1) of the African Human Rights Court Protocol.
48 Art. 30.   **49** Art. 29(2). The Constitutive Act of the African Union does not provide for a Council of Ministers, but it is assumed that the Executive Council of the AU will take over that role (art. 16 of the Constitutive Act).   **50** Art. 31 of the African Human Rights Court Protocol.

The Court shall submit to each regular session of the Assembly, a report on its work during the previous year. The report shall specify, in particular, the cases in which a State has not complied with the Court's judgement.

THE LIKELY IMPACT OF THE COURT ON THE PROTECTION OF HUMAN RIGHTS IN AFRICA

If properly managed, the Court could become a bastion of strength for human rights on a continent where these norms are often flouted. The Court could in the first place give the necessary teeth to the African Charter, also reinforcing the work done by the Commission. Moreover, the jurisprudence developed by the Court in respect of those rights which are widely recognised in the domestic legal systems of most African countries could provide a powerful point of reference and inspiration in terms of which the national courts, governments and civil society in the different jurisdictions could interpret these rights.[51]

Proper management of the introduction of the Court would in my view include the following:

- ensuring that both the Commission and the Court are properly resourced;
- selecting the seat of the Court with care, to ensure that it is easily accessible, well equipped and the judges have access to information and literature;
- selecting wise and courageous judges;
- the creation of stronger trade, diplomatic and other links between African States, which could form the basis of peer pressure to ensure the execution of the judgments of the Court.

Only States with a minimum level of protection of human rights should be encouraged to ratify the Court Protocol. There must be a widespread acceptance among those States that subject themselves to the jurisdiction of the Court that the Court will operate broadly within the framework of internationally recognised human rights, and that its judgments need to be executed. The ratification of the Protocol by States that do not share this view will render the Court ineffective. The absence of a tradition of respect for the judicial enforcement of human rights on the domestic level in any State does not augur well for its acceptance of the authority of a regional court with such a function.

---

51 See Frans Viljoen, 'Application of the African Charter on Human and Peoples' Rights by domestic courts in Africa' 1 43 *Journal of African Law* (1991)

The promotion of administrative justice in South Africa: a milestone for administrative law or a millstone for public administration: some comparative perspectives on codification[1]

J.M. HLOPHE

In 1993, at a workshop convened to discuss administrative law reform, Christopher Forsyth sounded a cautionary note about the need to balance the measures required to reform the administration through the promotion of administrative justice with the practical realties burdening the new government. He warned that our 'troubled world was littered with intended utopias', grand visions that ultimately mutated into 'little hells.'[2] At the same time the former Chief Justice of India, P.N. Bhagwati urged South Africans to 'forge new tools, fashion new remedies and devise new strategies for bringing administrative justice within easy reach'.[3]

A decade later and with the codification of administrative law in the shape of the Promotion of Administrative Justice Act are we perched on the abyss of a little hell, or is this one of those new tools destined to promote fair, just and reasonable procedures that are consistent with the rule of law, democratic values and natural justice?

The Promotion of Administrative Justice Act is unquestionably a milestone in the evolution of administrative law. It marks the beginning of a journey, the end goal of which is to develop an integrated system of administrative justice. The fact that this legislation was mandated for enactment through section 33(3) of the Bill of Rights, and strict time limits were set for its implementation, means that there has been limited time to prepare for the demands its implementation will place on the administration and the justice system. This should not, however, detract from the fact that for the first time uniform rules and principles of administrative procedure have been defined in a statute that binds the entire administration at all levels of government.

It is the first step towards developing a comprehensive code of administrative law. Without this codification process there is a danger that broad appli-

1 I am grateful to Gillian Nesbitt, Research Assistant at the Cape Provincial Division, for her assistance in the preparation of this paper. The flaws herein are entirely mine. 2 See C. Forsyth, 'Speaking truth unto power: the reform of administrative law' (1994) *SALJ* 408. 3 See H. Corder, 'Introduction: administrative law reform' (1993) *Acta Juridica* 1.

cation of section 33 of the Bill of Rights might have tended to overproceduralize government action, which in turn might thwart the implementation of wide ranging and ambitious redevelopment programmes. In this way it signals a move beyond the broad scope of section 33 of the constitution, to provide certainty with regard to the procedural requirements of administrative decision-making.

Its primary objective then is clearly to give effect to the right to just administrative action as detailed in section 33 of the 1996 South African Constitution of the Republic of South Africa No. 108 of 1996. The drafters of the Act have had to balance a number of competing demands. On one hand there was a need to allay the concerns of those who feared section 33 would be used to hinder the Government, as it addressed the socio-economic imbalances that have indelibly scarred the country. On the other hand clear requirements needed to be set out for procedurally fair administrative action as well as for the consequences of contravention of those actions by administrators. This has made the Act a creature of compromise. It would have been naïve in the extreme to believe that, with the time constraints imposed on the drafting process and given the historical context, it could have been otherwise.

It is quite clear that the Act and its regulations seek to give form to the obvious requirement that administrative justice must flow from the administration itself by defining the procedural parameters within which the administration can and must function. Ultimately and ideally this should allow for increased public participation and for administrative accountability. In addition it must compel the administration to take account of the values enshrined in the Constitution.

The Constitutional Court in the case of *Premier, Mpumalanga v. Executive Committee of the Association of Governing Bodies of State Aided Schools: Eastern Transvaal* 1999 (2) SA 91 (CC) emphasised the need for a young democracy, faced with the immense challenges of transformation, to be aware of two main constitutional principles. The first is the eradication of discrimination. The second is the need for procedural fairness. Both these principles are, of course, based on separate notions of fairness:

> the first on fairness of goals; the second on fairness of action or procedural fairness; and both need to be honoured.[4]

The preamble to the Promotion of Administrative Justice Act emphasizes the need for efficiency, effectiveness and legitimacy. Clearly this attempts to cover a broad spectrum of requirements and once again it is a question of maintaining a balance. It is important to avoid the over-proceduralisation which

---

4 See *Premier, Mpumalanga v. Executive Committee of the Association of Governing Bodies of State Aided Schools*: Eastern Transvaal 1999 (2) SA 91 (CC).

will reduce efficiency, but, at the same time, to limit cursory decision-making which will impact on legitimacy.

A number of critics remain unimpressed by the attempts of the Act to meet these apparently contradictory requirements. Some critics maintain that it is unrealistic to expect inadequately trained administrators to conform with the act's detailed procedural requirements, while others have levelled criticism at its intensive focus on judicial review.[5] In addition, some commentators have queried the inclusion of the German idea of 'direct, external, legal effect' which as a concept alien to South African administrators and judicial officers alike, might hinder the effective application of the Act.

It is true that judicial review has played a prominent role in South African administrative law. At the time it was seen as a limited but reasonably effective means of attempting to combat political and legal acts of government repression. Opponents of judicial review maintain that it is over-rated as a means of curbing abuses of power. The argument is that it should not have maintained such a significant presence in the Promotion of Administrative Justice Act because it simply, 'insulates and shields the real sources of bureaucratic maladministration from sustained exposure and eradication.'[6]

The focus on judicial review is undoubtedly a reflection of the role it played in the past but it is also indicative of an intention to establish codified grounds of review. This is a deliberate effort to contrast with the situation as it existed before the enactment of the Constitution, when judges who had the courage to stand against the system could only look to the common law and amorphous notions of natural justice for assistance. The fear that this will lead to an uncontrollable wave of judicial activism lacks substance.

Judges have and will continue to be wary of trespassing on the polycentric expertise of administrative agencies. Furthermore this concern about the place of judicial review in the Act fails to recognise that the primary purpose and focus of the act is to provide the administration itself with a greater understanding of the requirements of procedurally fair administrative action.

The objections raised regarding the inability of the administration to cope with the detailed procedural demands of the Act, and the fear that this will be a millstone around the necks of administrators, fails to take into account the strict ethos of constitutional integrity which should be permeating our entire political, legal and administrative systems.

Section 195 of the Constitution of the Republic of South Africa No. 108 of 1996 refers to the need for the following principles to govern public administration: fair and equitable service; accountability; transparency and public participation. The Department of Public Service and Administration policy doc-

---

5 See C. Hoexter, 'The future of judicial review in south african administrative law' (2000) 117 *SALJ* 498.   6 See Allan Hutchinson, 'The rise and ruse of administrative law and scholarship' (1985) 48 *MLR* 293.

ument, *The Batho Pele White Paper*, acknowledges the need for reformation of the public service to ensure that the administration gives due attention to the rights and interests of individuals and groups. The intention must be for these elements to complement each other and to encourage good decision-making in the first instance. Such a conclusion will avoid endless recourse to the courts.

There is perhaps an element in the Act of the 'judge over your shoulder'[7] attitude, but this does not mean an over-judicialisation of the administration. It is rather an opportunity for public servants to make a concerted effort to incorporate an ethic of integrity into the impersonal workings of government bureaucracy, which contrasts with that held in the past. Then the administration was an eager servant of the State, ensuring that the constant flow of oppressive rules and regulations that restricted the lives of the majority of the population at that time were maintained. They are no longer immune from scrutiny by the courts as a result of piecemeal legislation and ouster clauses which left the judge to develop a case by case interpretation of administrative justice through common law. Now public servants have clear procedural boundaries within which they are compelled to operate.

It would seem appropriate then to examine some of the steps taken by foreign jurisdictions to deal with the effects of a codified administrative law. German law, for example, has had a strong influence on various aspects of the Act; I have already mentioned one aspect. The German Government took around 20 years to fine tune and then enact, still amid much debate, their Code of General Administrative Procedure. Contrast this with the position of the South African Law Commission, which had less than a year to prepare a draft bill.

The incorporation of the German concept of 'direct, external legal effect' is another attempt at striking a balance between contrasting interests, namely protecting individual rights without hampering the workings of the administration. If this is then linked with the determinative theory of rights, it should allow for a broader interpretation of 'administrative action.'

The German legal system has established a separate structure of specialised administrative courts. The general rules of administrative law are uniform through out the country and govern the validity, invalidity or revocability of administrative acts and liability for damages in relation to the conduct of public authorities. A great deal of emphasis is placed on pre-court procedures. A large number of the cases dealt with, in the form of rescissory actions and actions for a mandatory injunction, require preliminary proceedings.[8] These are handled through an internal appeal mechanism applicable to all branches of administrative law.[9] The main purpose of this system has been to avoid establishing tri-

---

7 See C. Forsyth, 'Speaking truth unto power: the reform of administrative law' (1994) *SALJ* 410.
8 See R. Pfaff and H. Schneider, 'The Promotion of Administrative Justice Act from a German perspective' (2000) *SAJHR* 63.   9 See Pfaff and Schneider (note 2 above) 59.

bunals for specific areas of public administration. The result is cheap, effective
action with easy access to such mechanisms. This has led to increased efficiency
by avoiding recourse to expensive and time-consuming judicial remedies

It is important, given the limitation on resources which exists, to investigate the possibility of creating a generalised system of internal appeal procedures in South Africa. It is unfortunate that no provision has been made in the
act similar to that of the German administration to reconsider its own decisions. The Promotion of Administrative Justice Act, however, does provide
for the Minister to make regulations in respect of strengthening internal appeal
mechanisms and even establishing a system of tribunals.

It is unlikely, however, given financial constraints, that it will be possible
to establish a solid system of tribunals. In consequence every effort must be
directed at bolstering those participatory mechanisms that the act outlines. Draft
regulations already detail the requirements for notice and comment procedures,
and for public inquiries and hearings. These regulations also make provision
for special assistance to be given to members of the community who may be
illiterate. These are fairly revolutionary concepts for the administration to deal
with, and it is clear that a comprehensive education programme must be put
in place. The Code of Good Administrative Conduct outlined in section
10(1)(e) of the Act will be a vital tool in this respect and should provide clarity where, at present, there may be confusion.

One of the problems of codification is a danger that rules are not maintained in line with modern procedural standards. The French have a standing
commission on codification, which has expressed a concern that there is a possibility under a rule-based system that

> the focus tends to be on compliance with the rules rather than with
> the quality of the results.[10]

It is to be hoped that the advisory council which may be established in
terms of section 10(2)(a) of the Act, will take the form of an Administrative
Review Council. This will advise the Minister and ideally will ensure that we
learn from the extensive experiences of other legal systems, not only European
but also Canadian and Australian, so such problems are avoided. This monitoring capacity of the Council will be important to guarantee that administrative procedure is user friendly, responsive and effective. So that eventually
it becomes possible to say

> that this society is one which now accords to the individual an oppor-
> tunity to meet on more equal terms the institutions of the State.[11]

10 See C. Harlow 'European administrative law and the global challenge', 1998 European
University Institute, Working Paper RSC 98/23.   **11** See M. Kirby 'Effective review of

The Act will not be a panacea for the ills that have crippled administrative justice in this country. Administrative law is far from achieving integration and in this sense is a fair reflection of South African society. Nonetheless, even with its flaws, it is a step towards a more accountable and responsive public administration.

In conclusion, however, it is vital to be aware of one indisputable fact, regardless of how good or integrated our system of administrative law becomes, it will not solve the problems facing the South African judiciary. Given our history it is not surprising that large sections of the public still view the judiciary with a great deal of mistrust. There remains a fundamental need to improve our image, given our past and the perceived and actual role played by some judges to keep apartheid alive. It will be impossible for us to maintain the legitimacy of our constitutional democracy if our own legitimacy as an institution continues to be questioned.

administrative acts: the hallmark of a free and fair society' (1993) *SAJHR*.

The administration of justice

FRANCIS MURPHY

INTRODUCTION

The Irish Constitution of 1937, like most other constitutions, adopts the Montesquieu principle of the separation of powers. Power is divided equally between the three organs of government – the legislative, the executive and the judiciary – and each enjoys its own area of exclusive competence. Whilst few doubt the wisdom of this principle, we have experienced in Ireland growing problems with its application in practice. These problems include:

1. the legitimacy of the delegation of the law–making powers of the legislature to the government or to a particular minister;

2. the administration of justice by bodies other than the courts;

3. the administration of justice otherwise than in public or *in camera;* and

4. the nature and scope of the orders which can and should be made by the judiciary against the legislature or the executive in vindicating the constitutional rights of individual litigants.

These problems are not unique to the constitutional system established in Ireland, but are shared by other jurisdictions.

DELEGATION OF LAW–MAKING POWER

As between Parliament (Oireachtas) and the Government, or its Ministers, a common problem has been the extent to which the legislature can delegate some measure of law-making power to the Government or individual Ministers. These problems have been considered in a number of cases involving legislation ranging from the Social Welfare Act, 1952[1] to the Aliens Order, 1946.[2] The courts have consistently held that, where the delegation in question is more than the giving effect of principles and policies contained in the primary leg-

---

1 *Harvey v. The Minister for Social Welfare* [1990] 2 IR 232.   2 *Laurentiu v. The Minister for Justice* [1999] 4 IR 26.

islation or where what is done constitutes the making, repealing or amending of the law, such action is unconstitutional.[3] The difficulties encountered in the delegation of law-making power have not been restricted to Irish legislation but have included the manner in which directives in regulations of the European Union are given full force and effect in Ireland.[4] However, the most obvious and most common form of delegated legislation is the power conferred on a Minister of Government to fix the date on which an Act or some part thereof is to come into operation. In the *State (Sheehan) v. The Government of Ireland*[5] the courts had to consider the effect of such delegation, and more particularly, the refusal of the Minister to exercise the power so conferred on him, thus postponing indefinitely material legislation having operative effect. Were such postponement to achieve the virtual repeal of the legislation in question, such action would be unconstitutional.

THE ADMINISTRATION OF JUSTICE BY BODIES OTHER THAN THE COURTS

I mention the problems of the legislature only in the general context of diffi-culties encountered with the separation of powers. My concern here is with the administration of justice: not the enactment of laws. The judiciary faces two problems. First, the identification of the area in which it has exclusive juris-diction and, secondly, the extent or circumstances in which it should exer-cise that jurisdiction so as to require a particular response from either the leg-islature or the executive.

The crucial provision of the Constitution is Article 34.1 which provides: 'Justice shall be administered in courts established by law by judges appointed in the manner provided for in this Constitution and, save in such special and limited cases as may be prescribed by law, shall be administered in public.' That Article confers on the Judiciary an exclusive role in the administration of jus-tice. The problem is how it should be defined. As Kingsmill Moore J pointed out in *In re Solicitors Act 1954*[6] that:

> From none of the pronouncements as to the nature of judicial power which have been quoted can a definition at once exhaustive and pre-cise be extracted, and probably no such definition can be framed. The varieties and combinations of powers with which the legislature may

---

3 See for example: *Cityview Press Ltd v. An Chomhairle Oiliúna* [1980] IR 381; *The State (Gilliland) v. Governor of Mountjoy Prison* [1987] IR 213; *Cassidy v. The Minister for Industry and Commerce* [1978] IR 297; *O'Neill v. The Minister for Agriculture and Food* [1997] 2 ILRM 435; and *Maher v. The Minister for Agriculture and Food* [1994] 1 IR 329. **4** See *Maher v. The Minister for Agriculture and Food* [2001] 2 IR 139. **5** [1987] IR 550. **6** [1960] IR 239, at 271.

equip a tribunal are infinite, and in each case the particular powers must be considered in their totality and separately to see if a tribunal so endowed is invested with powers of such nature and extent that their exercise is in effect administering that justice which appertains to the judicial organ ...

However, it is widely accepted that the five characteristic features of the administration of justice – outlined by Kenny J in *McDonald v. Bord na gCon (No. 2)*[7] – provide the best definition of this important concept. He identified them as follows:

(1) a dispute or controversy as to the existence of legal rights or a violation of the law;
(2) the determination or ascertainment of the rights of parties or the imposition of liabilities or the infliction of a penalty;
(3) the final determination (subject to appeal) of legal rights or liabilities or the imposition of penalties;
(4) the enforcement of those rights or liabilities or the imposition of a penalty by the court or by the executive power of the State which is called in by the court to enforce its judgment;
(5) the making of an order by the court which as a matter of history is an order characteristic of courts in this country.

In deciding who is entitled and empowered to administer justice, regard must also be had to the provisions of Article 37.1 of the Constitution:

Nothing in this Constitution shall operate to invalidate the exercise of limited functions and powers of a judicial nature, in matters other than criminal matters, by any person or body of persons duly authorised by law to exercise such functions and powers, notwithstanding that such person or such body of persons is not a judge or court appointed or established as such under the Constitution.

Thus, a body which is not a court and would be prohibited from administering justice will not fall foul of the Constitution if it satisfies the limited exception contained in Article 37.1.

This article and the question of 'limited powers' was considered in *In re Solicitors Act 1954*[8] when the appellants, who had been struck off the roll of solicitors by order of the Disciplinary Committee of the Incorporated Law Society, contended that this function was unconstitutional since the Committee was not a court nor were its members judges, and that the function of striking off was

7 [1965] IR 217. 8 [1960] IR 239.

not a 'limited' one. The Supreme Court agreed with this contention and declared the relevant part of the Act to be invalid. Kingsmill Moore J declared that:

> Here we are dealing with a tribunal which depends for its existence and its powers on a legislative act of the State. If the effect of such legislation is to confer the power to administer justice on persons who are not regularly appointed as judges it is by Article 34 unconstitutional, unless it can be brought within some of the saving provisions of the Constitution.[9]

Thus, the question for the Court to decide was whether the tribunal in question could be said to be exercising powers of a 'limited' nature. The Court held that the powers and functions conferred by the Act were of such a far-reaching nature that their exercise amounted to the administration of justice and could not fall within the 'limited' functions exception in Article 37.

> A tribunal having but a few powers and functions but those of far-reaching effect and importance could not properly be regarded as exercising 'limited' powers and functions ... If the exercise of the assigned powers and functions is calculated ordinarily to affect in the most profound and far-reaching way the lives, liberties, fortunes or reputations of those against whom they are exercised they cannot properly be described as 'limited' ... The power to strike a solicitor off the rolls is a 'disciplinary' and 'punitive' power ... It is a sanction of such severity that in its consequences it may be much more serious than a term of imprisonment.[10]

That decision had far-reaching consequences. The legislation governing a number of professional and vocational bodies had to be reviewed. This test was later applied by Finlay P in *M v. Medical Council*[11] where the plaintiff had challenged the constitutionality of sections 45 to 48 of the Medical Practitioners Act 1978, on the ground that those provisions purported to give the defendants judicial powers of a non-limited nature in relation to certain disciplinary matters. Finlay P. held that there was a 'very striking difference' between the extent and nature of the powers conferred on the disciplinary committee of the Law Society in the above mentioned case and those conferred on the defendants in this case since neither the Medical Council nor the Committee had any power to:

erase the name of a practitioner from the register;

suspend him from his practice;

attach conditions to the continuation of his practice;

make him pay compensation or to award costs against him.

9 Ibid., at 264. 10 Ibid., at 263–4, 274. 11 [1984] IR 485.

The court found that the only power vested in these bodies under the Act was to initiate proceedings in the High Court which might lead to an order being made in respect of any of those matters. The court concluded, therefore, that the powers in question were not judicial in nature and that, if they were, they were 'limited' pursuant to Article 37.1.[12]

It is worth remembering, however, that the definition of the judicial power is not fixed and is capable of expansion, as Kenny J stated in *McDonald v. Bord na gCon*:[13]

> Every exercise of the judicial power referred to in Article 6 is not an administration of justice, for the courts in this country have jurisdiction and powers the exercise of which is not an administration of justice, and new powers and functions may be conferred on courts and judges although the exercise of these powers and functions is not an administration of justice.

THE ADMINISTRATION OF JUSTICE OTHERWISE THAN IN PUBLIC

Some of the work performed by the judiciary is more properly described as administrative rather than the administration of justice and, where this is the case, it is permissible for procedures to be followed which may not comply with Article 34.1 of the Constitution[14] since that provision only applies where justice is being administered. It is the nature of the act and not the identity of the individual which determines whether its performance may constitute the administration of justice. This is of special importance in relation to the constitutional obligation to administer justice in public. In *In re Singer*,[15] the Court held that Article 34.1 did not require that the dates for trials should be fixed in open court rather than by the registrar in consultation with the judge. Maguire CJ held: 'This work is purely administrative and, while necessary as a preliminary towards preparing for a sitting of the court, is not in any sense the administration of justice referred to in Article 34.1 of the Constitution.'

In civil matters, the principal exception to the requirement of publicity is to be found in section 45 of the Courts (Supplemental Provisions) Act 1961 which provides that justice may be administered otherwise than in public:

12 *M v. Medical Council* [1984] IR 485 at 499: '[T]he only powers of the Committee or the Council which could be said to be final and, in a sense, binding are the publication of a finding by the Committee of misconduct or unfitness to practice and the Council's power to advise, admonish or censure a practitioner. Even if it could be said that [such powers were] something affecting the rights of a practitioner...these would be functions so clearly limited in their effect and consequence that they would be within the exception provided by Article 37 ... even if ... they constituted the administration of justice.'   13 [1965] IR 217.   14 Such as where some matters are dealt with in the judge's chambers and not in public as required of the administration of justice under Article 34.1 of the Constitution.   15 (1963) 97 ILTR 130.

(a) in applications of an urgent nature for relief by way of habeas corpus, bail, prohibition or injunction;
(b) in matrimonial causes and matters;
(c) in lunacy and matters involving minors; or
(d) proceedings involving the disclosure of a secret manufacturing process.

It should be noted, however, that the first exception may only be made where urgency is established. Kelly, in *The Irish Constitution* describes the operation of the section thus:

> The fact that s 45(1) allows such interim relief to be granted otherwise than in public is designed to allow for urgent applications to be made outside of ordinary sitting hours (e.g. where a judge makes an interim order at his own home) where the exigencies of the situation might not conveniently allow for reporters to be present.[16]

Applications for hearings to be conducted *in camera* are not often successful. In *In re R. Ltd*[17] a former chief executive brought a petition under section 205 of the Companies Act 1963 claiming oppression. His grounding affidavit included sensitive business information and the company applied for, and was granted, an *ex parte* order by Johnson J directing that the petition be heard *in camera*. However, a majority of the Supreme Court held that these facts did not afford any justification for such an order. Walsh J observed:

> It is difficult to see why the disclosure of evidence of this type must necessarily be deemed to be a failure to do justice in the case of a juristic person where it would not be such in the case of a human person or of any unincorporated body of persons...A limited company is the creature of the law and by its very nature and by the provisions of the law under which it is created it is open to public scrutiny.[18]

A more interesting example of the difficulties involved in upholding the publicity requirement is *In re Countyglen plc*.[19] An inspector was appointed under section 8 of the Companies Act 1990 by the High Court to investigate the affairs of Countyglen plc. The inspector applied to the High Court for directions under section 7(4) of the Companies Act 1990, seeking to engage a firm of lawyers in Guernsey and, at the hearing of the application, applied to have the proceedings heard *in camera*. The court acceded to this application on the

16 Kelly, *The Irish Constitution* (3rd ed., Dublin, 1994, Hogan & Whyte), p. 402.   17 [1989] IR 126.   18 Ibid., at 137–8. This case was subsequently followed in *Irish Press plc v. Ingersoll Publications Ltd* [1993] ILRM 747.   19 [1995] 1 IR 220.

condition that the Attorney General be given notice of the making of the order and be given an opportunity to present any objections to the making of the order. The Attorney General submitted that the appointment of an inspector under sections 7 or 8 of the Act of 1990 constituted the administration of justice and that such appointment affected the rights and interests of the company over which the inspector was appointed and the interests of its shareholders and creditors.

The court affirmed the *in camera* order and held that the order was made in pursuance of section 7(4) of the Act of 1990 as a direction to the inspector 'with a view to ensuring that the investigation is carried out as quickly and as inexpensively as possible.' It was stressed that the fact that orders giving directions must be made by a judge of the High Court did not itself determine whether such orders constituted the administration of justice[20] since many important decisions made by judges are of a purely administrative nature.[21] Murphy J stated:

> Not only do I agree with the view tentatively expressed by Walsh J ... but I believe that it is generally accepted in practice, though not tested formally, that many orders made in the course of the winding-up of companies by the court are merely administrative directions and not the administration of justice. Indeed in recent years practice directions have been made by the President of the High Court which expressly recognise that orders for the extension of time for the lodgment of a statement of affairs; a direction to the Taxing Master to tax costs already awarded and other similar matters can and should be made informally and *in camera*.[22]

The Court concluded that the giving of directions in pursuance of section 7(4) did not constitute the administration of justice; accordingly Article 34 of the Constitution did not require that the proceedings be heard in public.

MANDATORY INJUNCTIONS

Another problem which the separation of powers has created for the judiciary concerns the nature of the orders which can and should be made by the judiciary against the legislature or executive in vindicating the constitutional

---

20 In *The State (O.) v. O'Brien* [1973] IR 50 at 67, Walsh J. pointed out that: 'The quality of the act is to be determined by the act itself, not by the person who is doing the act.'   **21** *In re Singer* (1963) 97 ILTR 130; and *McGlinchey v. The Governor of Portlaoise Prison* [1988] IR 671. Furthermore in *In re R Ltd*, [1989] IR 126 at 135, Walsh J adverted to the fact that 'many matters which come under the heading "lunacy and minor matters" probably do not constitute the administration of justice but simply the administration of the estates and affairs of the wards of court.'   **22** [1995] 1 IR, at 225.

rights of individual litigants. In a series of judgments[23] culminating in the decision of the full Supreme Court in *Sinnott v. The Minister for Education*[24] it has been held that an order for *mandamus* against the Oireachtas would violate the separation of powers, but that such an order might be made in an appropriate case against a Minister. However, even then, as the Chief Justice explained in *Sinnott,* it should be presumed that where the Supreme Court grants a declaration, the Minister will meet his or her obligations and take appropriate steps to comply with the law laid down by the Courts. Accordingly, mandatory relief would not ordinarily be granted. What is clear[25] is that the courts have no jurisdiction to substitute for an impugned enactment a form of legislation which it considers desirable or to indicate to the Oireachtas the appropriate form of enactment which should be substituted for the enactment.

The nature and scope of orders to be made by the Courts have been tested in particular in relation to the vindication of the express or implied rights of children under the Irish Constitution. A number of very tragic cases have arisen in which proceedings were brought on behalf of children who were severely mentally handicapped asserting their constitutional rights to be educated, and other proceedings have been brought even more frequently in which a constitutional right to what is described as 'secure accommodation' is asserted on behalf of particular children.

It is perhaps a surprising feature of the Irish Constitution that it *does* contain a lengthy and detailed provision (Article 42) which sets out with apparent clarity the rights, duties and powers of parents and the State in relation to the provision of education and the right – and to a certain extent the duty – of a child to receive it. Despite its apparent clarity, this express constitutional provision has given rise to intense political and legal controversy. Even greater difficulty arises in relation to the provision of secure or any accommodation as that right is not the subject matter of any express provision. It has been identified, however, in a number of cases – culminating in *F.N. v. The Minister for Education*[26] – as one of the implicit or unremunerated rights granted by the Constitution.

Perhaps it is not the absence of any welfare provision in the Irish Constitution that causes surprise; rather, it is the inclusion of the educational provision. That occurred, it would appear, for historical reasons. When religious emancipation was granted in 1829 by Parliament of Westminster, a logical accompaniment of the open practice of religion was the education of its

23 *Byrne v. Ireland* [1972] IR 241; *McKenna v. An Taoiseach (No. 2)* [1995] 2 IR 10; *O'Donoghue v. The Minister for Health* [1996] 2 IR 20; and *F.N. v. The Minister for Education* [1995] 1 IR 409. **24** [2001] 2 IR 505. **25** This was stated by Keane J in the High Court in *Somjee v. The Minister for Justice* [1981] ILRM 324 and was reiterated by O'Higgins CJ in *Norris v. Attorney General* [1984] IR 36. **26** [1995] IR 409.

adherents. It was in 1831 that the United Kingdom Parliament enacted what were indeed revolutionary provisions in relation to education, granting – perhaps for the first time in Europe – free education for children within the ages of six and twelve years. As that system had been continued and strengthened through the nineteenth century, it was logical that it should be continued and perhaps reinforced by the original Constitution in 1922 and the existing Constitution in 1937. However, provisions in relation to housing, health or social services were not catered for in either Constitution and to a significant extent would have been anathema to the moral philosophy on which they were based. More recent analysis of the Irish Constitution detecting the existence of such rights represents a re-evaluation of the philosophy on which the Constitution was based and the terms in which it was expressed. The most significant feature of the Irish Constitution in this respect is negative rather than positive: it contains no provisions comparable to Article 17, 26 and 28 of the Bill of Rights enshrined in the Constitution of the Republic of South Africa, 1996. If any such provisions are to be found they represent judicial ingenuity. Certainly they do not represent the wishes of the Irish electorate as and when expressed in the year 1937.

Decisions of the Constitutional Court of South Africa in *Soobramoney v. The Minister for Health*[27] and *Government of RSA v. Grootboom*[28] in relation to Articles 26 and 27 of the Constitution of the Republic of South Africa illustrate the difficulties in construing and applying express constitutional provisions. The identification and application of implicit rights is even more problematic. As I understand it, the problem with which the constitutional courts here are presented is not dissimilar to our own. On my reading of *Soobramoney,* it would appear that the plaintiff, who was in desperate need of admission to a hospital to receive renal dialysis treatment, claimed the constitutional right of access to health care services provided by the State. In *Grootboom* the applicant was one of a substantial group of children and adults living in extremely bad conditions who sought to rely on their constitutional right to have access to adequate housing. How should these constitutional demands be addressed in your jurisdiction or mine? To direct, if one may do it, the executive or the minister to provide the resources required by a particular plaintiff may mean depriving another equally or even more deserving claimant of a similar benefit.

In Ireland we have never fully addressed the question. In *Sinnott*[29] the applicant (suing through his mother) was a 23-year-old man who suffered from severe autism. Article 42(4) of the Irish Constitution imposes an express obligation on the State to 'provide for free primary education'. The State contended that whatever obligation it had to provide primary education – and it was accepted that

---

27 [1998] (1) SA 765. **28** 2001 (1) SA 46 (CC). **29** *Sinnott v. The Minister for Education* [2001] 2 IR 505.

the obligation extended to autistic children – terminated when the child attained the age of 18 years. That contention was rejected in the High Court but upheld on appeal. In the result, the Supreme Court decision does not indicate the precise nature of the right enjoyed by the plaintiff with disabilities. In the High Court, the trial judge (Barr J) had in fact laid down very precise details of the education to be received by Jamie Sinnott; the ratio of teachers to pupils and the scholastic year over which it was to be provided – there being in the case of autism a tragic propensity to regression. Whether Mr. Justice Barr would have been correct in making such an order in relation to a younger plaintiff is a question which remains unanswered but in general it would seem that a detailed mandatory order of that nature would require very exceptional circumstances and even then it would seem to represent a trespass by the judiciary on the functions of the legislature. Certainly when it was argued in the High Court in Ireland[30] that Travellers had a constitutional right to be housed, the High Court judge dismissed the constitutional claim on the basis that this was a claim that would have to made to *politicians* rather than judges as it would require a consideration of the fairness or otherwise of the manner in which the organs of State administer public resources: a task which the Court would be unable to perform.

As I read the judgment of Justice Yacoob in *Grootboom,* it is recognised by the Constitutional Court of the Republic of South Africa that all of the rights in the Bill of Rights are interrelated and mutually supporting, so that the rights themselves and the claims of individuals cannot be seen in isolation one from another. It was accepted, as I understand it, that it would not be possible economically to realise all rights immediately but that the State was bound to give effect to the rights and that, in appropriate circumstances, the Court would enforce them. It was pointed out that the question which was posed for the Judiciary was always whether the measures taken to realise the rights afforded[31] were reasonable. To be reasonable, regard had to be made to those whose needs were most urgent and whose ability to enjoy their rights was most in peril. At the end of the day, the Court issued a declaratory order which required the State to devise and implement a programme which included measures to provide relief for people in desperate circumstances who had not been adequately catered for in the programme applicable to the area in which their problems had arisen.

CONCLUSION

In the brief period in which I have had the opportunity of drawing down these thoughtful decisions from the Internet, I have been fascinated by the similar-

---

30 In *O'Reilly v. Limerick Corporation* [1989] ILRM 181.   **31** Article 26 of the Constitution of the Republic of South Africa, 1996.

ity of our problems and excited by the fact that the South African courts have – within the terms of the Constitution – found a solution to them. As soon as the opportunity arises, I will look forward to inviting counsel appearing in my Court to ask why we should not adopt the same prudent solutions as you have done. If you are kind enough to invite me back here in two years time I will give you their answer to that question.

The review by the Supreme Court of the constitutionality of bills passed by the legislature in Ireland prior to their promulgation[1]

AINDRIAS Ó CAOIMH

Article 26 of the Constitution of Ireland provides that the President may refer a Bill to the Supreme Court for a decision on the question as to whether such Bill or any specified provision or provisions is or are repugnant to the Constitution or any provision thereof. The provision is such that it must be exercised within strict time limits and while it has many features which are attractive, the exercise of this jurisdiction by the President has a number of drawbacks.

THE CONSTITUTIONAL FRAMEWORK

It is necessary to set the provisions of Article 26 in context with other provisions of the Constitution. The parliamentary system in Ireland is one modelled on the British system insofar as it is a bicameral system with most of the power residing with the lower house of parliament (Oireachtas) which is known as Dáil Éireann (comprising at present 148 members). The second house of parliament is the Seanad (Senate) which is composed of 60 members; due to its composition it is almost invariably guaranteed to have a majority of its members who support the government of the day. Dáil Éireann elects the Taoiseach (Prime Minister) and approves the members of the Government nominated by the Taoiseach for appointment by the President who is vested with very limited powers under the Constitution.

In practice legislation is generally introduced by Ministers of the Government and passed by both houses of parliament. An exception is a Money Bill (which includes all fiscal legislation) which is required to be initiated in Dáil Éireann only and is deemed to be passed by both houses of the Oireachtas if

[1] While this paper is confined to a consideration of provisions of Article 26 of the Constitution which provides for references of Bills passed by the Houses of the Oireachtas for decision as to whether any such Bill or any specified provision or provisions thereof is or are repugnant to the Constitution or any provision thereof, it has to be stated that in the case of laws passed and promulgated, that the High Court and on appeal the Supreme Court has jurisdiction to consider the validity of any law having regard to the provisions of the Constitution.

not returned by Seanad Éireann within a period of 21 days. Accordingly legislation may be deemed to be passed by both houses of the Oireachtas without, in fact, obtaining the approval in real terms of both houses. Furthermore, the Government may certify certain legislation as urgent such that the time for its consideration by both houses of parliament may be curtailed.

Having been passed (or deemed to be passed) by both houses of the Oireachtas the President is required to sign same and promulgate same as a law (Act of the Oireachtas). The Bill is presented by the Taoiseach to the President for signing and must be signed by the President not earlier than the fifth and not later that the seventh day after presentation for signing. However, at the request of the Government with the prior concurrence of Seanad Éireann the President may sign a Bill earlier than the fifth day after its presentation for signing, in which event the Bill must be signed and promulgated by the President on the day of its presentation for signing. A Bill becomes law on and from the date of its signing unless the contrary intention appears and will come into operation on the date of its signing unless the Bill otherwise provides.

THE ARTICLE 26 PROCEDURE

Article 26 of the Constitution relates to any Bill other than a Money Bill, a Bill to amend the Constitution (which must be approved by the People by Referendum) or a Bill the time for consideration of which by Seanad Éireann shall have been abridged under the Constitution. Under Article 26 the President may, after consultation with an advisory body called the Council of State, refer any Bill to which Article 26 applies to the Supreme Court for a decision on its conformity with the Constitution.

A reference to the Supreme Court must be made not later that seven days after a Bill has been presented to the President for signing. Where a reference to the Supreme Court is made pursuant to Article 26 the President is precluded from signing the Bill until the decision of the Supreme Court is pronounced. The Supreme Court is required to consider every question referred to it by the President for decision and, having heard arguments by or on behalf of the Attorney General (in defence of the Bill) and by counsel assigned by the Court, it is required to pronounce its decision in open court on such question as soon as may be and not later that 60 days after the date of such reference.

The Constitution was originally enacted on 1 July 1937, and the first President of Ireland entered office on 25 June 1938. Under a transitory provision[2] of the Constitution as initially enacted, it was provided that within a period of three years after the date on which the first President shall have entered upon

2 Article 51.

his office, any provision of the Constitution with the exception of Article 51 and Article 46[3] could be amended by the Oireachtas. Article 26 was amended under this procedure in 1941 by the second amendment of the Constitution Act. The changes effected at that time included a slight adjustment in relation to the time frame in which the President may make reference to the Supreme Court; further, it is provided, in the context of a decision by the Supreme Court, that the decision of the majority shall be the decision of the Court and that no other opinion whether assenting or dissenting shall be pronounced nor shall the existence of any such other opinion be disclosed.

Of greater import than the amendments previously referred to was an amendment effected to Article 34 of the Constitution by the insertion at paragraph 3 thereof of the following:

> No court whatever shall have jurisdiction to question the validity of the law, or any provision of a law the Bill for which shall have been referred to the Supreme Court by the President under Article 26 of this Constitution, or to question the validity of a provision of the law where the corresponding provision in the Bill for such law shall have been referred to the Supreme Court by the President under the said Article 26.

It is this amendment to the Constitution that has given rise to the most controversy in the context of the powers exercisable by the President under Article 26.

Article 26 had no counterpart in the earlier Constitution of the Irish Free State of 1922, nor does any comparable provision exist in the Constitution of the United States of America. Somewhat comparable provisions exist in Germany, in France and in Canada.

The provisions for Article 26 of the Constitution have been exercised somewhat sparingly by Presidents in the 63 years that it has been in force. The use of this provision has resulted in 14 decisions being given resulting in eight decisions in favour of the validity of the Bill and six decisions holding the provision or provisions of such Bills to be repugnant to the Constitution or a provision thereof.

The use so far made of Article 26 can be illustrated by the table [overleaf], which is set out in Professor James Casey's, *Constitutional Law in Ireland* (3rd ed., Dublin, 2001), pp 332–3 and supplemented by two more recent references.

The purpose of Article 26 is to provide for a speedy decision on the validity of legislative measures that have been passed by both Houses of the Oireachtas. Its limited use may be attributed in part to some of the disadvantages associated with it. In the first place the Court is being asked to examine

---

3 Providing for an amendment of the Constitution by way of plebiscite in the ordinary way.

	Bill	Judgment	Referred by	Result
1	Offences Against the State (Amendment) Bill 1940	[1940]IR 470	President Hyde	Valid
2	School Attendance Bill 1942	[1943] IR 334	President Hyde	Valid
3	Electoral (Amendment) Bill 1961	[1961] IR 169	President de Valera	Valid
4	Criminal Law (Jurisdiction) Bill 1975	[1977] IR 129	President Ó Dálaigh	Valid
5	Emergency Powers Bill 1976	[1977] IR 159	President Ó Dálaigh	Valid
6	Housing (Private Rented Dwellings) Bill 1981	[1983] IR 181	President Hillery	Invalid
7	Electoral (Amendment) Bill 1983	[1984] IR 268	President Hillery	Invalid
8	Adoption (No. 2) Bill 1987	[1989] IR 656	President Hillery	Invalid
9	Matrimonial Property Bill 1993	[1994] IR 305	President Robinson	Invalid
10	Regulation of Information (Services outside the State for Termination of Pregnancies) Bill 1995	[1995] IR 1	President Robinson	Valid
11	Employment Equality Bill 1996	[1997]2 IR 321	President Robinson	Invalid
12	Equal Status Bill 1997	[1997] 2IR 387	President Robinson	Invalid
13	The Planning and Development Bill 1999	[2000] 2 IR 321	President McAleese	Valid
14	The Illegal Immigrants (Trafficking) Bill 1999	[2000] 2 IR 360	President McAleese	Valid

the Bill without any concrete application of the legislation in any given situation. Therefore, it must make a judgment on the Bill in the abstract.

Secondly, the decision of the President to refer a Bill to the Supreme Court must be reached within a very short time frame. Thirdly, the Supreme Court has a very limited time within which to examine a particular Bill in light of the fact that it must arrange for a hearing in open court, assign a team to argue against the constitutionality of a Bill, and having concluded the hearing, having given adequate time for the preparation of arguments by Counsel on both sides, the Court must then deliver its judgment as stated within a period of sixty days.

Furthermore, a situation may arise where more than one Bill is referred to the Supreme Court pursuant to Article 26 at one and the same time. This happened most recently in the year 2000 in relation to the Bills previously referred to at points (13) and (14) in the list. However, in these cases only defined parts of each Bill were the subject matter of the reference.

Moreover, in considering a Bill the Court will have no evidence before it as to how a Bill will operate in practice. If the Supreme Court finds that any provision of a referred Bill or of the referred provisions is repugnant, then the whole Bill fails. In 1982, dealing with the Housing (Private Rented Dwellings) Bill 1981 the Supreme Court stated as follows:

> Article 26, s.2 sub-s.1 says that the Court's decision is to be reached after hearing arguments by, or on behalf of, the Attorney General and by counsel assigned by the Court. That Article makes no reference to the hearing of evidence. In fact, in none of the references that have come to the Court so far has evidence been heard. The difficulties that could confront a court of at least five judges in reaching a unitary decision on the basis of conflicting evidence is too obvious to need elaboration. It is not necessary in this case to decide whether evidence may, or should be, heard when considering a reference under Article 26. In this, as in all earlier references, the matters argued have had, in the absence of evidence, to be dealt with as abstract problems, to the extent that, unlike practically all other cases that come before the Court, there is an absence or shortage of concrete facts proven, admitted, or projected as a matter of probability. The Court, therefore in a case such as this, has to act on abstract materials in order to cope with the social, economic, fiscal and other features that may be crucial to an understanding of the working and the consequences of a referred Bill. Whether the Constitutionality of a legislative measure of that nature which has been passed, or deemed to have been passed, by both Houses of the Oireachtas is better determined within a fixed and immutable period of time by means of reference under Article 26 (in which case, if no repugnancy is found, the decision may never be questioned again in a court) rather than by means of an action with specific imputations of unconstitutionality would fall to be determined primarily on proven or admitted facts, is a question on which we refrain from expressing an opinion.[4]

4 [1983] IR 181 at 186.

In the case of that particular reference the Supreme Court referred to an earlier decision of that Court and of the High Court upholding the constitutionality of the law providing for the fluoridation of water.[5] That case depended on findings of fact based on lengthy oral evidence which was largely scientific in nature and complex in character. The Supreme Court pointed out that in reaching its conclusion the Court had made it clear that, if in the future the scientific evidence should be such as to warrant a different conclusion on the facts, the question of the validity of the Act could be reopened. In the context of the reference under Article 26, the Supreme Court stated that if the Bill for that Act had been referred to the Court under Article 26 of the Constitution, the case for invalidity would have been broadly the same; yet, it is doubtful in the extreme if it would have been possible for the Court not later than sixty days after such reference, to have heard and determined all the matters which necessarily fell to determined in that case. Furthermore, the Court's decision on such a reference would thereafter be immune from further challenge had it upheld the constitutionality of the Bill in the first instance.

In 1997, in dealing with the Employment Equality Bill of 1996 the Supreme Court stated *inter alia* as follows:

> If, in the present case, the Court were to find one provision of the Bill unconstitutional and say no more the Court might not have addressed the problem or problems which is or are causing the present concerns. The result in the event of the Legislature attempting to introduce amending legislation could be a second reference or a series of references which would be singularly unsatisfactory for the President and to the Legislature. Moreover counsel assigned by the Court have attacked several provisions of the Bill. Under these circumstances the Court is obliged to consider the whole Bill and all its provisions particularly those which have been impugned by counsel as being repugnant to the provisions of the Constitution.[6]

However, in the case of the Equal Status Bill of 1997 the Supreme Court stated the situation where counsel for the Attorney General conceded two particular provisions of the Bill to be repugnant to the Constitution. In the circumstances, the Court stated *inter alia* as follows:

> Once the Court, at the outset of its deliberations, knows that portions of the Bill are indisputably repugnant to the Constitution, it is difficult to see why the Court should embark on a consideration of other provisions of the Bill. In this context the fact that among these other provisions are many provisions which are admittedly inoperable seems to illustrate the futility of any such exercise.[7]

5 *Ryan v. Attorney General* [1965] IR 294.   6 [1997] 2 IR 321 at 333.   7 [1997] 2 IR 387 at 402

While the President has a discretion as to the terms of any reference and may refer an entire Bill or, alternatively, a specified provision or provisions for referral, in all references up to the year 2000 with the exception of the School Attendance Bill 1942 the reference was of the entire Bill. However, in the two most recent references, in the case of the Planning and Development Bill 1999 the President referred to a portion of the Act (being Part V of the Act) and in the case of the Illegal Immigrants (Trafficking) Bill 1999 the President referred to two distinct sections of the Bill. In taking this approach President McAleese may have had regard to what was stated by the Supreme Court in its decision on the then latest reference by her predecessor, namely, the reference of the Employment Equality Bill 1996 where the Court stated as follows:

> The form of the reference in this case raises certain practical problems for the Court. The President has referred for the Court's decision 'the question as to whether the said Bill or any provision or provisions thereof is or are repugnant to the Constitution ... '. When one considers that the Bill consists of seventy-four sections and either amends or refers to thirty-three other statutes one can see that the task confronting the Court is a formidable one. The task is not made lighter by the fact that the Court is constitutionally obliged to give its decision on the Bill within sixty days of the date on which the Bill was referred to the Court by the President. Within this time the Court must assign counsel, give them time to prepare their written submissions, hold an oral hearing at which the issues are debated in open court, make its decision and deliver its judgment.[8]

It would have been possible for the President to specify some specific provision or provisions of the Bill on which she needed the Court's decision but she was not obliged to do that. Article 26.1.1° of the Constitution provides that the President may, after consultation with the Council of State, refer any Bill to which the Article applies to the Supreme Court for a decision 'on the question as to whether such Bill or any specified provision or provisions of such Bill is or are repugnant to this Constitution'. Article 26.2 provides that the Supreme Court 'shall consider every question referred to by the President' and that it 'shall pronounce its decision on such questions'. Article 26.3 provides that if the Supreme Court decides that ''any provision' of a Bill the subject matter of a reference is repugnant to the Constitution the President 'shall decline to sign the Bill'.

If, therefore, the Supreme Court finds that any provision of a Bill referred to it by the President under Article 26 is repugnant to the Constitution, that is a sufficient, and indeed, compelling reason for the President to refuse to sign

---

8 [1997] 2 IR 321 at 331

the Bill. But if the President has referred to the Supreme Court 'the question as to whether the said Bill or any provision or provisions thereof is or are repugnant to the Constitution', the problem remains whether the Supreme Court by deciding that one provision was repugnant to the Constitution and remaining silent about the others, would have fulfilled its constitutional duty under Article 26.1.1° to consider 'every question referred to it by the President' and to 'pronounce its decision on such question'.

Professor James Casey in *Constitutional Law in Ireland* states: 'Clearly, if the President could identify the core provisions of a Bill and refer only those to the Court, this would be advantageous – not least in affording a clear focus for the oral argument.'[9] Professor Casey continues:

> The difficulty, however, is illustrated by the case of the Employment Equality Bill itself. The section which caused most controversy – section 37 – was upheld; the provisions condemned as invalid included section 15, which was found to impose vicarious criminal liability on an employer who was devoid of guilty intent. Section 15 had engendered no controversy in the course of the Bill's passage. If, therefore, the President had sought the Supreme Court's opinion only on section 37, the Bill would have been upheld – merely, as an Act, to fall in Article 34 proceedings by reason of the presence of section 15.[10]

The most controversial aspect of Article 26 of the Constitution is that created by the amendment effected by the Second Amendment to the Constitution Act in 1941. This precludes any subsequent challenge to the provisions of an Act where the provisions of the Act as a Bill have been subject matter of a reference by the President under Article 26.

THE CONSTITUTION REVIEW GROUP'S RECOMMENDATIONS

In 1995 the Government of Ireland established a review group to examine the Constitution and to establish those areas where constitutional change may be desirable or necessary with a view to assisting the Oireachtas All Party Review Group on the Constitution in its work. In reviewing Article 26 the Review Group came to the conclusion that Article 26 should be retained.

However, in the context of its retention the Review Group examined Article 34.3.3° insofar as it provides for unchallengeability of a provision or provisions of an Act previously referred under Article 26 of the Constitution. The Review Group stated as follows:

9 J. Casey, *Constitutional Law in Ireland* (Dublin, 3rd ed., 2000), p.337. 10 Ibid., p.338.

The possibility of referring a Bill, before it becomes law, for a decision by the Supreme Court on its constitutionality is a valuable democratic safeguard. It prevents an unconstitutional law being in force until successfully challenged, a situation which could have consequences difficult ever to put right. On the other hand, the decision confirming the constitutionality of a Bill gives it an initial stamp of validity of which, even if it were open to challenge later, it could be deprived only on strong and persuasive considerations.[11]

The Review Group indicated that the previous references had dealt with important issues. It stated that had Article 26 not existed the resulting uncertainty as to the constitutionality of the Bills could have caused serious difficulties such, for example, as electoral procedures being invalidated, adoptions lacking permanence and property rights being invaded.

Dealing with the generality of Article 26 the Review Group stated:

Generally, it appears desirable to be able to test the constitutionality of legislation before it comes into force where there is a serious body of legal opinion that a proposed Bill is open to constitutional doubt, the proposed legislation affects in an important way the rights of individuals or the institutions of the State, and a finding of unconstitutionality after people had acted in reliance on the law would have serious consequences.[12]

The Review Group considered the President to be the appropriate constitutional officer to make the decision about referring Bills and recommended no change in this regard.

Proposed deletion of article 34.3.3°

Having referred to the enactment of the Second Amendment to the Constitution Act 1941, the Review Group concluded that the language of Article 34.3.3° suggested that the drafters wished to ensure that internment provisions of the Offences against the State (Amendment) Act 1940 should enjoy a permanent immunity from constitutional attack where a somewhat similar provision had previously been struck down by the High Court. The Review Group pointed out that at the time of the enactment of Article 34.3.3° in 1941 it had been assumed that the Supreme Court was strictly bound by its own previous decisions and could not overrule them by reason of the doctrine of *stare decisis*. This doctrine had since been relaxed such that the Supreme Court was free to overrule previous decisions. A second argument put forward by the Review Group in favour of the change to the unchallengeability rule was that

---

11 *Report of the Constitution Review Group* (1996), p. 75.   **12** Ibid., at p. 76.

it could be assumed that a subsequent successful challenge to the Act could only be brought by a person prejudicially affected in a manner not envisaged at the time of the reference or because of some other significant change of circumstances. In this context the argument was put that it appeared undesirable that anyone so affected should be delayed from challenging the constitutionality of the Act by a seven-year period. Thirdly, it was argued that any period specified would of necessity be arbitrary and different time limits might be appropriate to different types of legislation. It was stated that such detailed selective provision would not be appropriate to the Constitution.

The Review Group, having considered the arguments in relation to Article 34.3.3°, stated that on balance it should be deleted in its entirety. It said as follows:

> Such a deletion would impact only marginally upon legal certainty, inasmuch as a decision of the Supreme Court upholding the constitutionality of the Bill would still be an authoritative ruling on the Bill which would bind all the lower courts and be difficult to dislodge. It is to be expected that the Supreme Court would not, save in exceptional circumstances, readily depart from its earlier decision to uphold the constitutionality of the Bill. Such exceptional circumstances might be found to exist where the Constitution had been later amended in a manner material to the law in question, or where the operation of the law in practice had produced an injustice which had not been apparent at the time of the Article 26 reference, or possibly what constitutional thinking had significantly changed.[13]

The one-judgment rule

Article 26.2.2° of the Constitution provides: 'The decision of the majority of the judges of the Supreme Court shall, for the purposes of this Article be a decision of the Court and shall be pronounced by such one of those judges as that Court shall direct, and no other opinion, whether assenting or dissenting, shall be pronounced, nor shall the existence of any such other opinion be disclosed.'[14] The present form of Article 26.2.2.° incorporates an amendment introduced to ensure a degree of legal certainty in the decision of the Supreme Court. The operation of the rule may also be designed to protect individual members of the Court from untoward pressures. It is to be noted that a similar rule applies in the case of the European Court of Justice which stems from the influence of French law on the jurisprudence of the Court. The Review Group considered the arguments for and against the deletion of Article 26.2.2° but was unable to reach a consensus that this Article should be deleted, some members of the Review Group being of the view that the special character of the Article 26

13 Ibid., at p. 80.   14 Cf. ibid.

reference procedure justifies the retention of Article 26.2.2° and others clearly in favour of its deletion.

The sixty-day time limit
The Review Committee considered that the period of sixty days should be extended to ninety days in order to enable counsel appointed by the Supreme Court to put arguments against the Bill in circumstances where they have too little time.

The five-judge rule
The Review Committee considered that no change should be made in this regard in circumstances where the membership of the Court has been increased from a President and four Ordinary Judges to a President and seven Ordinary Judges.

The effect of a decision of unconstitutionality
Where a law enacted by the Oireachtas is subsequently held by the Courts to be unconstitutional the decision operates *ab initio*. Were Article 26 to be amended by the abolition of the unchallengeability rule, the Review Committee considered that there seems to be a case for not allowing a subsequent judgment of invalidity to fulfil automatic retrospectivity but rather to take effect from a recent, current or prospective date.

RESPONSE OF THE ALL–PARTY OIREACHTAS COMMITTEE

The Report of the Review Group on the Constitution was considered by the All-Party Oireachtas Committee on the Constitution. It issued its First Progress Report in April 1997. Unlike the Review Group, it considered that a decision of the Supreme Court in a reference under Article 26 of the Constitution should be a decision of the Court consisting of not less than seven judges. However, the Committee considered that the period of sixty days should be enlarged to ninety days as proposed by the Review Group but appears not to have accepted all of the reasons put forward by the Review Group.

With regard to the one judgment rule the Committee favoured the deletion of Article 26.2.2° to enable dissenting judgments to be delivered. With regard to the immutability of the Supreme Court's decision, the Committee also agreed with the recommendation made by the Review Group that Article 34.3.3° be deleted. In the context of the effect of a declaration of invalidity of a law, the Committee concluded that the constitutional provision should be replaced with the following wording: 'Where a law has been found to be invalid having regard to the provisions of this Constitution, the High Court or the

Supreme Court (as the case may be) shall have jurisdiction to determine in the interests of justice the consequences of such a finding of invalidity.'[15]

CONCLUSIONS

With the experience of the exercise of Article 26 of the Constitution for over 60 years it can be seen that a clear consensus exists in Ireland that such a power should be retained. In the context of other States considering amending their constitutions to provide for a like power the following matters might be considered to be appropriate.

In the first place it is considered desirable that the power to make a reference should be vested in an officer who is constitutionally independent of the executive and other arms of Government. In this regard it will ensure that the decision to refer a Bill will be taken independently and not subject to political pressure. Secondly, the power to refer Bills should be exercised sparingly and, in the context of the exercise of the power, it is best to refer distinct provisions of a Bill as opposed to the whole Bill for consideration by Court. Thirdly, adequate time must be given to the Court to entertain arguments both in favour of and against the Bill and to enable it to reach a decision without any undue time pressure. Fourthly, consideration should be given to whether a decision of a court in these circumstances should be immune from further challenge once the Bill has been signed into law and promulgated. Further consideration should be given to the number of judges comprising the Court to make the decision and whether the decision of the Court should be one in which dissenting judgments are precluded or one which allows for dissenting judgments to be delivered. Finally, consideration should be given to what the appropriate effect should be of a declaration of unconstitutionality of an Act where Acts are subject to review by the courts in relation to their constitutionality and in particular where powers such as those contained in Article 26 are provided for under the Constitution.

Overall it must be emphasised that the essential view reached by the Review Committee on the Constitution, which commands almost universal support in Ireland, is that the possibility of referring a Bill before it becomes law for a decision by the Supreme Court on its constitutionality is a valuable democratic safeguard.

15 All-Party Oireachtas Committee on the Constitution, *First Progress Report* (1997), p. 65.

Index